THE EVERYWHERE CLASSROOM

THE EVERYWHERE CLASSROOM

How One Family Turned Wanderlust into Worldschooling and How You Can Too

Andi Almond

Rowman & Littlefield
Lanham • Boulder • New York • London

Published by Rowman & Littlefield
An imprint of The Rowman & Littlefield Publishing Group, Inc.
4501 Forbes Boulevard, Suite 200, Lanham, Maryland 20706
www.rowman.com

86-90 Paul Street, London EC2A 4NE, United Kingdom

Copyright © 2025 by Andi Almond

All rights reserved. No part of this book may be reproduced in any form or by any electronic or mechanical means, including information storage and retrieval systems, without written permission from the publisher, except by a reviewer who may quote passages in a review.

British Library Cataloguing in Publication Information Available

Library of Congress Cataloging-in-Publication Data
Names: Almond, Andi, 1977– author.
Title: The everywhere classroom : how one family turned wanderlust into worldschooling and how you can too / Andi Almond.
Description: Lanham, Maryland : Rowman & Littlefield, [2025] | Summary: "The Everywhere Classroom is the story of one family's worldschooling adventure, with tips and inspiration for those who wish to teach their kids through travel-whether on a weekend excursion or a year on the road. Spanning twenty-two countries, each chapter features a lively mix of experiences and insights into using the world as a classroom"— Provided by publisher.
Identifiers: LCCN 2024034939 (print) | LCCN 2024034940 (ebook) | ISBN 9798881801847 (cloth ; acid-free paper) | ISBN 9798881801854 (epub)
Subjects: LCSH: Worldschooling. | Home schooling. | Experiential learning. | Almond, Andi, 1977—Travel.
Classification: LCC LC40.5.W6 A56 2025 (print) | LCC LC40.5.W6 (ebook) | DDC 370.116—dc23/eng/20240924
LC record available at https://lccn.loc.gov/2024034939
LC ebook record available at https://lccn.loc.gov/2024034940

∞™ The paper used in this publication meets the minimum requirements of American National Standard for Information Sciences—Permanence of Paper for Printed Library Materials, ANSI/NISO Z39.48-1992.

To Finn and Aria
May you always treasure exploration,
approach life with a sense of wonder,
and relentlessly pursue your dreams

CONTENTS

Foreword *by Eric Weiner*   ix
Map of Our Journey: June 2022–July 2023   xiii
Preface: What Is Worldschooling Anyway?   xv

1   The Crazy Idea   1
2   Setting an Epic Out-of-Office Message   11

PART I: FIRST-QUARTER WORLDSCHOOLING GOALS (JUNE–AUGUST)   21

3   In Search of Magic: Morocco   25
4   *Parlez-Vous* Journaling?: France   40
5   The Music of Africa: Zanzibar   53
6   No Gnus Is Good Gnus: Tanzania   65
7   The Essay Fiasco of Joburg: South Africa   82
8   Trapped by a Rhino: Namibia   96

PART II: SECOND-QUARTER WORLDSCHOOLING GOALS (SEPTEMBER–DECEMBER)   111

9   Wisdom Begins in Wonder: Greece   117

10	The Deathstalker: Jordan	130
11	Are We Responsible Tourists?: Egypt	144
12	Found in Translation: Brazil	156
13	No Bravery without Madness: Antarctica	168
14	Champions of the World: Argentina	184

PART III: THIRD-QUARTER WORLDSCHOOLING GOALS (JANUARY–MARCH) — 197

15	And That, My Friends, Is Karma: India	201
16	No Mango Sticky Rice for You: Thailand	219
17	Happy Life, Happy Love: Cambodia	231
18	Good Morning, Vietnam: Vietnam	246
19	Mountains and Momos: Nepal	259

PART IV: FOURTH-QUARTER WORLDSCHOOLING GOALS (APRIL–JULY) — 281

20	Chasing Ikigai: Japan	285
21	Drenched at the DMZ: South Korea	300
22	The Family Mart Gang: Taiwan and the Philippines	311
23	Underwater Classroom: Indonesia	332
24	Seventh Continent: Australia	343

Epilogue: Homeward Bound: French Polynesia and the United States	355
Appendix: Worldschooling FAQs	365
Acknowledgments	369
About the Author	373

FOREWORD

by Eric Weiner

Most journalists view the world as a collage of calamities. I view it as a laboratory of ideas—good ideas—and a series of enticing what-ifs. What if we made prisons with no walls (Denmark)? What if we lived in the wealthiest country in the world (Qatar)? Andi Almond and family embark on their own intriguing what-if. What if we spent a year traveling with our children and the world was their classroom?

One word that appears often in Andi's delightful *The Everywhere Classroom* is "magic"—and for good reason. Travel is magic. Or, rather, it can be magic, if you travel well.

Traveling well has little to do with the number of stamps in your passport or photos on your Instagram feed. More important than where you travel is *how*. Do you breeze through cities, checking off sights seen and tours taken, or do you slow down and savor each moment? Do you ensconce yourself in five-star hotels or rough it at hostels?

Andi travels well. *The Everywhere Classroom* chronicles her year abroad with her husband and two children, ages thirteen and ten. It is a combination of travelogue and how-to guide. Each chapter ends with pointers and a report card. What went well and what needs work. Traveling well, like anything else, is always a work in progress.

Children are natural travelers, as any parent wrangling a wayward toddler can attest. Children explore. And they don't need five-star hotels or plutonium status on their favorite airline. They care not one whit for airline lounges or Michelin-starred restaurants. Children know magic can be found anywhere.

I've traveled widely with my own daughter—to France, India, and beyond—and I'm always struck by how much more she sees than I do. There's nothing wrong with my vision. My eyes just aren't fully open. I'm sure Andi and her husband had a richer, albeit more complex, journey traveling with their children; they saw these places through the eyes of a child.

Therein lies the reason we travel. As Henry Miller said, "One's destination is never a place, but a new way of looking at things." Do you see, in the broadest sense of the word, what is around you, what is inside of you? Have you embarked on your journey with an open mind and open heart? By this measure, a person who has visited only one country could be said to be very well traveled indeed.

No one knew this better than Henry David Thoreau, who lived nearly all of his too-short life in Concord, Massachusetts. But, for him, that was plenty. He observed Walden Pond from every conceivable vantage point: from a hilltop, on its shores, underwater. Sometimes he'd bend over and peer through his legs, marveling at the inverted world. "From the right point of view, every storm and every drop in it is a rainbow," he wrote.

Out there, on the road, we encounter much—for lack of a better word—weirdness. The Almond family is no exception; witness their brushes with snake charmers in Morocco and hungry kangaroos in Australia. Typically, there are two reactions to such oddities. One is to deny the weirdness. Thais eat fried insects. It is their way. Who am I to judge? Another reaction is to reject the weirdness out of hand. Eating insects is gross. I can't believe they do that. There is a third way. Acknowledge the weirdness—eating insects is gross—but then ask yourself what they get from this custom. There is always a reason. And who knows, you might learn something from it.

When we travel, we expand ourselves not by turning inward but by looking outward, interacting with other people. Do we see only differences—language, cuisine, customs—or do we also identify commonalities, a shared humanity? This is empathy. If we don't empathize, at least a little, with those we encounter, we never really see them.

The empathetic traveler doesn't try to fit in. She knows that is impossible and that there are advantages to seeing places at an angle. One of the best books about U.S. democracy was written by a Frenchman, Alexis de Tocqueville. This is no coincidence. An observant outsider often sees what insiders do not.

Empathizing with other people, though, doesn't mean becoming them. I know it's fashionable to brag that you "travel like a local." No, you don't. You travel like a foreigner. That's because you are one. And that's OK.

The kind of traveling classroom the Almonds invented was not easy. Teaching their children on the road, they encountered obstacles that don't exist back home, such as jet lag and wobbly Wi-Fi. Travel is hard, and always has been. Traveling for leisure is a relatively recent phenomenon. For most of human history, people traveled for a reason. They traveled to flee a war (or start one), to seek God or treasure, to chart new sea routes, or explore new wonders. There's a reason the words "travel" and "travail" share a common route—to travel is to travail.

It is this difficulty, though, the encountering and overcoming of obstacles, that supplies meaning. Purpose-driven travel. When we take a vacation, we vacate ourselves. When we travel with purpose, we fill ourselves. Social-science research tells us the happiest people are those who lead the most meaningful lives. So too with travelers. Travel meaningfully—on purpose and with purpose.

The purpose needn't be grand. You needn't save the world or the dolphins or anything else. We can't all be Mother Teresa. But we all can travel for good. That "good" might manifest as a kind word exchanged with a taxi driver or a collaborative journey with climate scientists. Whatever the form the "good" takes, what's needed is a fundamental shift in attitude, from one of getting to giving. To borrow from John F. Kennedy Jr., "Ask not what a place can do for you; ask what you can do for the place."

Much of the advice Andi dispenses to her children applies to adults equally. The importance of keeping a journal while traveling. We humans have terrible memories. Photos are poor substitutes for a written chronicle. As the French diarist Anais Nin said, "We write to taste life twice, in the moment and in retrospect."

I was five years old when I took my first solo journey. I roamed some two miles from my Towson, Maryland, home before police put an end to my adventure. What drove me? Curiosity?

Yes.

But it was not only an intense desire to know what lies around the next corner that propelled me. It was the firm belief that whatever it was would be pure magic.

Eric Weiner is a leading voice in the realm of travel literature, a renowned journalist, author, and speaker. Best known for his international bestsellers such as The Geography of Bliss *and* The Geography of Genius, *Eric has contributed to NPR as a correspondent and his work has appeared in prestigious publications including* National Geographic, *the* New York Times, *the* Washington Post, *and BBC, among others.*

MAP OF OUR JOURNEY

June 2022–July 2023

102,000 miles (~164,153 km). Four hundred days. Twenty-seven countries. Seven continents. Four travelers. One transformational journey.*

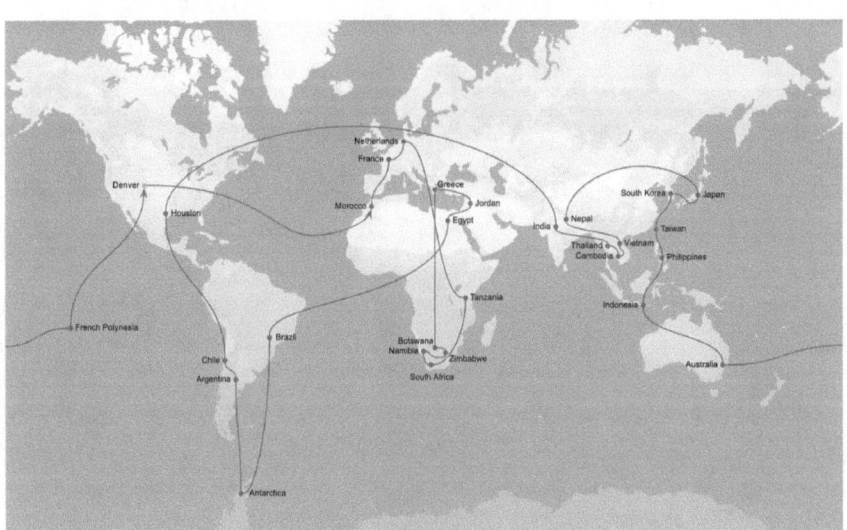

What will *your* journey look like?
The Everywhere Classroom. Let's go explore.

---

* Countries we visited on this trip, which are not featured, for length: The Netherlands, Botswana, Zimbabwe, Chile

PREFACE

What Is Worldschooling Anyway?

Education is the kindling of a flame, not the filling of a vessel.

—Socrates

A few months into our family trip around the world, our thirteen-year-old son, Finn, talked to a friend back home over video chat.

"So, are you having fun on your year-long vacation?" his buddy asked, but not in a malicious way, he was genuinely curious. Seeing photos of Finn and his younger sister, Aria, touring Greece or posing with penguins in Antarctica, it was understandable. To many, it probably seemed like they were ditching middle school.

"It's not a vacation. We're worldschooling," Finn replied.

"Okay, but it still sounds like a year off. You don't go to class five days a week, right?"

"True." Finn didn't elaborate, knowing it would be hard for his friend to understand. And he did raise a valid question: was this genuine schooling or just travel?

It was a fair confusion. Worldschooling felt mildly gimmicky to us too when we first considered educational options for our middle schoolers during our year abroad. Part of the challenge is that worldschooling lacks a single definition, though it is often likened to homeschooling without the home. Some call it roadschooling, lifeschooling, or self-directed learning; some families embrace the concept full time, others part time; some are child-led, while others follow more structured curricula.

At the core, though, is a focus on real-world experiences. Worldschooling as we define it is an educational approach where the world serves as the classroom, blending travel with learning to provide immersive experiences that enhance traditional academic subjects. This extends beyond conventional classrooms to incorporate cultural, historical, social, and practical lessons that are often overlooked in standard curricula. On trips of any length, it's a way to emphasize experiential learning, flexibility based on children's interests, global citizenship, and the development of life skills like navigating public transit systems, managing budgets, and communicating respectfully across language barriers.

For my husband, Randy, and me, worldschooling our children was never a rejection of traditional learning. It was a chance to travel as a family and make our on-the-road experiences the core of our kids' education for a time. We started small—a road trip through the American southwest one spring break; two weeks backpacking through northern Europe; three weeks in Ecuador one summer where we worked remotely, lived with a local host family, and the kids did Spanish immersion school. For our longer, year-long journey, we crafted a curriculum tailored to our travels, collaborating with their teachers to identify subjects that would naturally integrate into our explorations, like reading, history, and geography; and others, such as math and science, which would require supplemental materials.

Before leaving home, we made sure we understood what was required for the kids to bridge an entire school year. Different countries—and even different states—have differing approaches to alternate schooling arrangements. In Colorado, it was relatively simple. We worked with the school administrators in our district to align on the curriculum we planned to follow and formally defer the kids' enrollment for a year.

While traveling, we aimed to create immersive experiences, contextualizing learning with what we saw. In Greece, we explored ancient sites, used virtual reality to bring history to life, listened to the *Iliad*, watched documentaries, and incorporated practical math lessons in daily adventures. In Antarctica, we focused on science and sustainability, adding field projects to journaling and relevant literature for our middle schoolers.

Our worldschooling approach evolved over time, as we adapted to our children's learning styles, preferences, and family dynamics—and in response to bumps along the way. We had meltdowns and blowups as we figured out what worked—and what didn't—for our family. We got better at carving out dedicated time for writing and math, more calibrated at what to expect from essay writing and how to use rubrics to make expectations clearer, and alternating reading and audio books.

Are we the best teachers? Definitely not. After a year of worldschooling, I have vastly increased respect for our kids' amazing educators back home. Both Randy and I lost our shit more than once trying to get Finn and Aria to do the worldschooling we assigned, let alone do it well. There were times none of us wanted to tackle math or write—or grade—an essay. But the education they got on the road? I am positive it was unparalleled and worth the minor hiccups along the way.

Travel changes us. For kids (and adults!), it broadens their horizons, helps them unplug, and cultivates skills like flexibility, problem solving, empathy, and resilience. The good news is, worldschooling isn't limited to extended journeys; anyone can use travel as a tool for learning, on a local weekend getaway or a longer trip. The Everywhere Classroom is all around, for anyone to experience, simply by being intentional about incorporating worldschooling into travel plans.

Over the course of our adventures, we have seen the benefits of worldschooling firsthand and will continue to seek opportunities to use future travel—whether close to home or farther afield—as a springboard for learning. To kindle in our children a flame and fuel their curiosity, which will hopefully carry over for the rest of their lives.

HOW TO TURN COUNTRIES INTO CLASSROOMS ON TRAVEL OF ANY LENGTH

You have a family trip coming up. It might be within driving distance or an airplane ride away, a weekend escape or a longer adventure. You may simply want to relax, and that's okay! But if you want to use your travels as an opportunity for learning for your children, there are many ways to incorporate worldschooling that don't require much extra time, resources, or investment. Here are a few ideas:

- *Involve your kids in trip planning.* Encourage them to read a guidebook and help choose your destination. They'll learn more if they have skin in the game.
- *Let them be tour guides for a day.* Give them a budget and parameters. Then have them research, plan your activities, map out where to go, how to get there, and how much it will cost. Our kids love taking ownership of the planning for a time and getting to tell us what we're doing for a change.
- *Read a relevant book by a local author.* Check out a book from your library set in the country you're visiting or related to your trip in some way.
- *Watch a relevant documentary or movie.* Have a family movie night and enjoy a documentary or film about wherever you're heading.

- *If headed abroad, learn key words and phrases in the local language.* Even if English is widely spoken, saying hello, good morning, please, and thank you in a city's native language will light up people's faces and can be a window into the culture.
- *Engage a local guide for a walking tour.* Seeing a new place through the eyes of a resident is a great way to get a deeper sense of a country, find local haunts and street food recommendations, and learn about the culture in an engaging way.
- *Select where you stay for an authentic experience.* Book locally owned bed and breakfasts, hotels, hostels, or Airbnbs in a cool neighborhood, or go further and opt for a homestay with a local family for a true cultural immersive experience.
- *Take public transportation when possible.* Show the kids how to read a subway map, get tokens, navigate the bus system, or ride the rails. Experience cities as the locals do for a more authentic experience.
- *Eat local street food, sampling traditional specialties.* Or consider taking a cooking class as a family to get a flavor for the country's culture, literally.
- *Explain currency conversion, if applicable.* Help your kids understand local money and the conversion rate. Let them take the lead in ordering, getting a practical math lesson as they calculate the change in local currency.

THE CRAZY IDEA

Five years before our big trip, we flew to Europe for our first family backpacking adventure.

Caminante, no hay camino; se hace camino al andar.
(Traveler, there is no road; you make your own path as you walk.)

—Antonio Machado

One day in February 2017, shortly after I turned forty, I was browsing our library's travel section in search of a new book and inspiration. Randy and I planned to backpack through northern Europe that summer with our two young children, then five and eight. In anticipation of that adventure, I planned to check out a travel memoir à la Bill Bryson or *Eat, Pray, Love*. Instead, I stumbled upon a copy of *One Year Off: Leaving It All Behind for a Round-the-World Journey with Our Children* by David Elliot Cohen.

Intriguing.

Fifteen years and seemingly a lifetime earlier, Randy and I had done a round-the-world trip in our mid-twenties. We spent six months in South America and another six in Southeast Asia. The whole journey—and in particular the two months we spent living and working on an ecotourism cooperative in the cloud forests of northern Ecuador—was a deeply formative part of our young adult lives. Could we pull off something like that again? And this time with two kids in tow? It was a crazy idea. But it started to take root.

As I read Cohen's book one night, I turned to Randy and asked, "What do you think about taking a year to travel the world as a family at some point?"

Without a hitch, like he'd been thinking about it too and come to the same conclusion, he answered, "Absolutely. We'll do that."

I was excited, but also needed to clarify, only half-jokingly. "Cool! Let the record show, though, this was my idea."

Randy and I met in New York in 1999, shortly after college. We were both consultants at Accenture. Nine months after we started dating, he took a job with a start-up in northern Germany. I was able to get an overseas assignment with a client in Frankfurt. This kicked off an amazing period in our lives. As ex-pats, we partook in the generous European

THE CRAZY IDEA

vacation policies and cheap travel options to explore as much as we could. Our favorite thing to do was go to the *Hauptbahnhof*, or central train station, see where the next train was going, hop on it, and end up wherever it took us.

After about a year and a half, my client engagement was wrapping up, and Randy's start-up was imploding. It was time to move on, but to what? We didn't have strong ties to anywhere back in the States and no idea what we wanted next career-wise. We didn't have kids or a house or a car—all our belongings fit in a couple of suitcases. After working for a few years, we had each built up a small amount of savings.

We decided to use it to channel Frost and take the road less traveled. At least for Americans. For Brits, Kiwis, and Aussies, among others, taking a gap year as a twenty-something-year-old is a fairly common rite of passage. But when we announced to friends and family that we had bought backpacks and were going to spend the next year hostel hopping and volunteering around the world, we got a *lot* of raised eyebrows and head tilts that silently—and some not so silently—said, *Really? You think this is a good idea? Why?*

We did it anyway. And it was incredible. We grew up a lot. Got engaged halfway through the trip. Reflected on what we wanted for our future. I wanted to make a difference in the world and decided to become a reporter, applying for grad school in journalism. Randy applied to business school, both to begin when we returned. Along the road, we met kindred spirits who we believed in the depths of our souls we'd stay close to for life. We had stomach bugs, wild hallucinations from our Malaria medication, periods of deep homesickness, and stretches when we thought we'd travel forever. At the end of it all, we came home changed.

I will always remember the reverse culture shock after a year away. My dad and stepmom picked me up at the airport in Houston and, as we walked through the parking lot to their car, I realized I had to pee. My first thought was to pop behind a truck and squat down right then and there. I went to the public restroom instead, feeling profoundly grateful for a real toilet—with a seat! And warm, running water in the sink! I realized how much we take for granted in the United States. There would be more moments of dissonance like that for months while we reintegrated back into "normal" life.

None of the fears that our well-intentioned friends and family had once voiced came to fruition. Our gap year, rather than being a hindrance to our careers, was always a unique talking point—and made us more well-rounded individuals with a broader global perspective than we would have had otherwise. Over the next fifteen years, we built successful careers. Randy gravitated toward marketing roles at tech start-ups. I pursued my interest in writing, becoming a reporter before shifting to communications roles and later leading diversity and inclusion efforts for consulting firm McKinsey & Company.

In 2010, when our son, Finn, was two, we moved from California to Colorado. By then, we had lived and worked in two countries, five states, nine cities, and as nomads in countless places around the globe. We were ready to put down roots, and the Boulder area fit our personalities perfectly. When our daughter, Aria, was born the following year, we felt complete, at peace, and settled.

We introduced the kids early to traveling, flying with Finn as an infant to Hawaii then to Italy when he was eighteen months old. Aria was a baby when we visited my hometown of San Juan, Puerto Rico; she did her first backpacking trip with us at age five, trekking with her small purple pack through Iceland, Finland, Sweden, Norway, and Scotland. We spent a spring break driving through the southwest, visiting the Grand Canyon in Arizona and learning about the Ancestral Puebloans, who built thriving communities on the cliffs in Mesa Verde, Colorado. In the summer of 2019, we lived at a homestay in Cuenca, Ecuador, working remotely as digital nomads while the kids spent their days learning Spanish. They caught the travel bug from us, and always eagerly looked forward to our next adventure.

But it never occurred to us to travel more. After all, Finn and Aria were in school. And Randy and I enjoyed our jobs, which were not only fulfilling but allowed us good work–life balance. Plus, gap years seemed like things young adults did. It wasn't something people in their forties with teens and tweens did—or was it?

After reading *One Year Off* and having our late-night conversation in 2017, we resolved to make an extended family trip happen. Our ideal year to go, we decided, was the summer of 2022 through 2023. The kids would be in sixth and eighth grades—old enough to remember the experience and do adventurous activities, young enough to keep high

THE CRAZY IDEA

school intact and not mind traveling with their parents (too much!). That would also give us five years to save for the journey.

The question of their education loomed large in my mind, though. There is a reason I didn't become a teacher—many, actually. I have very high expectations, limited subject-matter expertise, and I am not particularly patient. Randy is good at breaking down complex concepts into simple explanations, but he's not an educator either. So, how we were going to tackle Finn and Aria's schooling was an open question—and a potential sticking point. Cohen was vague on the topic in his book, plus his kids were a lot younger when they traveled. I searched for other resources about family travel but came up short.

"Could we put them in local public schools for a month here, a month there?" I wondered aloud to Randy. "Like, maybe we travel to twelve places in twelve months and bounce from school to school. Do people do that?"

"No idea," he replied, unhelpfully.

"Maybe there are online resources, or they could just do a real gap year, like not school at all and then drop a grade," I suggested hopefully. "Is that even legal?"

"Even if it is, they will *not* like that idea," he said.

"Okay, well, what are your suggestions, Mr. Negativity?"

"I suggest we figure out if we can do it at all financially first, then we'll sort the rest of it out. Deal?"

I hate it when he's logical. "Fine," I grumbled, and dropped it—for a bit, anyway. First things first, I supposed.

Over the next few years, we made conscious trade-offs, prioritizing experiences over things, and saving as much as we could. Then COVID-19 shut everything down in early 2020 and the world was thrown into upheaval. But timing was on our side. Countries slowly emerged from the crisis, and it felt like we'd be able to take the leap as planned.

So, in June 2022, we set off, bound for Morocco.

Many people likely think we're crazy or irresponsible for upending our lives like this. To (*gasp*) travel at length with our teen and tween—and voluntarily worldschool them while exploring far-flung lands. To take a big risk in stepping temporarily out of the workforce at what is, at ages forty-eight and forty-five for Randy and me, respectively, the peak of our careers. To rent our house, say goodbye to friends and family, live on a much tighter budget and out of a seventy-liter pack for thirteen months.

I get that. It's not the typical path.

It's also, we realize, a privilege to be able to hit the pause button on real life and travel for a year. It requires savings and resources to step out of the workforce for a time. A trip like ours may not be for everyone, but there are countless ways to travel as a family and use the world as a classroom—and likely more doable than many realize.

As we talked to friends and colleagues, many said they were intrigued and inspired by what we were doing. They could envision pursuing something similar in the future—maybe not in the same way, but in some incarnation. They wanted to know more. They wanted details. They wanted stories. They wanted a how-to guide.

Greater remote work opportunities post-COVID and the normalization of alternate forms of education has facilitated a level of location independence for many that opens exciting new possibilities for living, working, and educating. We met other families traveling for long periods of time on a range of budgets and tackling schooling in different ways depending on length of trip and age of kids, and it's a trend that will only continue.

We met a family from Austin, Texas, with two boys who left home for a year around the time we did. They were on a very tight budget, often eating Ramen noodles and Swedish meatballs at IKEA to stretch their dollars. They opted for slow travel, spending three months living in the countryside in Hawaii before traveling to Indonesia, Australia, and New Zealand. With a background in education, the mom shaped her boys' worldschooling curriculum.

In Fez, Morocco, we met a U.S. military family traveling with their three teens "all summer long or until the money runs out," hopping on standby flights to extend their travel funds. Because they took their annual pilgrimages during summer vacations, they didn't need to focus as much on formal schooling. They noted, though, how much their children had learned in their travels over the years, in ways that can't be measured by letter grades.

We spent time in Paris with a worldschooling family who spent eighteen months driving an RV across Japan. They had two kids, ages thirteen and ten like ours at the time. The mom worked as a digital nomad, continuing her job remotely, while the dad assumed the role of full-time teacher, using online resources to keep up the kids' education.

And, in Buenos Aires, we bonded with a family of five from Indiana who I'd met through my Instagram travel community. They were in the midst of a seven-month trip to see the seven continents. They had originally planned a year-long trip, but their kids wanted to experience part of the school year back home, so they shortened their timeline. The parents arranged a virtual semester through the kids' school, bridging the gap with online schooling to when they would rejoin their classes in person in the spring.

Most of us saved for years to afford our trip. And all of us felt deeply that any uncertainty upon return or minor gaps to a traditional education would be far outweighed by the lasting memories we made and the worldschooling lessons learned along the way.

We watched as our kids matured through our journey and became more comfortable in their own skins. When we first landed in Morocco, a country so different from our own, the bustle of the medinas sent them skittering and reaching for our hands. Foreign noises made them jump. They sniffed warily at unfamiliar tastes and wrinkled their noses at the pungent smells of local spices. They held back and let us do most of the talking when meeting new people.

Over time, they walked farther in front of us, confident they could navigate whatever city we were in fairly independently. They came to appreciate great works of art and learned how to say thank you in more than a dozen languages. They got an immersive lesson in plate tectonics as we crossed the Great Rift Valley in East Africa and the birthplace of humankind in Botswana. In the Namib Desert, they tested how a magnet attracts the black iron flecks hidden in the sands before they oxidize, giving the dunes their rust-colored hue. They learned about great explorers like Sir Francis Drake and Ernest Shackleton as we crossed the Drake Passage and set foot on the Antarctic peninsula. And when they wanted ice cream on a hot day in Cambodia, they learned to calculate the conversion rate and ask for correct change as they bought themselves their treats.

They grew better at recognizing their own limits, which at times meant pushing through fear to reach an apex and, at others, knowing when to turn around even if that meant foregoing a summit. They became comfortable chatting with Uber drivers from Cape Town to Buenos Aires about *futbol* (soccer) and American politics (which everyone, everywhere, asked us about) and can tell you what to do if you ever come face to face with a shark.

In our increasingly fragmented, polarized world, we go about our frenzied lives, rarely stopping to take a beat. There's an incomparable power that comes from stepping out of our routines, trying new things, learning a language, volunteering in a community, or experiencing a new way of life, whether for a weekend, a week, or longer.

I can't help but believe that's a good thing for us all.

This is our story of how we spent one year bumping along dirt roads, climbing mountains, and worldschooling our teen and tween. It's about how we navigated Plan Bs when flights were canceled and plans went awry. How we dealt with seasickness, stomach bugs, and scorpion stings. How we watched the shifting sands in the desert and dove the oceans, lay together under the stars, and pushed ourselves to our limits. And at the end of it all, came home with a deeper sense of the world, our place in it, and our ability to play a part—however small—in making it a better, more sustainable, inclusive place.

MAKING EXTENDED TRAVEL AFFORDABLE FOR FAMILIES

Extended travel and worldschooling might seem like luxuries for the super-rich, but they're achievable dreams for many families willing to plan strategically and make thoughtful, often long-term, trade-offs. Here are some ideas for preparing for an adventure like this:

Assessing and Redirecting Finances:

- Review and adjust your spending habits to prioritize savings for travel.

- Set aside funds regularly, as even small savings can accumulate over time. Kids can even contribute to this, making them feel part of the long-term family goal.

Making Lifestyle Choices and Trade-offs:

- Reduce nonessential expenses like frequent dining out, coffee runs, or luxury hobbies.
- Keep your current vehicle longer, saving the expense of a new purchase for travel.
- Embrace secondhand clothing and DIY beauty treatments for big savings.
- Sell unused items or downsize your living space to boost travel funds.

Leveraging Home Equity:

- Rent out (or sell) your home while traveling to generate additional income.

Evaluating Risk Comfort and Exploring Remote Work:

- Understand your family's readiness for travel uncertainties.
- Investigate remote work or freelancing opportunities to maintain income while abroad.

Embracing Savvy Trip Planning and Budget-Friendly Options:

- Consider less expensive countries and places off the typical tourist trail.
- Utilize travel hacking techniques, including credit card points, to maximize your budget.
- Compare flight prices, embracing off-peak hours and multiple connections for deals.

- Opt for longer stays in a single location to save on costs.
- Explore affordable lodging options like hostels, guesthouses, or house-sitting / swaps.
- Plan to shop locally, cook meals on the road, and try street food.

Planning a Comprehensive and Realistic Travel Budget:

- Ensure your budget accounts for all costs, including emergencies and travel insurance.

With these and other thoughtful strategies, families can embark on extended travel on budgets comparable—or even lower—than what they'd spend over the same period at home.

2

SETTING AN EPIC OUT-OF-OFFICE MESSAGE

Finn and Aria in front of our big world map in 2022, a few months before we set off.

Shortly after conceiving our wild idea in the spring of 2017, we met with a financial adviser. We wanted to talk through our plan early—years before we intended to leave—so we could begin saving toward our aspiration. We were starting from a good place, with strong dual incomes and solid reserves, but we would need to actively plan and make trade-offs to pull something like this off.

We discussed a range of scenarios, because there are many ways to make extended travel happen, and how much we'd need to save would be dictated by how we wanted to do it. Would we go for a full year, or would we consider nine months, half a year, or a summer abroad? Would we rent or sell our home? Would we continue working on the road, pursue leaves of absence, or quit our jobs altogether? Would we assume in our financial modeling that we'd be able to earn similar salaries upon our return or build in a buffer in case it took longer to find new jobs and they paid less? Would we opt for slow travel to a few countries to keep costs lower or did we want to explore more places?

From the start, Randy and I were aligned on our vision. Unfortunately, that vision put us on the higher end of what we'd need to save. Our ideal scenario was to travel as a family for a full year. We preferred not to work while backpacking, if possible. We would rent our home, earning enough in rental income to cover the mortgage. And we preferred to explore a wide range of countries to introduce our kids to different cultures and ways of life.

While achieving all of that might be a stretch, we walked away from our meeting with the financial planner optimistic that, with focused saving and belt tightening, we could make our vision—or something near it—happen in five years.

So, we shared our plan with the kids. Finn was eight at the time and Aria, five. They're very different kids. Finn takes time to warm up to new ideas that push him out of his comfort zone. Aria is happy to go with the flow. Characteristically, Finn had a lot of questions.

"When will we leave?" he asked.

"Not for another five years."

"Where will we go first?"

"Not sure yet. We can all brainstorm ideas together," we promised.

"Can I bring my stuffies?"

"You can bring one small stuffed animal if you want," I said.

"What will happen to our house?"

"We'll come back to it."

"What will happen to Sir Myles?" (Our cat.)

"Good question, buddy. We'll make sure he has a nice home while we're away."

"Oh, OK."

Aria just shrugged and said, "Cool, that sounds good."

Even though it was far in the future—five years to a five-year-old is an eternity (and, in fact, Aria doesn't remember us talking about the trip that long ago)—we wanted to plant the seed and get them used to the idea. We also wanted them to feel part of the planning from the start. If we had sprung it on them when they were middle schoolers shortly before leaving, they might have balked. But by building it into our family narrative early, it didn't occur to them that we'd ever do anything else. A year abroad? Sure. That's just what our crazy family will do.

Over the next few years, occasionally, and usually completely out of the blue, one of the kids—most of the time, Finn—would ask something like, "When we're on our round-the-world trip, will we go to Antarctica?" (Unlikely.) Or, "On our world trip, can we still talk to friends sometimes?" (Yes.) Or, "Is it time to buy a map and plan our route yet?" (Almost.) Or, "Can I finally get a cell phone like everyone else when we travel?" (Haha, but no.)

They had clearly been processing on their own time and were getting as excited about our adventure as we were.

Then COVID-19 sent us all into lockdown. For a while, it seemed insane to think we'd ever venture outside again, let alone travel to the other side of the world. Also, after a few months of forced homeschooling when schools shut down, I vowed, never again. Finn is a smart kid but can be lazy, dashing off his work as quickly as possible to play video games or whatever else he preferred to do. He got decent if not great grades with little effort, and he and I clashed as I tried to get him to focus on remote schoolwork during the COVID shutdowns. Aria was easier in that respect. A rule follower who tends to apply herself to whatever task is at hand, she was off and running independently with her assignments.

The idea of us continuing to homeschool through that uncertain 2020–2021 academic year if schools stayed shut kept me up at night. Randy and I both worked at demanding, full-time jobs that required long hours. Like many families, we were struggling, and it felt like it would be a nightmare to try to balance it all indefinitely. That July, we made the decision to enroll both kids in a nearby private school, because it had a better chance of continuing in-person classes. It was a fortuitous choice, first for that school year, and later as we geared up to leave on our trip.

Because—slowly, painstakingly—the world emerged from the pandemic, or at least we all learned to live with some level of endemicity in a new normal. We got vaccinated. Then boosted. Mask mandates eased. Travel resumed.

We dipped our toes into flying again in late 2021, backpacking through Spain as a family for two weeks. While we wore masks and planned activities more than we did pre-pandemic, we felt safe and able to experience the culture, beauty, and thrill of exploration again. It made us confident that we would be able to pull off our round-the-world adventure as planned.

In January 2022, six months before our expected departure, we bought a world map, mounted it on a cork board, and put pins in countries we were keen to visit. A pin didn't guarantee we'd go, but it gave a sense of where our collective interests lay. Over dinner, we talked as a family about the countries we were most excited about. Everyone picked their top three, did research, and made a case about why we should travel there.

Finn's top choices were Antarctica (because it's super cool and he wanted to say he'd been to all seven continents); China (he'd been studying Mandarin in school so was keen to further his language skills); and Greece (he was a big fan of the *Percy Jackson* series by Rick Riordan and wanted to study more Greek mythology firsthand).

Aria's three picks were Sri Lanka (she had a classmate whose family is from there and had shown her pictures of elephants. Elephants!); the Netherlands (a friend had moved there, and she wanted to visit her);

and Australia (she hoped to scuba dive on the Great Barrier Reef after getting certified. Also, koalas!).

Randy's wish list included Brazil (he'd been there years earlier on a work trip and was enchanted by Rio); Tanzania (drawn by the mystique of Zanzibar and the opportunity to go on safari); and Japan (fascinated by Japanese culture, he wanted to dig deeper in an extended stay than what's possible on a shorter trip).

And I hoped to visit Morocco (it's always held captive my imagination as a land of magic and spices, deserts and camels); India (friends warned us that it's chaotic, crazy, and we'd likely get a stomach bug, but if you can get over all that, it's a place that will burrow into your soul); and Thailand (a country Randy and I had visited years earlier and to which I wanted to return).

We began sharing our plan with friends and got going on the logistics. We researched COVID restrictions and geopolitical situations in different countries, Googled visa and vaccination requirements, explored health insurance options, and mapped potential itineraries. We told Finn that Antarctica was too expensive, but the rest of our choices were within the realm of possibility.

In February, Randy and I told our bosses that we were leaving, giving ample time for smooth transitions. Having worked for seven years at McKinsey & Company, a global consulting firm, I was eligible for an unpaid, year-long leave of absence, which I gladly took. Randy's tech company was also supportive of our life decision but didn't have as generous of a sabbatical option, so he ended up quitting on good terms.

There was still the thorny question of what to do about the kids' schooling while we were away, though, which loomed large over our heads.

"I'm super excited about our trip," was Finn's common refrain. "I just don't want to drop a grade."

"Me neither," Aria piped up every time this conversation arose.

"OK, so if we worldschool you, you'll need to work hard. It's not going to be a year-long vacation. We'll be tough teachers, and you'll have to listen to us and do what we say to do."

"We will, we promise," they chorused.

It made me nervous to take on a year of teaching without any kind of manual, especially after the debacle of our short stint at homeschooling during the pandemic. But, after researching alternatives, worldschooling seemed like the logical choice for us. Given that we planned to backpack extensively rather than picking a few places for extended stays and, knowing that cell coverage and Wi-Fi might be inconsistent, our best bet seemed to be to construct our own curriculum rather than tap into an online academy or put the kids in local schools.

In March, we broached our idea with the kids' teachers. They were supportive and excited for us. Finn and Aria would learn so much, they assured us, they had no doubt they would successfully bridge the year. They helped us think about our approach to subjects that might not come organically, like geometry and experimental science, and outlined the themes they would cover in literature so we could touch on similar topics in texts of our choosing, relevant to places we'd be traveling. After aligning on a full plan, we formally deferred the kids' enrollment so they could rejoin their classes in the fall of 2023.

It was all starting to come together. With jobs quit and schools deferred, we were locked in. There was no going back. This crazy, wild idea—five years in the making—was happening.

The next few months flew by. Every evening and on the weekends, we worked to check something off our endless list of to-dos. Randy has always been our travel planner. He's a whiz at research, price comparisons, finding budget options or connections no one else wants, and handling logistics. I am our photographer and documentarian, which is nice in the end but a bit useless in the actual making-it-happen department. Still, I tried to do my share in the run-up to our departure, as did the kids, because there were many moving pieces.

We read any books we could find on family and budget travel to get tips (though there weren't that many on family travel and none on worldschooling), renewed the kids' passports, got new credit cards from international banks, reviewed packing lists, bought *Lonely Planet* guidebooks on Kindle, and started honing our itinerary.

Our rough vision was to travel for the first three months to Morocco, France, the Netherlands, then Eastern and Southern Africa. From there, we'd head to the Eastern Mediterranean and Middle East before flying to South America. In 2023, we planned to explore Southeast Asia, India, Nepal, East Asia, and Australia.

We would stay loose and book as little as possible far in advance. We wanted to leave ourselves some flexibility to shift direction based on insights from locals, health and geopolitical situations, and simply how we were feeling. The only thing we knew for sure was that we needed to be back in Colorado by July 21, 2023, since that was when I started work again. Beyond that, Randy booked our first set of flights to Casablanca, the first two nights' Airbnb in Morocco, and our time on safari in east Africa (since that had to be locked in advance). Everything else, we would figure out on the go.

We made several visits to a health clinic to get the shots and vaccinations we needed. To Aria's dismay, there were a lot—yellow fever, Japanese encephalitis, typhoid, meningitis, malaria pills (Malarone), and more. We hired a property manager and rented our house to a couple who had lost their home in a huge Colorado wildfire earlier in the year. They were thrilled to have a furnished home, which reduced how much we needed to pack up. We boxed up our personal belongings, donated lightly used or outgrown items to Goodwill, and stored everything else in the basement.

In the last days before leaving the country, we canceled newspaper and magazine subscriptions, put a hold on the mail, locked down our credit, and shut down utilities. We stocked up on anti-diarrhea medications and electrolyte powders and made sure we had a fully stocked first-aid kit. I shoved extra Ziplock bags into a nook in my backpack, just for good measure, and did a final list check to make sure we hadn't missed anything.

The kids selected notebooks—as a journal for Finn and sketch book for Aria—and stocked their pencil cases with pencils, erasers, pens, rulers, and a protractor. After dithering for weeks about the decision, Aria selected the lucky stuffed animal that would make the trip, her tiny koala, Kaleb. She tucked him carefully in a pouch in her daypack. Finn, deeming himself above such things now, opted to travel stuffie-free.

We were ready. It was time to hit the road.

Randy's mom drove us to the airport on Friday, June 10. We were flying from Denver to Charlotte to New York and finally, at midnight, crossing the Atlantic to Casablanca.

It was an unforgettable feeling to set my out-of-office message that afternoon before shutting my laptop and switching off my work mobile, to gather dust in a secure spot for a year. "I'm out of office on a gap year, returning July 2023."

And so, the adventure began.

DECIDING ON AN EDUCATIONAL MODEL FOR YOUR FAMILY TRIP

When planning a trip with an educational focus, choose an approach that fits your family's objectives, preferences, and needs. Here are some things to keep in mind as you tailor your travel for learning:

Length of the Trip: Short vs. Longer

- *Short*: Focus on concise, impactful learning experiences, like visiting historical sites or participating in local events during brief stays.

- *Longer:* Provides opportunities for a thorough exploration of subjects and cultures. Ideal for immersing yourselves in the local community or undertaking extended projects.

Personalized vs. Online Curricula
- *Personalized:* Allows you to tailor the learning to your children's interests and trip specifics, offering a more engaging experience but one that requires more preparation.
- *Online Curricula* (e.g., through free online academies, learning apps, or virtual courses): Structured and varied, requires less prep but may lack relevance to specific travel destinations and needs reliable internet.

Outsourcing vs. Self-Teaching
- *Outsourcing* (e.g., with local tutors or guides, educational tour companies, study abroad programs, language learning, or worldschooling communities): Offers professional, structured learning but can be more costly.
- *Self-Teaching:* Promotes family bonding and flexibility, tailored to your children's needs but requires confidence in teaching (and plenty of patience).

Choosing the right educational approach depends on your trip's nature and duration, the desired depth of cultural immersion, your children's learning needs, and your preferred level of involvement. Combining different methods can create a rich, educational journey.

I

FIRST-QUARTER WORLDSCHOOLING GOALS
(June–August)

June 11, 2022
Dear Finn and Aria,

We are so excited to begin our round-the-world trip together! We will be traveling this summer to a lot of countries you (and, in some cases, we) have never been to before—Morocco, France, the Netherlands, and parts of eastern and southern Africa. We'll get to experience new cultures, foods, music, and art. It's going to be great!

As we have discussed, this is not a year-long vacation. :-) To continue with your classmates at the end of our travels and "graduate" from eighth and sixth grades, you'll need to focus on your education, even if it looks different from the schooling you have known.

A lot of learning comes from the act of traveling itself. But some will be more formal and focused, and we will work together as a family to make sure we have the right balance and time for you to get everything done. To start, we'll ease into worldschooling so you can have a summer break and get used to the new pace of travel.

These are the goals we have for you for our first three months on the road:

1. *Read the guidebooks for the countries in which we are traveling.* We have downloaded *Lonely Planet* guidebooks to your iPads. These are

packed with information about the places we'll be visiting, ideas for activities, safety tips, and cultural considerations. They have sections about each country's history, people and society, currency, food, language, art, music, and more. We want you to read these to get context about what we see and do in person.

2. *Read the books we have chosen for you by local authors or set in places we're going.* We spent time with your middle school teachers to understand the themes you would have explored in English literature this year. Themes of identity, coming of age, differences, and acceptance were important. Rather than reading the same books as your classmates back home, I (Mom) have found a mix of fiction and nonfiction books set in the countries we'll be visiting or by local authors that explore similar themes. Literature can be a powerful reflection of culture, and seeing the places through the authors' eyes will enhance our own experiences.

Here is our list for the next few months:

- Morocco: Nothing other than *Lonely Planet* guidebook
- France: *Genevieve's War* by Patricia Reilly Giff
- The Netherlands: *Diary of a Young Girl* by Anne Frank
- Tanzania: *Because of Khalid* by Carolyn Armstrong
- South Africa: *Born a Crime* by Trevor Noah (audiobook) and *Cry, The Beloved Country* by Alan Patton (audiobook)
- Namibia / Botswana / Zimbabwe: *Wild Life: Dispatches from a Childhood of Baboons and Button-Downs* by Keena Roberts

3. *Watch relevant films as a family to add context and depth to our experiences and understanding of the geographies we're visiting.* Here is a target list:

- Tanzania: *The Lion King* (yes, the Disney animated movie :-))
- South Africa: *Mandela: Long Walk to Freedom* (a film based on Nelson Mandela's autobiography); *The Power of One* (a drama about a young South African boy's coming of age); *Invictus* (a sports film about events in South Africa before and during the 1995 Rugby World Cup)
- Botswana: *Surviving Paradise: A Family Tale* (a wildlife documentary on the Okavango Delta)

4. *Begin the daily practice of writing in your blog or journal.* We deliberately planned our family adventure for when you are both old enough to remember a lot of the experience, but you won't remember everything. Writing down your impressions as we go will be something you look back on and will be grateful to have. It takes discipline to write on a regular basis and isn't something you're used to. So, for the summer, we simply want you to get into the habit. Write about what you see, hear, smell, and taste. Write about what you love, what you dislike, and what surprises you.

   You can choose your medium (though not social media)—an online blog, a journal, notes on your iPad. Wi-Fi and connectivity may be a challenge, but we can give it a try and modify, if needed.

5. *Write one long-form essay related to the places we're in.* Writing is an important part of life, and I (Mom) want to help you hone your skills. Over the course of our worldschooling year, you'll write a variety of types of assignments. We'll start with nonfiction. I'll assign different topics for each of you, and you'll have two weeks to complete your essay, including researching, outlining, rough draft, and final draft.

6. *Learn the basics of the languages in the places we'll be in.* American tourists have a terrible reputation for not bothering to learn any words in different languages when traveling abroad. That's not going to be us. We're lucky because English is a common denominator in much of the world, but you'll be amazed at how much richer an experience it is when we're able to converse with people in their language, even if only with a few words. So, in each country we visit, we'll learn *please*, *thank you*, *how are you*, *good*, and *delicious*. Even a few words go a long way.

   Here are languages we'll encounter this quarter:

   - Morocco: Arabic
   - France: French
   - The Netherlands: Dutch
   - Zanzibar / Tanzania: Swahili

7. *Be fully present in the experiences we are having.* A huge part of worldschooling will happen organically as we learn through our experiences about science, history, geography, culture, language, arts, and

music. You will gain practical life skills while navigating new places and interacting with new people. Take it all in with a sense of wonder and curiosity. Ask lots of questions. Try new foods with an open mind. This will be a year of new experiences for us all. Embrace the journey.

Let's have an awesome summer!
Love,
Your worldschooling teachers (Mom and Dad)

3

IN SEARCH OF MAGIC

Morocco

Excerpt from Finn's Journal
June 12, 2022 | Casablanca, Morocco

Today, we fly from Denver to Charlotte to New York, then catch one last plane to Casablanca, Morocco. We're on our way!! It is exciting being able to go on this world trip, and I think it's going to be a big adventure. I can't wait to get fully immersed in it. But I also feel a little sad and nervous to be leaving behind everything and everyone I know. Dad says it's normal to feel that way and that pushing our comfort zones is part of the experience. It's such a dad thing to say.

IN SEARCH OF MAGIC: MOROCCO

Within minutes of arriving at the crowded medina in Casablanca, a vendor beckoned us to his stand, calling, "My friends, come, let me show you magic."

He picked up an intricately carved cedar-wood box, then flexed his fingers with a flourish, like a magician. "Ali Baba boxes," he said, then leaned in closer, whispering, "They hold secrets."

He showed us a series of plank shifts that uncovered a hidden key, then another set of maneuvers to reveal the keyhole. We watched intently, trying to remember the combination. At thirteen, Finn loved puzzles. With the skill of a practiced Rubik's-cube aficionado, he leaped in to try to replicate the movements but needed a few more demonstrations before mastering the technique.

The vendor then motioned to our ten-year-old daughter, Aria, and me and showed us another, smaller box. We jumped at the secret hidden inside—a wooden snake that leaped out when he opened the lid. I was glad for the din of the medina, so no one heard my yelp.

Finn would have bought several Ali Baba boxes as souvenirs, but we reminded him we were on day one of our year-long adventure, so adding wooden chests to his backpack wasn't the best idea.

We arrived in Casablanca the night before after a twenty-hour transatlantic journey. When we first started mapping our route, we had gotten good, practical advice to start with someplace culturally similar to our own to ease the transition. In the end, though, we decided what the hell, threw logic to the wind, and booked flights to Morocco as our first stop.

It was number one on my wish list of travel destinations, holding a romantic allure as a fabled land of magic, mystery, and spices. It's a land of mint tea and camels, snake charmers and carpet vendors, crowded souqs and ancient, labyrinthine medinas. A place where the cultures of Europe, Africa, and Arabia collide.

But an easy port of entry for our family trip, it was not.

We were keeping our first couple of weeks light on the formal worldschooling front, knowing there would be a period of adjustment—and that a huge part of worldschooling would come naturally through the experiences themselves. The main expectations we had were for Finn and Aria to read the travel guide, focusing on the history and culture sections, and to start their daily journal writing. Beyond that, we simply wanted them to enjoy the start of our journey.

Part of that entailed getting over jet lag, and that was easier said than done. Despite our best efforts to get onto local time, when Randy's alarm went off at 9:30 a.m. on our first morning, we ignored it. When we finally roused, it was afternoon.

After showering, we headed out. Our immediate priorities were lunch and finding an ATM. We headed to the mall. Locals in a mix of traditional dress and headscarves, T-shirts and jeans waited in line at a McDonald's. We scoffed at the idea of eating at a fast-food chain but quickly changed our tune when we realized our credit cards didn't work in most of the food court, and we still hadn't found a functioning cash machine. Swallowing our pride, we approached the counter at Burger King, ordered chicken fingers and burgers, and vowed never to speak of it again.

Sustenance secured, we found an ATM near the exit and stocked up on dirham, Morocco's currency, then turned onto the main boulevard to walk toward the city center. Casablanca, a port city in western Morocco, is a stark juxtaposition of beautiful French-colonial architecture, which probably once stood grand and stately, and dilapidation and disrepair. Paint peeled off walls tagged with graffiti. The stale stench of trash, strewn in piles on the street, rose in the stagnant air of the heat wave we landed in, temperatures topping 102 degrees. Scrawny cats loitered on stoops, mewing mournfully and scavenging for scraps.

"Aw, look at the little guy," Aria cooed, bending toward a kitten, then recoiling. "Ugh, what is wrong with it? The poor thing has bugs crawling all over it."

"Yeah, it's probably best to avoid petting animals on the road," Randy told her.

Both kids gave the cat a wide berth and sad looks as we kept walking.

Nearing the city center, the smell of the fish market hit us before we entered it. Shelves rose to the rafters, packed with fresh catches—sole, eel, shrimp, tuna, and tiny live turtles, which lumbered around their crates. Touts crowded close, inviting us to eat at their stand, each claiming the title of Best in Casablanca. We shook our heads and kept going.

Aria grabbed my hand as we walked, scooting closer to me. Finn attached himself to Randy like a sidecar and rolled alongside him as we dodged the touts.

"Everyone keeps staring at us," Finn said quietly.

"Well, they're all hoping we'll visit their stalls and buy something," I answered.

"Do they always come so close?" asked Aria, hopping aside for the umpteenth time to avoid being run over by a motorbike, which had zoomed around a blind corner.

"Seems like it. Wow, every time I think a motorbike can't possibly go through that little opening with all these people in the alley, they do, at full speed," said Randy, as we wound our way through the medina.

"You'll be fine, guys," I told the kids. "Most people are just being friendly. I'm more worried about motorbikes. Just be aware of what's around you and keep on your toes."

The fish market soon gave way to a warren of tightly packed stalls with all manner of wares. Gold-lamé bound books piled high next to tables covered with beaded necklaces and bracelets, vibrant slipper stands, and pungent spices piled in tall, colorful towers. We craned our necks to try to take in everything at once.

We were admiring a particularly impressive display of rosebuds in woven baskets when a tall Black man with a wide, easy smile fell astride beside us.

"My friends, where you are from?"

"The United States," Randy replied.

"Ah, good, good. A very nice country. You need to come with me. I will take you to the best market in Casablanca. This is the tourist one," he said, flicking his wrist disdainfully as if to say this was no good, no good at all. "I will show you where the best bargains are found. Come."

Randy and I glanced at each other and shrugged. Having nothing better to do, we followed him, staying on the alert for a scam or any danger. He led us through the maze of stalls and into one of the houses in an open square.

"Is this safe?" Aria hissed at me as we climbed two flights of stairs behind the man.

"I think so, honey. There were a lot of people outside and this all seems OK," I said but was starting to have doubts about how good of a plan this was myself. I took stock of the exits, just in case.

On the second story, we entered a room filled to the ceiling with carpets. Here, our smiling friend left us with an older man called Hamid, who motioned for us to sit on the cushioned benches along the wall. He insisted we stay for mint tea.

"My friends, you are lucky. We are here only today from cities in the north. Other carpet vendors cheat you. But our carpets are made of the best wool and silk. Last for generations."

He unrolled a gorgeous scarlet rug. Then a blue runner. Then a soft carpet spanning the length of the room. He told me to take off my shoes and walk on it. (It was very soft, I conceded.) Hamid kept bringing down rugs, laying them flat atop one another, trying to guess our preference. A long one? Maybe a red one? Or perhaps a durable rug that's cat friendly?

"There are forty million people in Morocco and seventy million cats," Hamid informed us. "We like cats very much. I have twenty at home. This carpet is strong. It holds up well for the cats. Do you have cats?"

The kids nodded, eyes shining. Hamid had them at cat. They were mesmerized by him and his factoids.

His assistant arrived soon thereafter with our tea in a gleaming silver pot. We watched as he added sprigs of fresh mint and two sticks of sugar to the boiling water. He poured long, slow streams from high in the air into thin glasses before tipping the tea back into the pot, mixing it thoroughly before the final pour.

"Do you think it's poisoned?" Finn whispered under his breath.

"What? No, of course not, honey. This is a common ritual in Morocco. In fact, Dad and I experienced a very similar thing years ago in Egypt. It's all good," I promised him.

After being reassured that the tea wasn't going to kill us, Finn took a sip and sank back into the cushions. He declared softly with a smile, "This is such a cool experience."

As we drank our tea, Hamid tried to get us to name our price for one or more of the rugs. We politely but insistently declined, and once he understood that bargaining was not going to happen, he abruptly left the room, grumbling about us giving up the best deals. We gathered our things and left, finding him outside, all smiles again. He took a deep drag on a cigarette, then motioned us to his friend's apothecary shop next door, another place of unparalleled bargains. This time, we held our ground, saying we needed to be on our way, and resumed our walk toward the Hassan II Mosque.

I exchanged smiles with Randy as we listened to the kids chatter to one another about how fantastic it must be to be a cat in Hamid's home and how they wanted to try pouring tea like the locals do, from high in the air, getting it to tinkle without a spill into glasses on the table.

LOST AND FOUND: FAMILY STRATEGIES FOR STAYING CONNECTED IN UNFAMILIAR PLACES

When exploring new places as a family, it's helpful to be prepared for the unexpected, including getting separated. Here are some strategies to ensure safety and peace of mind:

- *Pre-Trip Discussion*: Talk about regrouping strategies in case someone gets lost or separated, particularly in crowded, non-English-speaking cities.
- *Contact Information*: Make sure kids carry a card with your accommodation's address.
- *Regrouping Strategy*: Set up a city-specific plan, like staying put for ten minutes, returning to the last known location, or heading to a familiar landmark.
- *Stay Calm*: Teach and role-play with your kids about staying calm and what to do if they're alone (we used to practice getting lost in a mall in the United States).
- *Seeking Help*: Advise on who to approach for help, such as a police officer, a mother with children, or a store or restaurant owner.
- *Phone Use*: Show your kids how to dial your number from a different country's phone.

Additional Points:
- Create a distinctive meeting point in each new city.
- Consider wearable GPS trackers for younger children.
- Practice key phrases in the local language for asking for help.
- Keep a recent photo of each child on your phone for identification.

The following day, we took the train south from Casablanca to Marrakesh, crammed into a sweltering compartment with five other people.

Navigating the tight, bustling streets on foot upon arrival, we found ourselves squeezing against the sunbaked, pink earthen walls to avoid the motorbikes that whizzed past. Aria, narrowly missing being clipped a few times, remarked with a hint of disappointment, "Oh, so that wasn't just a Casablanca thing."

Crossing the threshold of our riad was like stepping into an oasis. The stifling heat was replaced by a cool, open-air courtyard. A small plunge pool sat at the center, surrounded by cushioned benches and a low table. Our hosts greeted us with mint tea as we checked in. After unpacking, we grabbed seats in the shade on the roof deck, listening to the street sounds of Marrakesh from above.

"Why don't you use this time to write in your journals or read more about Marrakesh in the *Lonely Planet* guide?" I suggested to Finn and Aria, who were lounging.

"Can we do it later?" they asked.

I agreed, then settled back to watch them dart about the riad with their iPads, excitedly giving their friends in the States a virtual tour.

Before we headed out for the night, I handed each kid a slip of paper with the riad's address, a safety precaution in case we got separated. We had discussed what to do in a scenario like that—how to dial our cell numbers from abroad, approach strangers for help in a non-English-speaking country, and tactics for borrowing a phone, since they didn't have their own.

Finn looked affronted. "Mom, we don't need a cheat sheet."

"Just humor me," I said, tucking the paper into his pocket. "It's important that you know where home base is and how to find your way back since we'll be moving around quite a bit."

For dinner that night, we walked to a tiny restaurant near the medina, with just four low tables and no menu. We were served a family-style platter of chicken tagine over couscous by a woman from her tiny kitchen. With no individual plates, we all leaned over the huge dish, laughing as our forks clanged together.

"This tastes like sawdust," Aria announced, poking the couscous suspiciously.

"Huh," Randy said. "You've had couscous before."

"This is different," she said.

"Well, it's what's for dinner. It's delicious."

Never a big eater anyway, Aria picked her way through the tagine and, in the end, gave it a rave review, for her anyway.

"It was better than sawdust," she conceded.

From the restaurant, we strolled to check out the souqs, or shops, in the medina. A man in his early twenties caught our attention, inviting us to smell the spices in his stall, piled high into vibrant pyramids. Hamza was his name, he said. He had a huge smile, and he made the kids laugh with his easy manner.

We held out our arms as Hamza rubbed bars of amber, jasmine, and sandalwood on our wrists, telling us to breathe in deeply. He showed us the differences in varieties of Argan oil and let us sniff the fresh spices compared to the pre-ground towers, which were far less aromatic.

"Watch," he said, putting black cumin, rosemary, and lavender into a thin cloth and holding it tight to our nostrils. "This will clear your airways and cure you of snoring."

"Dad could use that!" Finn joked.

We took turns smelling and being knocked back by the strength of the concoction, laughing at everyone's reaction after inhaling, like sniffing a massive dose of Vick's VapoRub.

The kids would have, yet again, bought much of what we sampled but settled on using their allowance money to buy a tiny bar of honey soap (Finn) and an amber rock (Aria) to perfume her clothes.

"Hamza was super nice," Finn said, turning to leave.

"Can we come back tomorrow?" chirped Aria, grabbing my hand as we leaped aside in tandem to avoid a motorbike.

"We'll see," said Randy, and we walked back to our riad in the warm Moroccan night.

On Tuesday, we took a guided tour of Marrakesh with a local man, Aziz. We had met him the day before at the train station upon arriving from Casablanca and arranged for him to show us around. Our day began at the Jardin Majorelle, a lush botanical garden once owned by fashion designer Yves Saint-Laurent. Next, we visited the Saadian tombs, a historic royal necropolis, impressive with its Italian marble, intricate gold detailing, and delicate plasterwork.

Our final stop was a traditional leather tannery on Rue de Bab Debbagh. As we approached, Aziz handed us sprigs of mint, jokingly calling them "Berber gas masks," which he insisted would combat the tannery's acrid smell.

"Ugh, this barely helps," Finn complained, pressing the mint against his nose.

Aria coughed. "It's so strong! How can people work here all day?"

Randy, already discarding his mint, said, "You'd be surprised how quickly you adapt."

Aziz led us along dirt paths, past stray sheep, cats, dogs, chickens, rusted bicycles and machinery parts, and weathered wooden shacks. A local tradesman took over, guiding us through the tanning process. We watched in fascination as hides from various animals were stripped, soaked in vats of pigeon excrement (explaining the smell), and then dyed in large stone wells. At the end of the tour, we were shown the finished products—soft suede and leather items in a vast showroom.

"That's amazing, how it goes from that," Aria said, nodding to the operation outside, "to this. It almost makes you forget the time it spent in pigeon poop." She was trying on a soft, red leather jacket and trying to justify why it made sense to add it to her backpack.

After prying her away leather-free, we mentioned to Aziz our interest in visiting the Sahara. He took us to a tour agency, where we arranged a multiday trip, set to start in a couple of days. With that secured, Aziz returned us to our riad.

After sundown, we walked to Jemaa el-Fna, Marrakesh's vibrant main square, which comes alive in the evenings. It was a sensory overload: the aroma of grilled meats, the loud cries of touts, the whirl of colors and music, the energy of dozens of dancers, acrobats, comedians, and fortune tellers all vying for attention.

Even through the din, we heard the low hum of a *pungi* flute. "Come look at the cobra, my friends. See the magic!" the snake charmer called. He gestured us over with great theatricality then resumed playing his flute. The cobra at his feet, however, seemed wholly uninterested in his antics, only stirring when the man prodded him with a baseball cap.

Later, at a café high above the square, we discussed the ethics of practices like snake charming and exploiting monkeys for entertainment.

"It's sad to think about," Aria said, clearly troubled.

"We'll see monkeys in the wild later on our trip anyway, right?" Finn asked.

"Definitely," said Randy.

"I'm really happy to be traveling," Finn said. "This is awesome."

As night fell, a full moon rose above Marrakesh, round, bright, and beautiful. Light cigarette smoke wafted on the breeze, which Aria wrinkled her nose at. We sat together on the deck and took in the sounds of the square unfolding far below us.

A couple of days later, we met our new guide for the next leg of our journey. A Berber nomad with seven brothers and sisters, Ayoub introduced himself saying, "I am happy to take you to my home in the Sahara. Brother, sister, there, in the desert, you will see real magic."

Our trip would take us eastward over the High Atlas Mountains, to the ancient *ksar*, or fortified tribal village, of Ait-Ben-Haddou with its red clay brick structures dating to the seventeenth century, down into the Dades Gorge, and, finally, on to the Sahara. We quickly left behind the crowded streets of the city for vast, open flatlands. We passed lemon, olive, and date groves, then summited the high pass of Col Du Tichka before descending to the eastern plains. Dry hillsides dotted with scrub brush stretched before us. We snaked beside a river lined with cherry trees and Berber villages. Ayoub pulled over at a roadside stand, bringing us a bunch of cherries, which burst in our mouths, fresh and sweet.

"This is so good, Ayoub, thank you," Finn said.

"You are welcome, little brother," Ayoub replied. "We are family now. Anything you want, you ask me."

After a twelve-hour day, we stopped at the *Dar Ahlam* hotel along the Dades river, tucked into the gorge of the same name. We had dinner on the deck and chatted into the night with one of the owners. He told us *Dar Ahlam* means House of Dreams, and later, as we drifted to sleep, we thought it seemed perfectly fitting.

CHAPTER 3

Early the next morning, we met Ayoub to continue toward the town of Merzouga, a gateway to the Sahara Desert on the eastern edge of Morocco. Temperatures were scorching. We had known it would be hot in Morocco in June, but we arrived in a heat wave; it topped 106 degrees that day, a dry, unforgiving heat. Locals in flowing dress and head wraps avoided the streets at midday when the sun was highest. Everyone emerged at dusk when it was less violently hot.

"I want to invite you to visit my family before we arrive at the Sahara," Ayoub said. While he grew up a nomad, Ayoub told us his family had settled years earlier in the oasis town of Erfoud. "My sister will do henna on your hands," he offered. "Would you like this?"

"We'd love to," we replied instantly.

At Erfoud, we followed him inside a white building into a large open room covered in red carpet. Plush red cushions lined the walls. A low, round table with a lace tablecloth sat in the middle, the only piece of furniture.

We left our shoes at the door and sat cross-legged on the floor. Ayoub's mother came out to greet us, followed by his sister and sister-in-law carrying a baby, ten months old. None of them spoke English, so Ayoub translated. Another sister soon followed with a huge plate of freshly baked bread, olive oil, and peanuts.

Ayoub's sister brought her henna dye and needles and motioned for Aria to extend her hand over the pillow she placed on her lap. Her head scarf blocked her face to us as she bent low, drawing intricate swirls along the back of Aria's hand and palms.

"It's beautiful," Aria said, then thanked her using the Arabic we had learned. "*Shukran*."

"That's so detailed," Finn said, coming over to look. "Is it going to stay green?"

Ayoub explained that the dye would darken as it dried and oxidized, deepening from olive green to orange and eventually to a terra-cotta hue.

"Ah, that makes sense," I nodded, while she repeated the process for me.

We visited with Ayoub's family while our henna dried. Given the language barrier, it was quiet but not uncomfortable. There was a sense of comfort and warmth that needed no words. Finn and Aria had fun playing with the baby, who kept crawling across the carpet, trying to yank the lace tablecloth. They giggled every time his mother pulled him back, only to watch him beeline forward again, mesmerized by the tantalizing cloth.

"Ayoub, that was great, thank you," Randy said after we said our goodbyes.

"Yes, that was so special," I added.

Ayoub shook his head. "You are family now. It makes me happy we could visit together. Brother, sister, come, let's go now to the desert."

Brown plains gave way to a rust-colored hue as we approached the Sahara. To our excitement, we soon spotted a caravan of camels on the side of the road.

"They are actually dromedaries, not camels," Ayoub clarified. "Camels have two humps; dromedaries have one. In Morocco, we don't have camels, but there isn't a word in Arabic for dromedary, so we just call them all camels."

"Oh, yeah, I remember that from a Dr. Seuss book, *Why, oh why, are deserts dry?*" exclaimed Finn. "Opa gave us that book, remember?"

"Mmm," Aria replied, noncommittally, her eyes still glued to the animals.

Shortly before sunset, we arrived in Merzouga, just thirty miles from the Algerian border. The Sahara spread out before us, soft and reddish in the late afternoon sun. It was as breathtaking as we had imagined, and even more beautiful, raw, and vast.

Our dromedaries were waiting for us, three dun colored and one creamy white. We decided to name our steeds: Dobby for me, Harry Potter for Aria, Marvin for Randy. Finn, who kept changing his mind, first dubbed his ride Camel, then Melvin, and finally settled on Mario.

We mounted Dobby, Harry, Marvin, and Mario and set off with a guide into the desert. Ayoub was driving the van and dropping off our packs at the tent camp where we'd stay for the night, and we'd see him the following day. We hadn't been sure how comfortable it would be to ride the dromedaries but quickly adjusted, the uphills less daunting than the steep downhills.

Close to camp, after an hour's ride, our guide stopped and let us dismount to climb the dunes on foot and enjoy the sunset at our leisure. We gladly took him up on the offer after clumsily figuring out how to get off our ride. (Have you ever dismounted a dromedary? It's nerve racking as you brace yourself, leaning back, while they lurch down in front then abruptly plunk down their backside.)

Once down, we set off across the dunes, reveling in the feel of the silky sand against our bare feet. The kids thrilled at running downhill, slip sliding with each step. Randy and I walked, hand in hand, in awe by the immensity of it all. From the ridgeline, we sat to watch the sun set across the desert, which stretched as far as we could see in all directions. The shifting sands were spectacular, shades morphing with the changing of the day, amber to ocher to dusty rose.

We stayed at a desert camp that night, glamping in a tent made for four. Our Berber hosts served us a traditional dinner including Moroccan salad, tagine, an eggplant and parmesan side dish, followed by fresh fruit. After dinner, they played Berber music on drums outside under the stars, inviting us to dance and join in, which we eagerly did. The music and our laughter filled the night.

"It's so nice and cool out here," I said as we started to walk back to our tent, which I knew would be sweltering. "Can we sleep outdoors on the sand?"

"You can," said one of our hosts tentatively. "I wouldn't, though. Scorpions come out at night."

"Ah," I replied quickly. "Right then. No scorpions for us. Do you think we're safe to just lie out for a bit under the stars?"

"Yes, that should be fine. Sleep well."

Before retiring to our tent, we hiked to the top of the nearest dune and spread out on the sand to look at the stars and spin stories about the Milky Way. Finn and Aria both took turns inventing tales about the constellations. Finn's was a particularly sweet and intricate story about a girl who made a wish to change the sky. She traveled far to find an old man who had long ago become the granter of happiness. He created a bridge to the sky, knowing it would make the girl happy, and welcomed her to ask her wish. Immortal, he granted it, and, in so doing, she became part of the heavens, a new constellation, forever.

For our normally taciturn teen, it was a deeply moving story, which I didn't want to end. It was incomparably special to lie together in the dark night, spotting falling stars and feeling like the only people in the world.

Shortly before dawn, we rose to climb the dunes again, now cool and pillowy soft under foot. The sun rose over the far hills, tinting the sky rose gold. Awed by the true magic of Morocco, I lightly traced my henna tattoo, now terra-cotta against my hand, and buried my toes in the sand. I thought about the countless footsteps left over years only to be wiped away each night by the desert breezes in an endless dance that stretched to the horizon.

ALMOND FAMILY REPORT CARD ON MOROCCO

- *Top Marks*: Don't miss riding dromedaries at sunset into the Sahara and staying overnight in a desert camp—a true highlight.
- *Needs Work*: Ensure your credit cards are compatible with the local system and carry some local currency. This helps avoid the scramble for cash and unexpected fast-food stops.
- *Learning Tips*: Fully engage with every aspect of Morocco as part of the educational journey. From navigating medinas to exploring local crafts, Morocco provides immersive and enlightening experiences that are both fun and educational.

4

PARLEZ-VOUS JOURNALING?

France

Excerpt from Aria's Journal
June 27, 2022 | Paris, France

It's our last day in Paris, and we visit a crepe place for breakfast that our friend told us about. I order a crepe with Nutella. I can get used to Parisian food! Tonight, we're visiting the Eiffel Tower. I'm looking forward to that because it's something you hear so much about. But I am scared of heights, and Finn wants to climb to the top, so we'll see how that goes.

CHAPTER 4

It was after 3 a.m. when Aria padded into our bedroom, her panda bear sleep mask askew atop her tousled hair.

"Finn is vomiting in the bathroom," she whispered. "It's loud and gross. Can I sleep with you?"

We groggily tried to get our bearings. It was our first night at an Airbnb in Provence, southern France, and we were all exhausted from a long travel day. Half-asleep, I shuffled to the bathroom to check on Finn.

"Are you OK, buddy?" I asked through the door.

He vomited in reply. It was going to be a long night.

We expected that there would be stomach bugs, illnesses, cuts, and bruises on a year-long trip. We just didn't think it would happen so quickly. We'd been gone a little over a week. From the heat of Morocco, we'd flown to Marseilles, then rented a tiny black Citroen to drive through lush countryside to Haute Provence, which was eighty degrees Fahrenheit (twenty-seven degrees Celsius) and felt like heaven. Our Airbnb was tucked off a dirt road outside the quaint town of Greoux Les Bains.

Jean-Marc, the owner, came to greet us and give us a tour. I strained to resurrect my high school French and instantly wished I'd brushed up more.

"*Parlez-vous français?*" he asked brightly.

"*Oui, un peu,*" I said confidently, then realized I had exhausted my ready vocabulary.

"We need to add Duolingo lessons to our worldschooling, stat," I grumbled under my breath as Jean-Marc chattered away happily, and I tried to look like I understood.

"How many times did I suggest you take refresher French before we left?" Randy teased.

"Shush, I'm trying to focus," I said, turning my attention to our host.

His English was nonexistent, but, with exuberant hand signaling and a wild mixing of Romance languages, we managed just fine. He was thrilled to have us stay at his country cottage, giving us a chilled bottle of rosé and a jar of local lavender honey as welcome gifts.

He showed us a lazy river winding through the property. Two plastic chairs and a table were set up along the banks—a perfect spot for a glass of wine, he told us with a wink. There was a pool, lounge chairs, and hammock next to a koi pond. Randy and I looked at each other and smiled. "That'll do, pig, that'll do." Randy said, quoting his favorite movie, *Babe*.

After swimming and downtime, with me futilely trying to coax the kids to do their journaling, we drove at dusk across winding roads flanked by fields of lavender. We wandered through the fields, breathing in the delicate, sweet floral scent. Then we were awoken a few hours later by Aria reporting that her brother was throwing up.

We took it easy the following day. It was raining, and after the heat and bustle of Morocco, it felt nice to snuggle up in the cozy cottage. We listened to the raindrops on the roof, while Aria started reading her worldschooling book, *Genevieve's War*, and wrote in her blog.

We had let the kids decide what medium they wanted to use to chronicle the trip. Aria had chosen to create an online blog. Finn preferred to keep it old-school, writing journal entries in a spiral-bound notebook, into which he also planned to paste souvenirs and receipts. We were already running into connectivity issues for Aria's blog, though. While we had intermittent access to Wi-Fi, the signal across Morocco was weak, and it wasn't much better in rural France. She was struggling to take notes off-line then transfer them into posts. She vowed to stick with her plan for one more week and see if it got better; if not, she would switch to paper and pencil as well and started eyeing cute journals with lavender covers, just in case.

While Aria typed on her iPad, Finn alternated between cat naps and bathroom runs. He finally appeared in the early afternoon, bedraggled but feeling better. He kept down a slice of baguette and agreed to a drive to get fresh air.

We wound through the lavender fields, the unsettled sky and dark clouds a striking contrast against the deep purple blooms. I could have spent hours in the fields or visiting the hillside villages, sniffing bundles of dried lavender tied with twine, sampling local honey, and checking out quilted tablecloths I could never carry in my pack. Not long after we began wandering the cobblestone streets, though, Finn announced, a little too loudly, "I need a bathroom. Now!"

We began speed walking on a manic hunt for toilettes. Finn found one at a restaurant, and we waited outside until he finished, then called it a day. Thankfully, it was only a twenty-four-hour bug, and by the next morning, he felt up to exploring.

We headed to the Gorges du Verdon, a river canyon in southeastern France. It was raining, but since our plan was to kayak through the gorge, it wasn't a deal breaker. Finn and I partnered up in one kayak while Randy and Aria hopped into another.

"Can you guys paddle in sync this time?" Aria needled us, reminding us that the last time we paired up, Finn and I had been wildly spastic in our movements.

"Psh, we were born to paddle in sync," we replied and took off, daring them to catch us.

When Randy and Aria were out of earshot, I turned to Finn.

"Seriously, Finn we do need to paddle more in unison than last time. Why don't you take the lead, and I'll follow?"

"OK, keep up," he replied.

We set off toward the gorge, finding a good rhythm buoyed by the current and wind at our backs. Tall limestone cliffs rose out of the turquoise waters. Rock climbers scaled the canyon walls, making their way along the crags. Sunshine peeked through the clouds, then disappeared again under a curtain of rain.

The water was low because of lighter-than-usual snows, so we couldn't make it all the way up the gorge. When our paddles grazed the bottom, we turned and started back upstream. Paddling against the current was much more challenging than our ride into the gorge.

A brisk afternoon wind whipped at our faces and droplets of rain hammered us as the skies darkened. The current bore us backward, and we strained against it, working hard. White caps formed on little waves that rose out of nowhere, so different from the placid water from hours earlier. We summoned all our energy to paddle in sync, but we weren't making progress.

After realizing it was fruitless, we pulled up onto shore, a short walk from the boat house. As we started to carry our kayaks along the rocky beach, a couple of guys from the shop ran over to help us. "*Merci*," we called, then scurried to our car to change and get warm again.

By early afternoon, the wind died down and the skies cleared. We drove to another spot along the lake and laid out a picnic on the thin ribbon of pebble-strewn beach. Randy opened a bottle of burgundy, and we sipped wine from plastic cups. He tore off pieces of baguette for each of us, which we topped with cheese and local salami.

Finn grabbed a pebble and skipped it across the lake.

"Seven skips," he called. "Beat that!"

"You're on," retorted Aria, never one to let a challenge go. She hopped up to find an acceptable stone, then gave it a hard throw. It landed with a loud kerplunk as Finn guffawed.

"Let me show you how it's done," said Randy, hiding a smile. He got up to show her how to side arm the pebble across the surface. "Eight skips! A new record."

I got up to join in, and we spent a lazy afternoon drinking wine, skipping stones, and enjoying the newfound rhythm of slower travel.

TRAVEL JOURNALING FOR KIDS: A PARENT'S GUIDE

Journaling is not just a way to record memories; it's a skill that, when nurtured, can provide a lifelong means of expression and reflection. However, it often requires guidance to create meaningful entries. Here are some tips and prompts that we found helpful:

- *Encourage Regular Entries*: Set aside time each day for journaling, such as during a quiet evening or at a cafe. Consistency helps in forming a habit.
- *Provide a Special Journal*: Let your kid choose a special notebook or start a blog for their travels. This makes the act of journaling feel more significant and exciting.
- *Have It Double as a Scrapbook*: Encourage them to paste tickets, postcards, or photos into their journal, or to sketch in it. These tangible memories add depth to their entries.
- *Start with Simple Prompts*:
  - What was the most interesting thing you saw today?
  - Describe the tastiest food you tried.
  - What new words have you learned on this trip?
  - Draw a picture of a place or object that fascinated you today.

- *Encourage Descriptive Writing*: Teach them to describe not just what they see but also what they hear, smell, and feel. This makes their writing more immersive.
- *Share Your Own Experiences*: Sometimes, journaling together and sharing entries can inspire them. It shows that you value journaling too.
- *Ask Open-Ended Questions*: Encourage them to think deeper about their experiences. Questions like, "How did today's experiences make you feel?," "What did you learn?," or "What was different about today compared to home?" can provoke thoughtful responses.
- *Have Fun with It*: Remind them that their journal is a personal space for creativity. There's no right or wrong way to journal.

A few days later, we drove to Avignon to catch the TGV train to Paris. For two kids raised in suburban Colorado, Paris was Finn and Aria's first meaningful experience in a large city, and they were excited to take it all in. Randy had booked us an Airbnb apartment in the second *arrondissement*, on the Right Bank of the Seine. We took the metro to the Strasbourg Saint Denis stop and then walked to our third floor apartment. Before heading to dinner, we unpacked in the closet-sized apartment as best we could, which meant laying a few things in a corner on top of our packs, since shelf space was nonexistent.

The next morning, we took a family-oriented cruise along the Seine. The kids squealed as we passed the Eiffel Tower and Notre Dame Cathedral, its Gothic architecture still visible through scaffolding as rebuilding continued following a deadly fire in 2019. The guide pointed out the Musée d'Orsay, explaining its transformation from a railway station to a museum, and kept the kids engaged with tales of revolutions and artistic movements. It was an ideal blend of sightseeing and education, kickstarting our immersion into Paris's culture and history.

In the afternoon, we walked to the Bois de Boulogne, a public park just outside the city. About two-and-a-half times the size of New York City's Central Park, it has botanical gardens, a zoo, lakes with row boats and canoes, and miles of well-tended dirt paths.

"Ooh, let's rent bicycles for the afternoon," Finn suggested, eyeing a stand of bikes.

"One step ahead of you," Randy said. He had already downloaded the Velib app.

"We don't have helmets, though," Aria pointed out. She cast deeply unimpressed looks at the helmet-less children zooming past, as though they had just robbed a bank and were making a quick getaway.

"Part of embracing new cultures is doing as the locals do," I told her. "Do you know the expression, 'When in Rome . . .'"?

"Yes," she said. "Do as the Romans do. I know. But, what if I fall?"

"Don't fall, and you'll be fine," Randy said. "Let's ride!"

We spent the afternoon peddling around the park. Tentative at first, Aria quickly gained confidence and eased into the experience.

"I still don't want to bike on the street without a helmet," she announced. "But that was fun!"

In the metro station, we showed the kids where we were on the map and had them purchase tickets for us to get back to our stop.

"You remember the address?" I asked.

"Yes, Mom," they replied, rolling their eyes at my "in-case-of-separation" check.

"OK, good. Just making sure."

Randy woke multiple times that night, felled by the same stomach bug Finn had earlier. Still weak the next morning, he decided to stay in, at least for the morning.

Our plan was to see the Arc de Triomphe then have tea and macarons at Ladurée Maison. With our usual chief navigator down for the count, it was the perfect opportunity for a practical worldschooling lesson.

"All right, Finn. You're in charge of getting us around Paris today. Since Dad is out of commission, Aria and I will look to you to figure out the way, buy metro tickets, check what stops we need to make, and how to walk there when we get off."

"Cool," he shouted, already charging out the door. "Bye, Dad, feel better!"

Finn shares Randy's ease with geospatial relations, plus he is keenly observant. I was sure that this wouldn't be an insurmountable challenge for him, but it also wouldn't be easy. It would be his first time navigating a big city by himself. Unfortunately for Aria, she inherited my nonexistent sense of direction; I wasn't going to be of much help to Finn.

We stopped in front of the metro map, and Finn swiftly mapped out our route.

"We'll start on the M4 then transfer to the M1," he declared. "Then, it's a short walk down the *Champs Elysees* to Ladurée."

"Great; that looks good to me. It's pronounced 'shonz uh lee zay,' though, buddy."

"Ah, I did not know that," he said. "It is totally not spelled that way."

"French can be a tough language," I replied. "All right, *après vous*, as they say."

He strode down into the metro and, using my credit card, bought a package of ten tickets. He then whisked us all around the city without a hitch.

"I told you, Mom, it was simple," Finn said later, waving off my praise.

"Still, well done. It's impressive to be able to navigate a foreign city on your own. I'm quite sure I wouldn't have done it as well."

I gave him a hug, surprised to notice that I was nose to nose with him now.

"Did you grow more?" I asked, accusingly.

He smiled smugly. "Maybe. I might start calling you 'shorty,' Mom." He patted me on the head as we crossed to take in the Arc de Triomphe with hundreds of other tourists.

At Ladurée, an iconic Parisian restaurant and dessert bar decorated with marble and intricate floral patterns, Finn, Aria, and I had fun pretending to be posh. We tried exotic-sounding macarons, like lavender, orange blossom, and our favorite, Marie Antoinette tea. Randy, feeling better, joined us shortly thereafter. He and Finn decided to spend the afternoon wandering on their own while Aria and I went to the Louvre, which she was keen to visit.

Of all the exhibits in the museum, Aria was most excited to see the Mona Lisa. I was less enthused, knowing it would be a mob scene, but was happy to take her. I downloaded a free app, which guided us through a two-hour tour of museum highlights. When we got to the room with the Mona Lisa, we joined a long line to see the small painting at the far end of the room.

"You still want to do this?" I asked.

"Yeah, I mean, we're here, so we might as well see it, right?"

"Sure. I love that you care so much and are excited."

We learned while in line from our handy app that the Mona Lisa only became famous in the early 1900s when it was stolen by a museum handyman. The ensuing media frenzy captured worldwide attention, catapulting it into fame.

"That makes sense," Aria said thoughtfully after we had our turn to view the painting up close. "It's fine, but there are so many other paintings I thought were better. I can't wait to tell Dad and Finn that it's only famous because it was stolen! I bet they didn't know that."

She chatted away as we walked. She took the lead, determined to prove that she too, knew where we were going, which she did—more or less and with only a little help.

"You guys, these journal entries are not very descriptive," I said. "In fact, you don't say much of anything in them."

We were hanging out in a coffee shop, working on journaling while Randy was price shopping for flights to Africa. I was trying to keep my cool with Finn and Aria, while being annoyed.

"We talked about the kinds of things you should be writing about, right?" I pressed. "I suggested that you focus on what you're learning, what's new and different, what surprises you, what makes you laugh or is disappointing or exciting. But, in almost every entry since we left home you both just mainly list what we did each day and what you had for breakfast."

They looked at me blankly. I tried to put my frustration in check and channel a patient person.

"OK, let me ask you this—what sounds better to you? 'Today, I had yogurt for breakfast. Then we did a river cruise and saw a lot of cool monuments including the Eiffel Tower. We learned a lot. The guide was great. It was a fun day.'"

"Or," I gave an alternative. "'Today, on our first day in Paris, we had yogurt with fresh berries that we bought from a street vendor outside our awful, cramped Airbnb. Then, we went on a cruise on the Seine. The guide made us laugh with her jokes. We saw many sites like Notre Dame, the Eiffel Tower, and museums on the shore. I was surprised to learn about the fire in 2019 and am glad to see Notre Dame being restored.' Which of those entries do you think Future You will appreciate reading more?"

They grudgingly agreed that the second was better and promised to try to take more time to write more reflective entries in the future.

Satisfied and quite pleased with myself, I finished my cappuccino.

On our last night in Paris, we ate a late dinner, then walked to the Eiffel Tower. One of Finn's wish list activities had been to climb the famous iron lattice tower at night, to experience from on high the twinkling lights of Paris, like he'd seen in postcards of the city. It was just a few days past the summer solstice, so it was light until late in the evening.

Randy reviewed ticket prices. There were three levels accessible to visitors. "Shall we just walk up the first two stories? It's pricey to go all the way up."

"Aw, I really hoped to see the lights from the top. Can we walk the first two stories and then take the elevator the rest of the way?" countered Finn.

Aria looked worried. "Finn, the tour guide on our Seine cruise said the Eiffel Tower sways at the top. She said people can feel it and sometimes get sick."

"Come on, Aria, the views will be unbelievable! You'll be fine."

We decided to go to the top; when in Paris, after all. I gave Aria a reassuring hug.

"Most tall buildings sway a little; that's totally normal," I said. "They're designed to do that. Allowing some movement lets them withstand high winds and earthquakes."

"Okay. I'm just not going to look down," she replied, jutting out her chin. "I'll look straight ahead. Will you stay with me?"

I assured her I would, and we set off. As we ascended the stairs toward the first story, surrounded by the structure of the famous tower's pillars, she walked in front of me, gripping the railing tightly with both hands. She slowly, methodically, stepped up each stair. She kept chanting to herself quietly, "It's like climbing the stairs to my bedroom back home; it's like climbing the stairs to my bedroom back home."

When we arrived at the first floor, we told her she had this. Randy explained how the architects constructed the tower and that iron is very durable and safe. She told us she felt a bit better as we walked around the wide landing, gazing in awe at the city.

Night started to fall, and the lights of Paris twinkled far below as we climbed to the second story. From there, we rode the elevator to the top. Aria squeezed my hand and gave a tentative smile as we got off onto the narrow last platform. We took a family selfie with the City of Lights unfolding around us, far below, and I could see that her eyes had regained their usual gleam now that it was literally, all down from here.

Having conquered the apex, Aria darted off onto the second-floor landing after descending in the elevator. She ran to a set of swings that she'd spotted earlier but had been too scared to use. With newfound confidence, she jumped on and asked me to take her photo so she could share it with friends back home.

As we walked back to the metro station just before midnight, Aria talked a mile a minute, her mojo completely returned.

"I'm so proud of myself for making it to the top. I would have regretted it if I'd stopped," she said as she skipped along. "That was really special. And now I've done it! I wonder if my fear of heights is gone completely. Did you know that we climbed 674 steps? That's a lot of steps!"

As Aria danced on the sidewalk, Finn guided us to our Airbnb. We followed a step behind, glancing back now and then, until the tower faded into the distance.

ALMOND FAMILY REPORT CARD ON FRANCE

- *Top Marks*: While Paris has undeniable allure, allow time for other areas. Catching the high-speed TGV train to see the lavender fields in Provence is one of many unforgettable experiences on a France itinerary.
- *Needs Work*: Brush up on basic French to ease communication challenges and enhance your interactions with locals.
- *Learning Tips*: Use city environments like Paris as living classrooms. Engage in guided tours, use public transport, and visit museums to transform everyday sightseeing into rich educational opportunities.

THE MUSIC OF AFRICA

Zanzibar

Excerpt from Finn's Journal
July 8, 2022 | Zanzibar

As I do my controlled roll out of the boat into the shallow waters of the reef, a shiver goes down my spine. I hadn't realized until now how nervous I am. I know that Aria is nervous too, so I try to stay calm and collected. After all of us are in the water, the dive master briefs us on the plan for our first-ever scuba dive. As we descend, I get this feeling in my stomach that's a bit like the opposite of butterflies—as if the butterflies snapped out of existence just like that. Under the water, we see moray eels, starfish, and countless fish. It's beautiful. I wish we could dive for hours. Sadly, all good things come to an end. So, when we get the signal to ascend, I am disappointed but happy knowing we have another dive before we head back to land.

54 CHAPTER 5

We flew into the island of Unguja, also known as Zanzibar, around midnight after a twenty-hour travel day from Europe. We had arranged for a driver to meet us at the airport in Stone Town. He knew the way to the quiet coastal village of Matemwe on the northeastern shore, about an hour's drive away, but was not familiar with exactly where our small hotel was. Randy pulled up the address on Google maps, and the driver nodded, then pointed to Randy's mobile.

"You call hotel; I speak?" he asked, mimicking talking into the receiver.

Randy punched in the number for Seles Bungalows, then handed his phone to the driver, who spoke to someone in rapid-fire Swahili, the national language of Zanzibar, in the Tanzanian archipelago.

"OK," the driver said. "We go."

We quickly veered off the lit, paved street onto dirt roads pitted with potholes and gave silent thanks to GPS for some sense of where we were headed. There were no more streetlights, no little villages. It was just blackness. Several more times we had to call the hotel so our driver could get additional instructions. As it was close to 1 a.m., we had to try a few times before anyone answered.

"This will be interesting if we can't find it," I muttered to Randy, keeping my voice low so the kids couldn't hear.

"We might not find it?" Finn asked, perking up. I had thought he was asleep.

"What! What if we don't?" Aria piled on, suddenly awake.

"No, we'll find it. Don't worry," I said. Sheesh. When you yell at them to write in their journals, they can't hear a thing; but whisper about maybe being lost in the middle of nowhere in Africa and, suddenly, their hearing is perfect.

After another quarter of an hour, our driver stopped outside what seemed to be a wall. In the darkness, we couldn't make out a thing. He knocked on the door, then spoke in Swahili with someone whose shrug and bewildered expression were understood by all of us to mean, "No idea."

We drove on a little farther before doubling back; our driver seemed to think that the wall had, in fact, been the right place. He and Randy got out and pushed open the door. I started calculating our odds of sleeping on the side of who-knows-where-we-were that night.

Thankfully, one of the staff members finally appeared. She led us beyond the wall onto a sandy path, our cell phone lights illuminating thin beams in front of us. We climbed a steep wooden ladder propped on the outside of a wooden bungalow and stepped into a spacious circular room. It had three queen-size, four-poster beds swathed in mosquito netting. The woman smiled at us, swept her arms wide, and welcomed us to Matemwe.

"*Karibu sana*," she said warmly and told us we'd get the tour tomorrow. Gratefully, we nodded and said good night.

Exhausted, we flopped into our beds, pulled over the thin sheets, and fell fast asleep.

We awoke around 11 a.m. to the sound of waves and a pair of songbirds chirping from the frangipani tree outside our second-story window. Rays of sunshine streamed in from the windows on the balcony doors. I pulled back the netting around my bed and stepped onto the deck, breathing in the rich seaside air and taking stock of our surroundings. What a difference the morning made.

Tucked behind the stone wall that had looked so foreboding the night before was a tropical paradise. A handful of thatched-roof cottages ringed an open-air restaurant on the sand, a pool, and lush gardens. We were thrilled to settle down there and call it home for a week.

Our plan was to get Finn and Aria PADI (Professional Association of Diving Instructors) scuba certified so we could go diving as a family. We had signed up for their course with Eagle Ray divers, a short walking distance from our hotel.

After breakfast, we wandered over to meet the instructor and confirm that the kids would begin the following day. With that secured, we had the afternoon ahead of us to explore and catch up on reading and writing.

At low tide, we walked along the wide, quiet beach. The sand was soft underfoot save for a narrow strip of seaweed spiked with sea urchins stranded by the tide. Boats lay propped up on shore. Workers painted and did upkeep on them, taking advantage of the exposed hulls before the tide came back in. Local women harvested seaweed, and a herd of cows, utterly disinterested in us, cooled off in the shallows. Except for a few rustic hotels and wooden homes along the strip, there was little around and few other tourists about.

As we neared our hotel, two Maasai men in traditional *shukas*, or red robes, and stylish sunglasses greeted us in Swahili and broken English. They introduced themselves as Thomas and Daniel. We walked with them to a leeward side of the beach, out of the wind, where they spread a brightly colored cloth on the sand and arranged an assortment of wooden trinkets, bowls, key chains, and jewelry. Finn, Aria, and I agreed to buy a couple of anklets, a bracelet, and a necklace. Using his tall walking stick, Thomas scratched the requested price in the sand. I negotiated to what we agreed was a fair compromise, and we said our goodbyes.

"*Asante sana*," I said, thanking him.

"*Hakuna matata*," Thomas replied. Thanks to Disney, I recognized the phrase.

"*Hakuna matata*, Thomas," I repeated, grinning.

We had been learning basic phrases in Swahili, but this one matched our vibe perfectly. It means, of course, no worries.

After a relaxing morning swimming in the Indian ocean and playing don't-step-on-a-sea-urchin, we all curled up in the shade with iPads and journals. The kids' literature assignment for our time in Zanzibar and mainland Tanzania was *Because of Khalid* by Carolyn Armstrong, a middle-grade novel about a boy who moves to the Serengeti and his ensuing friendship with a Maasai warrior.

"Mom, listen to me practice my Swahili," Aria called from her spot on the deck chair. She had carefully transcribed a number of words into the back of her notebook from the glossary of *Because of Khalid*.

"*Jambo*—Hello. *Asante*—Thank you. *Asante Sana*—Thank you very much. *Karibu*—You're welcome. *Mambo*—What's up? *Poa*—It's cool. *Lala salama*—sleep well."

"Nice, Aria! Those will come in handy. You can use them tomorrow if you see Thomas or Daniel again," I replied, mentally noting a few of the phrases myself.

She beamed and buried her head back in her notebook, curling her flip flops under her. She had officially given up on the idea of blogging and was now chronicling our travels in the black-and-red journal she had selected. Getting consistent internet had proved difficult, and she decided she was more of a pencil-and-paper kind of writer anyway.

That evening, a local band set up on Seles Bungalows' open-air patio. We had seen a sign promoting live Afro-roots music and grabbed a table on the sand. Our sleepy little hotel suddenly came alive; tourists and locals materialized out of nowhere. Musicians tuned their instruments and lounged on couches by the stage floor.

Then, they started to play. Different musicians rotated in for different songs, creating a diverse kaleidoscope of rhythms and beats. It was an eclectic group: a Russian electric guitarist; a singer named Sammy; a woman playing a shaker board, which made a sound like maracas; a bass guitarist; and a drummer. Each song felt unique, soulful, rich, drawing from a variety of African influences and styles.

We clapped and tapped our feet to the beat, whisked away by the range of melodies, so foreign to us and so artfully grounded in where we were. At 10 p.m., the band wrapped their set, and a gentle quiet settled into the darkness once more. Against the light chirping of crickets in the palms, we climbed the stairs again to our room in the treetops.

Aria and Finn began their scuba course the next morning, starting with a day of informational videos on DVDs in the dive shop, then textbook reading for more on the physics of diving. Worldschooling in action, I thought happily.

The dive master, Faridu, warned Finn and Aria at the outset that the material could be dense. "Some old people even fall asleep sometimes to the videos," he said with a grin, "So if you want a break, let me know."

"We'll be fine," they replied, already zoning out on the screen.

Randy and I were reading later that afternoon when the electricity across the entire eastern side of Zanzibar went out. Finn and Aria came running over to find us, telling us excitedly that they had been told by Faridu to simply read the textbooks for the rest of the day, since there was no power to finish watching the videos.

"When Faridu said old people fall asleep, I didn't believe him," Aria exclaimed. "I figured the videos would just be a few minutes long, so it didn't make any sense. But they are so long and boring, now we know why you'd conk out!"

Finn and Aria quickly claimed spots on chairs by the pool, propped up their PADI books, and studied with relatively impressive focus for the next few hours.

That night, Seles Bungalows hosted karaoke, an activity Aria was very excited about. A lively crowd appeared again. A few members of the band showed up, along with guests and staff, all gathered around the TV, singing along to the lyrics.

Throughout dinner, Aria brainstormed songs and tried to recruit us to join her. Finn was tired and uninterested. Randy and I were game, though. For our number, we chose "Hey There Delilah," by the Plain White T's. Sammy, the singer from the previous night, offered to play it with us live on his guitar. So, while he played the tune, we all sang along.

For the closing number, Sammy and the other locals chose Shakira's "Waka Waka," and everyone again joined in, belting out the chorus, "This time for Africa." As the music wound down, Sammy told us he'd be playing the next night with a different band at a hotel down the beach called Zanzibar Sunrise. It would be Zimbabwean music, upbeat, and fun.

"You should come; you'll like it," he invited.

No persuasion needed. "We'll be there."

DIVE INTO SCIENCE: HOW SCUBA CERTIFICATION MAKES PHYSICS AND BIOLOGY TANGIBLE FOR KIDS

Getting SCUBA certified isn't just about exploring the depths of the ocean; it's an immersive journey through the world of science. The process makes the abstract concepts of physics and biology tangible and engaging for kids, transforming learning into an adventure.

- *Understanding Pressure and Buoyancy*: Learning about the principles of buoyancy, atmospheric pressure, and wavelength becomes more than just a chapter in a physics textbook. Kids experience

these forces firsthand as they learn to control their buoyancy and manage the effects of water pressure.
- *Gas Laws in Real Life*: The study of gases under pressure, such as Boyle's Law and Charles's Law, comes to life as kids understand how these principles impact diving safety and the behavior of their SCUBA gear.
- *Marine Biology Up Close*: Instead of just reading about marine species, kids get to observe them in their natural habitats, learning about ecosystems, food chains, and biodiversity in a way that is interactive and memorable.
- *Environmental Science and Conservation*: During their training, kids learn about the impact of human activities on marine life and the importance of conservation, instilling a sense of responsibility toward the environment.
- *The Science of Dive Planning*: Dive planning teaches kids about the importance of calculations and forethought in science, including aspects like dive duration, depth limits, and nitrogen absorption based on dive tables or computers.
- *Encouraging Curiosity and Research Skills*: SCUBA diving nurtures kids' natural sense of curiosity. They learn to observe, question, and research the underwater world, developing essential skills for scientific inquiry.

The next morning, we boarded the Eagle Ray dive boat bound for Mnemba Island, just off the coast. Randy and I would be diving, while the kids snorkeled, as they still had more skill drills to complete before they could do a test dive. Also on the boat were a Brit, a Dutchman, a Swiss couple, two German women, and an Indian family who lived on the mainland.

For the first half hour, we paralleled the shore, enjoying a smooth ride. When we entered the channel toward the atoll, though, the choppy water sent our wooden boat on a rocky, wet roller coaster. As we rose and dipped in the swells, sea water pelting us, I started to feel horribly nauseated. I fixed my eyes on the horizon, trying to steady myself. After what felt like an eternity, we dropped anchor alongside other boats being tossed about in the waves.

Aria appeared equally sick, as did the Swiss woman, who was a new diver on her first-ever descent. She looked terribly unhappy about it. We suited up gamely, said goodbye to the kids, who would be snorkeling with one of the other instructors, and flopped backward off the side of the boat into the heaving water.

When we got the OK sign from our dive master, we let the air out of our buoyancy control devices (BCDs) and sank under the waves, then spent the next forty-five minutes fighting a strong current as we made our way to the reef. The visibility was decent, and we saw colorful schools of fish, a purple starfish, and a lionfish. Despite having layered on two long wetsuits, I got cold quickly and still felt seasick, so I was not disappointed when we got the signal to ascend to a safety stop and then to the surface.

Climbing into the boat, we learned from Finn and Aria that they had not, in the end, gone snorkeling. With the intense swells, visibility would have been abysmal, and they weren't feeling great either. I gave them hugs, wrapped myself in a towel, and went to huddle at the bow of the boat. Then I vomited over the side.

I wasn't the only one who had had enough of the expedition. Someone from Eagle Ray divers arrived like a rescuing knight on his dinghy steed. Faridu asked who wanted to head back versus doing the second dive. My hand shot up, as did the kids'. The Swiss woman bailed instantly as well, accompanied by the Indian family. Randy, who felt fine, opted to stay behind with the others.

We learned on the return that the Swiss woman had actually thrown up into her respirator while diving. I didn't even know that was possible and felt bad for her as she clung to the side of the boat and lost more of her breakfast as we zoomed toward Matemwe. Aria and I exchanged knowing glances; we didn't think diving was going to be her thing.

After showering and napping by the pool, I started to feel human again. Hours later, Randy returned from the afternoon dive. He said the water calmed a little and the second dive was good. But I didn't regret the early exit.

He had struck up a conversation on the ride back with the two German women, who were also at the start of a year-long backpacking trip. They had agreed to come over at happy hour, then would join us to listen to Sammy and his band play at the neighboring hotel.

When they arrived, we had fun swapping travel stories. They were starting their trip in Africa, camping and slow traveling. From there, they planned to head to India and Australia, where they intended to do a longer work-stay to stretch their budget. Like me, they were on leaves of absence from their jobs as a project manager and teacher.

After a round of drinks, we walked along the beach toward Zanzibar Sunset. The open-air restaurant and stage were lit with white lights strung from coconut palms. Cushions lined the sides of a pool in the courtyard. Sammy came around the corner and spotted us, greeting us like old friends. We plopped down on couches near the stage as the band began to play.

Sammy started with a solo song played on a traditional Zimbabwean instrument he told the audience was easy to remember because it sounds like, "Mmmm, beer, ahhhh." Finn really liked that, finding it hilarious, and kept repeating it through the night.

The *mbira*, as it's actually spelled, is a thumb piano, a wooden percussion instrument native to Africa. It was mesmerizing to watch Sammy's thumbs and forefingers fly across it as he plucked the tines.

Another musician soon joined him, playing the *hosho*, gourds filled with seeds. Then a woman came in, playing a huge xylophone called a *marimba*, then the drummer, and bass guitarist. The music was lively, and we sat for hours listening. As we left later in the evening, we waved to Sammy before strolling back to our bungalow under the light of a thin crescent moon.

Over the next two days, we went out on the dive boat again without further incident. The kids successfully completed their first-ever dives with us and passed their PADI exams. We officially became a family of divers.

As I pulled out my battered old dive logbook and wrote entries for the dives I did in Zanzibar, I flipped through past entries. Randy and

I were first certified in 2000 in Hurghada, Egypt. The last dive we had done was in Belize in 2004; we had done twenty-eight dives in between. Every partner I ever had was Randy.

"Look, you guys," I said as I wrote my description for our family dive. "For the first time ever, I get to put down a new dive partner—Finn Almond."

Finn's eyes lit up as he watched me write in his name and describe what we had seen together underwater in my log.

"And on the next dive," Aria piped up, "you can put another new dive partner, who will be Aria Almond."

On our final night in Matemwe, Seles Bungalows hosted another local band, the Lockdowners. We chatted with the Russian electric guitarist, who started the band in 2020 when COVID forced everyone to lock down. He started setting up socially distanced jam sessions with local musicians, and the name stuck. He had been booking gigs ever since, often featuring musicians from across Africa. That night's featured artist was a guitarist from Nairobi.

He played another instrument we'd never seen, which we were told was a *nyatiti*, a five-stringed bowl lute. It was huge—about three feet long—with a deep wooden resonator. He plucked the strings like a harp and sang soulful songs accompanied by a guitarist and drummer.

We had plunked down in a set of comfy chairs around a table by the stage and were playing the card game Hearts while we listened and waited for dinner. At some point, the electricity went out—clearly a common occurrence on the island. There was a low murmur and some light laughter, then cell phone flashlights lit up like candles around the courtyard. The band didn't miss a beat; they just kept on playing into the inky black night.

The kids put their hands behind their heads and leaned back, cards left to the wayside, content to listen to the music and simply *be*. As I watched them, I reflected on how much they had matured in the one month we'd been gone from home. Not long ago, they would undoubtedly have been twitchy about being plunged into darkness in a strange place. But now, they seemed perfectly happy to hang out, let themselves be carried away by the music, to take things as they came, at a slower pace.

As the locals say in Swahili, *"pole, pole."* It means, slowly, slowly.

I leaned back too and closed my eyes, listening to the music filling the dark night, and burrowed into it, completely content in the rhythms of Africa.

ALMOND FAMILY REPORT CARD ON ZANZIBAR

- *Top Marks*: Don't miss Stone Town with its rich history and vibrant markets, street art, and local vendors.
- *Needs Work*: Prepare for logistical challenges, especially if arriving at night. Ensure clear directions and local contacts are on hand to help navigate to accommodations, especially if staying at small guesthouses or in remote areas.
- *Learning Tips*: Enhance your trip by reading about the Maasai warriors, whom you're likely to encounter on the beaches.

6

NO GNUS IS GOOD GNUS

Tanzania

Excerpt from Aria's Journal
July 15, 2022 | Serengeti, Tanzania

We get up before sunrise in our tent in the savanna and pack our bags quickly. We are going on an early morning game drive with Freddie! It is cool but not cold as we set off. Soon, we come across a herd of wildebeests. They are grazing away happily. Suddenly, Finn spots movement in the grass to our right. Out darts a cheetah!!!! The whole wildebeest herd scatters. The cheetah chases a baby wildebeest, but the poor little guy is too slow, and the cheetah catches up to him and takes him down. Another cheetah comes running over to help. We watch from our jeep for a long time as they feast until there's nothing left of the wildebeest but bones. It is the craziest thing I've ever seen and something I know I'll never forget.

Our safari guide, Freddie, met us in the lobby of our hotel in Arusha, Tanzania, at 8:30 a.m. He was dressed in tan pants, a tan turtleneck topped with a tan T-shirt that read, "Only elephants should wear ivory," and a tan brimmed hat. Draped around his shoulders was a bright red Maasai scarf, offering a pop of color and added warmth in the crisp morning.

As we settled into the truck we'd be driving around in for the next few days, he asked us whether we'd ever been on safari before. We shook our heads.

"I am going to tell you the best and worst parts about going on your first safari in Tanzania," he said. "Which do you want to hear first?"

"The worst," Finn and Aria replied.

"The worst thing is that it only goes down from here," he said, grinning widely. "The best is that you've come to the most amazing place in the world for safaris."

We laughed, excited. It was safari time!

Freddie revved the beaten-up jeep into gear. "Let's go!"

Our weeks in Tanzania promised to be action packed. First, Randy had found us a good deal on a six-day safari. After that, we planned to climb Mount Meru, Kilimanjaro's "little sister" peak. Our adventures would start and end in the northeastern town of Arusha.

After Freddie came to get us, we headed off, discovering to the kids' glee that our jeep had a pop-top roof, which we could flip up to scout for animals. On day one, we would be driving through Tarangire National Park, between the Maasai Steppe and the Great Rift Valley.

Finn quizzed Freddie from the back seat. He wanted to be sure we wouldn't get stranded in the bush.

"How much gas do you have, Freddie?"

"Two tanks of 100 liters each."

"Oh, wow, that's a lot," Finn replied, looking to Randy for confirmation.

"Yep, that's a lot," Randy agreed.

"What happens if we get a flat tire?"

"We have two spares on the back of the jeep. And I am a good mechanic, so we would change it and keep going."

"Oh, OK. So, we'll be good?"

Freddie winked at him. "Yes, all good."

As we drove out of Arusha, small towns gave way to wide open plains where Maasai boys in red *shukas* and wooden walking sticks herded cows and goats. Thorny acacia trees and tall, thin sisal trees like Dr. Seuss creations popped up here and there across the barren earth. A dry riverbed cut through the lowlands, which extended until the imposing peak of Mount Meru in the distance.

"I can't believe we're going to climb that in a week," said Finn.

I peered out the window at the dark mountain, low clouds swirling around it. "It'll be an adventure, that's for sure."

"Did you know that it has that shape because of a massive volcanic blast, which blew away the whole eastern side about 250,000 years ago?" Randy asked.

"Cool!" Finn replied. "Like Vesuvius?"

"Kind of," Randy nodded. "Meru is dormant now, though."

"I am excited to see baboons and monkeys as we hike," Aria said. We had read that the multiday climb passes through many different vegetation zones, from dry forest to mountain rainforest and finally, drier scrubland.

Freddie peered at us in the rear-view mirror. "You will see many monkeys on safari too. You like baboons? They are naughty. Be careful; they'll steal your lunch and laugh."

"I can't wait to see that!" Finn laughed. "But, like, if they take someone else's lunch, I mean. Not mine."

Pointing out the Maasai herders in the plains, Freddie told us that the lifestyle of the Maasai people is not dissimilar to that of lions. In a Maasai family, women care for the children, find food and water, and manage the home. Same as mama lions, he said. The women also advise the men on whether to take another wife. The number of wives a Maasai man has depends on the size of his herd. A wife and children can only manage so many cattle, so if you want more, you need another wife and more children.

Freddie had only talked about the women and kids, so I was curious, what do the men do all day?

"They just chill. Tell stories, have fun." Freddie replied. Randy grinned and glanced over at me.

"Don't get any ideas," I said dryly.

As we drove through the rugged, volcanic landscape, Randy talked to the kids about the history and geology of the area, explaining about the formation of Africa in the time of Pangea.

"What do you know already about plate tectonics?" he asked them.

"It's what caused the breakup of Pangea and created the continents," said Finn.

"Is it what causes volcanoes and earthquakes?" Aria asked.

"You're both on the right track," Randy answered. "Billions of years ago, all the continents on earth were together in one supercontinent, Pangea or Gondwana. What's interesting is the way the earth works; it's not one solid ball of mass. The continents are at the surface, kind of 'floating' on top of the layers below. They're able to move very slowly. We don't notice it in our lifetimes, but over hundreds of millions of years, the continents are always moving. That's what led Pangea to break up into the continents we see today.

"Think about South America and Africa," he continued. "You can see how South America once nestled into the side of Africa. And all that leads us to where we are now—the Great Rift valley, which runs from Lebanon through the Red Sea, down through Kenya, Uganda, Tanzania, and farther south to Mozambique, ending in the Zambezi valley."

He explained that this activity led to the volcano forming around the Ngorongoro crater, where we would go on the last day of our safari in Tanzania. That formed from a side explosion that spread debris across the land and formed a hard pan, which made it easier for grasses to grow even while trees struggled to get nutrients.

Approaching Tarangire National Park, Freddie looked back at us again.

"Have you heard of the Big Five?" he asked. The kids nodded enthusiastically. "Good! They are not the biggest animals, though that's what the name sounds like. Hunters gave them that name years ago. These are the animals that are hardest and most dangerous to hunt on foot. Can you name them?"

Finn and Aria rattled them off, having read about them in our guidebooks. "Lion, leopard, elephant, rhinoceros, and cape buffalo! Do you think we'll see them all, Freddie?"

"You have a good chance. Let me know if you see any animals, and I'll stop. Many eyes, great vision."

"Zebras!" Finn shouted soon after we entered the park. Not far from a watering hole, five zebras grazed in the grass. As they walked, they bopped their heads, as if to the beat of a drummer only they could hear.

"They're flicking flies off themselves," Freddie explained. I preferred the explanation I had conjured in my head, picturing the zebras strutting merrily to the tune of "That's the way, I like it (uh huh, uh huh)." I smiled as I watched them for long minutes.

"Pumbas!" Freddie called a short while later, pulling over again.

"What?" We asked.

"Warthogs," he said. "After *The Lion King*, we just call them Pumbas." We laughed and adopted the name instantly, watching a family of fat Pumbas race along, the babies trotting to keep up with their mama.

"Content?" Freddie asked us.

"Content," we replied, and he drove on.

Over the next few hours, we stopped often to watch the wildlife. A huge elephant lumbered out of the forest feet from our truck. Ignoring us completely, it wandered over to a watering hole. A giraffe was already drinking from the far bank, its front legs splayed out so she could reach the water.

"This is unreal," Aria murmured.

"Totally," agreed Finn, standing on his seat, his head poking out of the pop-top roof.

Later, we stopped to watch a herd of wildebeests—also called gnus— eating grass in the plains.

"That's a gnu one!" Randy deadpanned. We rolled our eyes.

"Ugh, this is going to be a regular thing for you, isn't it?" I asked him.

"Mm-hmm," he replied. "It'll always be a gnu joke to me."

WILD LEARNING: ANIMAL WATCHING AS A WORLDSCHOOLING ADVENTURE

Wildlife exploration and animal watching can be an exciting educational avenue for your family, regardless of location or budget. Here are some ideas for inspiration:

- *Local Wildlife Exploration*: Discover wildlife in your backyard, local parks, or nature reserves. Learn about native species and their habitats for free.
- *Visit Zoos and Animal Sanctuaries*: These places offer diverse animal encounters. Use discount days or family passes to learn about conservation and animal protection.
- *Library Resources*: Borrow books on wildlife and habitats from your local library to enhance understanding and complement your animal-watching experiences.
- *Nature Documentaries*: Watch documentaries as a family related to the animals or regions you're interested in.
- *Safari Adventures*: If accessible, safaris offer a unique learning experience. Study the ecosystem, animal behaviors, and conservation efforts before and after the trip. Book early as spots fill up, especially on budget trips.
- *Citizen Science Projects*: Get involved in local or online wildlife observation projects. These encourage learning scientific methods and contributing to real research.
- *Online Educational Platforms*: Use websites and apps for interactive lessons or virtual tours about animals and habitats, many of which offer free resources.

At noon, we stopped for lunch at a rest area. Within minutes of spreading out our picnic on an open table, we heard a commotion and turned to look. A vervet monkey with bright blue balls darted to a nearby table and snatched a packet of cookies right out of a woman's hands then ran with it up a tree. The brazen monkey ripped open the wrapping and devoured the cookies while the woman yelled at him. Finn and Aria clutched their sides and howled with laughter. These blue-balled monkey thieves had just won their hearts for Most Epic Animals Ever.

They also presented a great worldschooling opportunity, one that I seized when we had a chance to talk in our tents later that night (and after I had had a chance to do some research).

"Any idea why those monkeys we saw today have blue balls?" I asked.

"No idea," Finn said, chuckling again at the memory of the cookie-stealing primate.

"It has to do with sexual selection and social status," I said. "Females like the brightest colored males. The larger and more colorful the balls, the more attractive they are, like a peacock's feathers."

"Blue balls for the win," Finn said.

I nodded, laughing. Science lesson for the day, check.

Over the next two days, we explored the Serengeti plain in north-central Tanzania. As we rumbled onto washboard dirt roads, Freddie quipped, "Now, you get a free African massage." He wasn't kidding. We felt well kneaded after clattering along at high speed, kicking up huge plumes of dust in our wake, and stopping when we spotted wildlife. We saw hippos lazing in a river, a cape buffalo, a caravan of giraffes eating leaves from the high boughs of acacia trees, and ostriches running in the distance.

It was late when we arrived at our tent camp, and the sun hung low on the horizon. Three women in traditional Tanzanian dress greeted us, singing and dancing to "*Jambo Bwana*," an East African song that means "Hello, sir," in Swahili. We recognized the tune from our time in Zanzibar and hummed along. After dropping our bags in our tents, we rushed back outside to catch the sunset over the savanna. The sun seemed overlarge, a cherry-red orb that hovered for long minutes in front of the wild date palm trees before melting into the horizon, staining the sky and endless plains scarlet and gold.

We grabbed beers in the fading light and joined other guests around a bonfire outside the main tent. After a buffet dinner, the staff put on a traditional cultural celebration, with dancing, singing, and drums on the sand. Finn and Aria were pulled from their chairs to join in. Finn, who would have shied away from that kind of performance before, danced wildly along with the lead Tanzanian dancer, like it was the most normal thing in the world.

When the show ended, quiet blanketed the camp, broken by occasional growls from the bushes around us. Armed guards accompanied guests to and from the tents. As we watched the guard's flashlight arc to our left and right, Finn spotted glowing red eyes in the bush.

"Hyenas?" He whispered excitedly.

"Yes," the guard said. "They are curious about you."

Finn flashed his headlamp toward them. "Wow, look at them, Mom!"

"I know, I see their eyes. Crazy, huh?"

"Do we need to be afraid?" Aria asked.

"No," said the guard simply.

That night, we went to sleep listening to the eerie cries of the hyenas outside our light canvas walls. I dreamed a hyena wearing a tan T-shirt reading, "I'm the mane attraction," stole my cake from the mess hall and ran off with it into the brush. I woke up sweating and craving chocolate, then spent hours trying in vain to fall back asleep.

Waking at dawn, we scarfed down a quick breakfast then rushed to meet Freddie for an early-morning game drive. We hurtled along desolate dirt roads, and before long, came upon a herd of wildebeest and zebras grazing on a grassy plain. We were the only people around and pulled over to watch the animals in the soft, golden light.

Suddenly, as one, the wildebeests bolted.

"A cheetah!" Finn exclaimed in a loud whisper, pointing to our right. Out of the corner of my eye, I saw what he had seen a split second earlier: a cheetah sprinting from the tall grass, straight into the heart of the herd.

"Oh my gosh," I murmured, whirling my camera around to catch the big cat darting across the road in front of us, clearly targeting one of the small gnus. "Wow!"

Within seconds, the cheetah caught up to its prey and took him down. We watched the gnu's legs flail as the cheetah wrestled it to the ground.

"Look, another cheetah!" exclaimed Randy, and we all swiveled to look toward the open meadow. A second cheetah bounded across the plain to help the first subdue the poor gnu.

"It's like something out of *National Geographic*," Finn murmured. "Except right in front of us."

We stayed for an hour watching as the cheetahs ate their fill. Two vultures circled overhead, eyeing the scene intently.

"They're waiting for the cheetahs to finish," Freddie commented.

"Will they chase the cheetahs away?" Randy asked. "Or will they move in after the cats have moved on?"

"They'll wait until it's clear, then make their move. Other scavengers will come too. Jackals, wild dogs, and hyenas will strip it to nothing. Hyenas can eat the whole body of their prey—skeleton, bones, teeth, horns."

"Ugh," Aria said. I nodded. I was already feeling bad for the gnu.

"Do you know what I have to say about all this?" Randy asked.

"Don't do it," I said, knowing what was coming.

"Oh, yes," he replied, then started singing from *The Lion King*, "It's the cirrrrcle of life, and it moves us all."

"Ha-ha," Finn said. "I gnu he was going to sing that."

In the far reaches of the northern Serengeti, we were on the lookout for the Great Migration. Considered one of the Seven Wonders of the Natural World, this is the annual movement of more than a million gnus as they migrate in a huge loop from Kenya to Tanzania at the end of rainy season. Freddie was hoping we would see a herd crossing the Mara river.

As we neared the river, Freddie explained the protocol. "Safari trucks can't park too close to the bank," he said. "We don't want to scare them off." So, we settled at a discreet distance, Freddie keeping an ear on his radio for any news of the wildebeest.

After thirty minutes, a group of zebras burst through the underbrush, followed by a line of jeeps, stirring us into action. Freddie's radio crackled to life, and we were suddenly part of a high-speed chase.

"Is that them? The gnus?" we asked, bracing ourselves against the bumpy ride.

"Yes, they're crossing!" Freddie yelled over the engine's roar. "Hold on!"

We joined a small handful of other trucks on a bluff overlooking the river. On the opposite shore, hundreds of wildebeest were stampeding down the steep embankment, kicking up massive dust clouds, only to stop abruptly at the water. Then, with another unified movement, they reversed back up the cliffs, as though suctioned by a cosmic vacuum cleaner.

"They are afraid of the river," Freddie said. "It can take a few tries for them to cross. They need the strength of the herd to get them to go."

"Huh," I said. "Wildebeest peer pressure."

Freddie laughed. "Something like that."

"What now?" Aria chimed in.

"We wait and see," Freddie replied.

We repositioned for a better view, discussing their possible strategies when, Freddie announced, "They're on the move again."

As we sped to a new spot, the herd was once more making its way down to the river, their movements synchronized and fluid. But again, they stopped short at the water's edge, as though slamming into an invisible barrier, and retreated to high ground.

Frustrated, Finn slumped in his seat. "They were so close!"

"Patience, grasshopper," Randy reminded him. "Did we spook them?"

"Maybe," Freddie conceded, pulling back further.

On their third attempt, we watched in awe as the wildebeest surged down the embankment and, this time, galloped across the river, continuing their grand migration. We cheered, feeling a sense of connection with their triumph. Witnessing such a massive and coordinated movement of life was an extraordinary testament to the relentless cycle of nature and the monumental journey these animals embark on each year.

Also, as Finn said, it was "crazy cool."

On our last safari day, dawn broke over the Ngorongoro Crater, a gigantic unbroken caldera, with mist curling along its ridges. In the pale morning light, we spotted two giraffes who seemed to nod a greeting before vanishing over a hill.

Descending into the crater, we saw zebras, gazelles, and eland roaming freely in the early morning. Through our binoculars, we spotted a leopard lounging in the shade and watched a male lion and his mate resting in the grass post-hunt, barely acknowledging the scavengers feasting nearby.

Finn was excited. "We've seen four of the Big Five now—elephant, cape buffalo, leopard, and lions! Just the rhino left. What do you think, Freddie?"

"Always possible. Keep looking."

But the rhinos remained elusive. We enjoyed other sights instead: hundreds of flamingos in the lake, a hippo grazing, and a cheetah surveying the plains from a rock.

As the shadows grew longer, Freddie turned and asked, for the last time, "Content?"

Gazing out at the wild, free animals, we replied, "Very content," then began the long drive back to Arusha.

After saying goodbye to Freddie and regrouping for a few days at a hostel in Arusha, we prepared for part two of our Tanzanian adventure: climbing Mount Meru. At 14,967 feet, it's the country's second-highest peak and fifth highest in Africa. We had chosen it over the more popular Kilimanjaro as a slightly shorter, less crowded, and more affordable option. We knew that it would be a challenging four-day trek, but one that we were excited for—especially after spending six days sitting in a safari truck.

The route would take us through dense jungle, high alpine desert, and misty cloud forests teeming with wildlife. When we told Finn and Aria that we'd likely see more baboons and monkeys along the way, along with bigger game, they couldn't wait to continue wildlife spotting. Due to the high possibility of animal encounters, an armed ranger must hike with each group.

As we prepared our packs and got bag lunches ready at the ranger station on our first day, we noticed other groups that had just come down the trail. One couple, looking dusty and exhausted, plopped onto benches nearby to chat with their guide. He congratulated them on their summit and pulled out official-looking certificates for each of them.

Aria sat up straighter and peered over. "Ooh, look, Mommy, we'll get certificates after summiting!" She does love a good memento after accomplishing something.

"Time to get started," our guide Sam said. He led us to where others in our group—ten in total—had gathered to meet the camouflaged, rifle-carrying ranger who would lead us up the mountain.

Finn looked uneasy at the sight of the weapon. "What's the rifle for?" he asked Sam.

"Mostly for cape buffalo," Sam replied. "Do not stray from the group. Let's go."

The first day was a manageable hike to Miriakamba Hut at 8,000 feet (2,438 m). We stayed in Baboon room, rolling out our rented sleeping bags on four bunk beds. Within minutes, one of the guides knocked on our door, calling, "Time for washy-washy!" and setting out bowls of warm water outside on the grass for us to rinse our hands and faces. It was the closest thing to a shower we would have for the next few days, and it felt wonderful.

After a dinner of noodles and fruit in the chilly main cabin, we donned headlamps and padded outside to brush our teeth in the open-air bathroom area, shivering in the cold, damp night. There was light rain falling, and mist descended over the camp. We used the toilets as quickly as possible, grateful for actual porcelain in the women's rooms (albeit with no seats) since the men's rooms only had holes in the ground. We then went back to Baboon room to cuddle into our sleeping bags and try to get some rest.

On day two, the wheels started coming off. Finn struggled with stomach issues but managed to push on. Aria, the youngest by far in our group, started lagging toward the afternoon. Before that, she had hiked at the front of the line just behind the ranger, whom she had befriended and who called her "Little Ranger." A Colorado girl at home in the mountains, she is a strong hiker who rarely tires, but the back-to-back long days and lack of sleep had started to catch up to her.

"My legs are so much shorter than everyone else's," she said in a little voice when we settled into our bunk room that afternoon at Saddle Hut, at 11,712 feet (3,570 m). "We've been hiking so long. And I slept so badly last night."

"Rest now, sweetie," I said. "You can choose to join us later for the hike to Little Meru or stay here—whatever you want to do is totally OK."

"I'll see," she said, worn out, and lay down to rest for a while in her sleeping bag.

Revived by a snack of hot cocoa, fresh mango, and bread with almond butter, Aria decided to join us for the acclimatization hike. The idea behind a hike like this is to gradually expose the body to higher altitudes, force it to adjust, and then descend to recuperate at an altitude that the body is already used to. It is a crucial step when hiking at high altitude. So even though we were tired and the idea of a "side hike" was not appealing to any of us, we gamely marched up the dirt path behind Sam and our other guide, Eli.

We were excited to see the green wooden sign at the apex of the mountain about an hour later, which proclaimed in bright yellow letters, "Little Meru, 3,820 m."

"We did it!" Aria exclaimed, having gotten a second wind. "Maybe we'll get two certificates now—one for Little Meru and one for Big Meru, if we get to the top!"

"Could be," Randy said. "Well done, team!"

We took a selfie of all six of us then sat on a boulder to take in the stunning panoramic views of Tanzania before heading back down to Saddle Hut. We needed to have an early dinner and try to get a few hours of rest before our attempt at the summit.

At midnight, we crawled out of our sleeping bags after a couple hours of restless sleep. We slipped into multiple layers of warm clothing, pulled on wool hats, switched on our headlamps, and stepped into the chilly night.

"How are you feeling?" Randy asked Aria.

"Not great. I have a headache, and I am so tired."

"Do you want to try to summit? Or do you prefer to stay here? Whatever you want is totally fine by us. One of us will stay with you if you want."

"No, I want to try," she said. "I can turn back if I need to, right?"

"Of course," I answered. "Three guides are coming with us for this last part—Sam, Eli, and Oscar. So, if any of us needs to turn back, the others can continue."

She nodded, and we set off. We walked quietly for hours in near total darkness, under a clear, starry sky. The rocky trail before us was illuminated only by the narrow beams from our headlamps until moonrise added its soft light. After four and a half hours of steady uphill climbing, Aria finally hit her limit.

"I need to go back," she told us. Her shoulders slumped. "I'm worried if I keep going, I won't be able to make it back."

"Aw, Aria, you've got this," Finn encouraged her. "Look how far you've come! We're probably close to the top now. It won't be the same without you."

"No. I can't do it. I need to go back." She sat down on the rocky ground.

"That's OK, honey," I said, squatting beside her. "Daddy and Eli will walk down with you in a few minutes. The sun is about to come up over Mount Kilimanjaro. Let's take in the view together. What you've already accomplished is incredible; you should be super proud of yourself." I gave her a big hug, then she curled up on my lap.

We sat together in the frosty, peach-hued dawn for a few minutes to watch the sun rise behind Kilimanjaro. Aria had reached a height of 13,808 feet (4,208 m), a personal best.

Randy and Eli then descended with Aria to Saddle Hut, while Finn and I continued on with Sam and Oscar. Two hours later, exhausted but exuberant, we made the summit of Mount Meru. We were the only ones there, alone above the clouds.

Hours later, we returned to Saddle Hut and reunited with Randy and Aria, who was feeling more rested and in better spirits.

"I'm disappointed I didn't make the summit," she admitted. "But Eli told me I'll still get a certificate for Little Meru! So that's good. I'd have been crushed if I hiked all this way and didn't get any certificate."

I laughed. "So true. I'm glad you'll get one for that accomplishment. It was a big one! And I'm proud of you for knowing your limits. You should be pleased with what you achieved."

"I am. I'm glad I tried. And happy you and Finn made it. I just feel badly that Daddy had to come down with me and didn't get to summit."

"Don't worry about that, honey. He was totally OK returning with you."

"I know, that's what he told me; I just wish he could have finished."

"Someday, we'll do another big climb and, I have no doubt, we'll summit," I said. "But even if we don't, I'll always remember the sunrise we saw together over Kilimanjaro."

"Me too, Mommy."

After a nap and lunch, we hiked another three hours down to Miriakamba Hut, where we spent the night in the now-familiar Baboon room. We splashed water on our face from our "washy-washy" bowls before eating some dinner and falling fast asleep in the bunks.

The next morning, we hiked out Momella Gate and piled our packs into an awaiting truck. Before we left the park, Eli and Sam handed out our certificates.

"Congratulations," Sam told each of us solemnly. We shook his hand and thanked the guides for their help. Aria beamed especially broadly, holding her certificate like it was made of delicate crystal, and gave Eli a big bear hug before we piled into the truck.

On the ride to the airport as we prepared to fly out to South Africa, the kids had fun recapping all the wildlife we had seen on safari and while climbing Mount Meru. The list was long—lions, leopards, cheetahs, giraffes, zebras, cape buffalo, eland, gnus, gazelle, flamingos, hippos, crocodiles, storks, hyenas, jackals, vultures, and oh-so-many monkeys and baboons.

"It's crazy how much we saw and learned with Freddie, Sam, and Eli," I said. "Freddie was totally right when he told us on the first day that there's no better place than Tanzania for a safari. It's going to be hard to ever top this."

"Unforgettable," Finn said, then added: "We never saw a rhino, though. Oh, well!"

"Yeah," I said. "Clearly, that'll be one for a gnu day."

ALMOND FAMILY REPORT CARD ON TANZANIA

- *Top Marks*: Book your safari well in advance, especially during peak seasons like the Great Migration in the Serengeti. Early booking ensures access to extraordinary wildlife experiences, even on a budget.
- *Needs Work*: Adopt a "go with the flow" mindset, particularly when using local or low-cost accommodations. Standards may vary from water pressure to cleanliness, but embracing these differences enhances the authenticity of the experience.
- *Learning Tips*: For treks like climbing Mount Meru, plan for contingencies. Using multiple guides allows flexibility if someone needs to turn back, accommodating families with varying endurance levels.

7

THE ESSAY FIASCO OF JOBURG

South Africa

Excerpt from Finn's Journal
August 17, 2022 | *Johannesburg, South Africa*

After seeing the living situation of the people in Alexandra township, I feel super privileged to live where I do in Colorado. When we first pull up to one of the neighborhoods in Alex, we see a little boy squatting to take a poo on newspaper, right in the open next to the houses. The river is filled with trash, and it smells horrible. Later, we see heaps of garbage on the streets, and goats wandering through traffic, eating plastic and scraps. When we get to our guide's house, he tells us that he has lived in Alex his whole life. His family shares one room, and they split the house with five other families. I feel lucky to have a clean and sanitary home with no other families, and Aria and I have our own rooms. I have never thought about it before.

> It is said that no one truly knows a nation until one has been inside its jails.
>
> Rolihlahla Nelson Mandela

CHAPTER 7

As we waited on the tarmac, ready for takeoff on our flight from Kigali, Rwanda, to Johannesburg, South Africa, the pilot came onto the loudspeaker. "Welcome to RwandAir. This flight is to Johannesburg, but it's not direct. We will stop in Harare to drop off cargo and stuff. Then we will continue to Joburg, landing at 4:30 a.m."

This came as an unwelcome surprise, as it was supposed to be a direct flight, landing three hours earlier. Now, we'd be cutting it close to make our connection on to Cape Town.

Luckily, there were no crowds in the pre-dawn hour when we landed, so we breezed through the Johannesburg airport and got to our gate with fifteen minutes to spare. We piled onto a bus, which drove onto the tarmac. When it stopped, everyone filed out toward a CemAir propeller plane. As we approached, the flight attendant leaned out of the plane's doorway and shooed us away. Confused, we crammed inside the bus again, and it promptly turned around.

An overhead voice confirmed what we'd already suspected: we weren't leaving for Cape Town anytime soon. There was a mechanical issue with the plane; we'd be delayed with a new departure time TBD.

"Well, maybe we can at least scrounge up a coffee," I said hopefully.

In the waiting area, Randy spotted a woman who was on our flight from Kigali to Johannesburg and now was also waiting to connect to Cape Town. He went over to chat with her. She was from Zimbabwe. Randy asked whether she had known ahead of time about the stopover in Harare. She shook her head. Then she shrugged, laughed, and held up her hands.

"That's Africa for you," she said.

The oldest city in South Africa and one of its three capitals, Cape Town was once nicknamed the "Tavern of the Seas," a respite for sailors looking for relaxation after months at sea. Built in the shadow of towering Table Mountain, it has white-sand beaches, rugged coastlines, mountains, museums, delicious food, and fantastic wine. It is a beautiful and complex place. The legacy of apartheid, which means literally "aparthood" in Afrikaans and was a system of racial segregation enforced from 1948 to 1994, hangs heavy, its dismantlement barely a generation old.

Crime is a real threat, especially at night, and locals reinforced what we read—we should not walk about after sunset but rather take Ubers, even if only a couple blocks away.

Randy had booked us an Airbnb apartment in Cape Town's business district. You had to pass two guards to enter the building. As the manager showed us to the condo, she stressed cheerfully that, in addition to being fairly safe, we wouldn't have to worry about load shedding.

"What's that?" Aria asked.

Randy explained. "In South Africa, there's not enough electricity for everyone to use it all at the same time. So, the power is turned off in different areas at different times. It's like taking turns to play a game; everyone gets a chance, just not all at once."

"Huh," replied Aria. There was clearly going to be a lot for us to learn here.

Our plan for the month in South Africa was to meet up with friends and immerse ourselves in Cape Town's history for a few days, then rent a car to drive the Garden Route along the coast, circle back and drive north to see the legendary Namaqualand daisies in bloom, before flying to Johannesburg. We would dive into worldschooling writing assignments, which I was very excited about. And we had to catch up on basic housekeeping. Having been on the road for two months, our clean clothes' situation was grim—we all looked shaggy and could use haircuts—and we needed to replenish supplies (shampoo for Aria, better walking shoes for me, and a new fleece for Finn, who kept losing things in every country we went, like a modern-day Hansel dropping a path of breadcrumbs).

Over the next few days, we eased into a routine, alternating between trips to the Victoria and Albert waterfront mall to tick off our mundane to-do list and explorations of some of the cultural and historical sites around Cape Town.

From the moment we stepped onto the ferry that took us to Robben Island, a former maximum-security prison where Nelson Mandela and other political prisoners were incarcerated during apartheid, it felt like stepping into a page of history. Our soft-spoken guide was himself a former political prisoner on the tiny island, located just five miles offshore. He showed us the sparse, eight-foot-by-seven-foot concrete cell where Mandela spent eighteen of his twenty-seven years in prison.

The space was so tight, Mandela had to roll out his bedding nightly and pack it away in the morning as the bulk of his cell was filled with a desk and bookshelves—a testament to his unyielding spirit and dedication to learning and writing, even in confinement.

In the courtyard, we saw the plot where Mandela gardened and secretly wrote his autobiography *Long Walk to Freedom*. The tour ended with a visit to the Blue Stone Quarry, where prisoners dating back to the seventeenth century endured hard labor in harsh conditions.

On another afternoon, we headed to the District Six Museum, which gave us a glimpse into another sobering chapter of Cape Town's history. It's a memorial to the vibrant community called District Six, which was dismantled during apartheid, displacing over sixty thousand residents. The exhibits, filled with personal stories and artifacts, conveyed a profound sense of loss and resilience.

Tired after long days, we spent time in the evenings relaxing, reflecting, and enriching our understanding of South African history and culture through audio books, reading, and films. We listened to Trevor Noah's *Born a Crime* and watched the film adaptation of Nelson Mandela's autobiography and *The Power of One*, a WWII drama set in South Africa.

After a few days, I decided it was time to layer on a longer form writing assignment to our curriculum.

"As you know," I told Finn and Aria, "you each have to write one nonfiction essay this quarter. For yours, Finn, I want you to expand on what we have been learning in South Africa. In the States, you studied civil rights leader Martin Luther King Jr. and have probably heard of Malcolm X. Now you have learned more about Nelson Mandela. I want you to compare and contrast the philosophies and approaches of these three leaders. You'll have two weeks to research, write an outline, rough draft, and then submit your final copy in Joburg. OK?"

He nodded.

"Any questions?"

"Nope."

"OK, good! Happy to bounce ideas along the way if you want, just let me know."

As I went to bed that night, I felt pleased with myself and what I thought was a genius essay topic. It was relevant, thought-provoking, and fascinating. Randy looked skeptical.

"That's a meaty assignment for an eighth grader. Not better to just have him compare two leaders?"

I brushed off his concern, breezily replying, "Nah, it'll be great."

After a week in Cape Town, we rented a white Toyota Starlet for a road trip across the Western Cape. Our first destination was the vineyard-lined town of Franschhoek, South Africa's food and wine capital. With its tree-lined streets and Cape Dutch architecture, it is quiet and quaint. It felt like the ideal spot to leave the kids for the evening while we went out for a date night. After two months of 24/7 togetherness, we were starting to wear on each other's nerves, so the kids practically pushed us out the door. We were only too happy to oblige.

Pulling on my jacket for the cool southern winter night, I called over to Finn. "How's your writing assignment coming?"

He was playing a video game on his iPad. "Fine. I'll finish the research tonight."

"I'd like to review a rough draft when you have one or talk through any ideas. Remember, it's due when we get to Joburg."

He grunted an acknowledgement, and we headed out the door.

The following day, we continued southeast to the fishing village of Gansbaai, where we checked into a bed and breakfast overlooking the ocean. Bundled into our jackets, we sat on the deck to watch the waves crash far below.

Karen, the owner of the little lodge, was talkative and helpful. She had lived in the area for years, having moved to escape the craziness of her native Johannesburg in search of a quieter life. We talked with her about race relations, South Africa's escalating electricity supply issues and deteriorating infrastructure, corruption, political parties, its history, and its future.

"For all our problems, there's a spirit here, in South Africa. It's hard to describe; it's like nowhere else in the world," she said. She told us she couldn't imagine living anyplace else. "I like the tension; it fosters creativity, entrepreneurship, scrappiness."

She said she feels South Africa is at a turning point. "It has its challenges. But that's what makes us hardy, like the desert trees that grow in the harshest of environments." She smiled with a sort of quiet reverence and then said, echoing the Zimbabwean passenger we'd met at the airport, "That's Africa for you."

COURSE CORRECTING WHEN WORLDSCHOOLING GOES AWRY

Embarking on the journey of worldschooling while traveling can be both exciting and daunting. As parents, you're likely not professional educators, and it's natural to face challenges and stumbles along the way. With planning and flexibility (and some humility, in my case!), you can create a rewarding educational experience for your children that's also enjoyable for you. Here are some tips that we found helpful after trial and error:

- *Set Clear Expectations*: Clearly define what you expect from your kids in terms of schoolwork. Discuss what assignments need to be completed, by when, and the standard of work you're looking for.
- *Create a Learning Schedule*: Draft a flexible yet structured calendar that balances educational activities with travel experiences. This helps maintain a routine and sets a pace for learning, one that can adapt to the rhythm of your travels.
- *Use Rubrics for Assessment*: Collaborate with your child's regular schoolteachers, if possible, to develop rubrics for evaluating assignments. This ensures that the work aligns with their curriculum and your expectations.
- *Embrace Technology or Online Tutors*: Use educational apps, online resources or even tutors to supplement learning. They can be especially helpful for subjects where you may not have expertise.
- *Stay Connected with Teachers*: If possible, maintain regular communication with your child's teachers for guidance and to ensure continuity in education.

- *Join a Community*: Connect with other worldschooling families. Online forums and communities can be great resources for advice and support, and you may even find opportunities to meet up in person, which can be highly rewarding.
- *Be Patient and Flexible*: Understand that there will be good and bad days. Adapt your plans according to your child's needs and the realities of travel.

Over the next few days, we continued our journey along the storied Garden Route in South Africa, a 190-mile (300 km) stretch bordered by dense forests on one side and the Indian Ocean on the other. We traveled through diverse scenery, from bright yellow canola fields to blue-gray mountains, coastal cliffs and serene lagoons, encountering small towns and exploring hidden beaches along the way. While driving, we listened to Alan Paton's 1948 classic, *Cry, the Beloved Country*, the story of a poor Black country priest and a wealthy white landowner whose lives intersect as they deal with a murder in the years leading up to apartheid.

"This is a heavy book," Aria commented about a third of the way into the novel.

Finn nodded. "I liked Trevor Noah's audio book way better. He's funny."

Randy looked at them in the rearview mirror. "We get it, but not every book is going to get five stars from you. This is relevant and a classic. Let's listen a little more, then we can do a *Daily Show*."

They nodded, and we settled once more into the drive, taking in the scenery and stopping as things caught our interest, while the sad tale unfolded in the background.

In Plettenburg Bay, we saw a sign for a primate sanctuary, a refuge dedicated to the rescue and rehabilitation of various monkey and ape species and decided to check it out. Set in a lush environment, the sanctuary featured dense canopies and natural enclosures interconnected by walkways and bridges. Following our guide through the forest, we came upon a suspension bridge spanning a deep gorge and began to cross. As we neared the middle, a huge gibbon came swinging toward us on the ropes, barreling along like a battering ram.

We stood frozen, unsure what to do. The gibbon didn't even break his stride. He simply dropped the rope on one side to swing past, then continued to hurtle toward the other bank before darting up and away into the trees.

Once across, I felt a sudden warmth spread across my shoulder. Glancing up, I caught a monkey mid-pee, directly above me on a branch overhead. Leaping aside, I scowled at him, but he had already scampered off into the canopy. Finn and Aria convulsed in giggles.

"Good luck when a monkey pees on you," said our guide, Andy, suppressing a grin.

"Mm-hmm," I said doubtfully, still glaring at the monkey's backside.

"Shh, you're going to like this," whispered Andy a little farther on. We rounded a bend and found two ring-tailed lemurs sitting cross-legged on the ground, hands on their little knees, eyes closed as they faced the sun. They looked like they were meditating in a Sukhasana pose.

"Don't block their sun," Andy warned. Right as he said it, someone from our group inadvertently cast a shadow over one of the lemurs. The creature instantly opened its eyes and trotted away on all fours, bushy tail raised as though in indignation.

Andy laughed. "I told you."

"I guess they don't like to 'move it, move it,'" I murmured, recalling the movie *Madagascar*.

Finn snorted. "Nice one, Mom."

Just north and west of Cape Town lies a region known for its stark and minimalistic beauty. Here, the landscape is defined by expansive skies and the austere hues of hills, rocks, and endless fields in shades of brown, gray, and muted purple. This tranquil, rugged terrain with its unadorned simplicity is often overlooked on travel itineraries.

But with the arrival of spring, the barren land undergoes a stunning transformation. The annual flowering of the wild Namaqualand daisies is a world-renowned environmental event, one which we were quite coincidentally there in time to witness. So, before returning our rental car, we ventured to the Northern Cape. There, the fields in early August burst into a vibrant array of orange, yellow, fuchsia, and white blossoms.

THE ESSAY FIASCO OF JOBURG: SOUTH AFRICA

The remote roads we drove along were quiet, lending a sense of discovery to our meanderings.

We hopped out to wander through field after field livid with color, leaving me reflective and awed by nature's power to dramatically change even the most unforgiving landscapes. As night fell, we settled into a small hotel for the night, watching the sky turn an otherworldly purple before fading to black under the glittering constellation of the Southern Cross.

With time to spare that evening, I checked in with Finn to review his essay progress. He handed over his iPad, on which he had typed out a rough draft. I read it silently, a crease forming between my brows.

"Finn, this doesn't feel very well structured. It's sort of a mishmash of facts that you seem to have copied and pasted into a document."

"I rewrote them from the original sources!"

"Fair enough, but you haven't logically structured your essay in any obvious way. It's more of a laundry list of facts about Mandela, Martin Luther King, Jr., and Malcolm X. You need to put more work into this to craft it into a compelling essay. Do more research into apartheid South Africa and race relations in America to set the context for each of these leaders. Give background on each of them, then devote a couple of paragraphs to comparing and contrasting their philosophies. Does that make sense?"

"I did do that," he said in a defensive tone.

Feeling frustrated, I tried again. "All right, so then take what you've done and spend time shaping it into another draft, with a CER structure. You've learned about that in school, right? Start with a claim or argument. Then, give evidence to support the claim. Finally, provide reasoning to explain how the evidence supports your claim. Got it?"

He replied with a terse, "Yes. Got it, Mom."

I could tell Aria was listening. "Your turn is next, kiddo. Are you hearing this feedback too? It'll be applicable when I assign you your essay."

She nodded, and I turned back to reading my book.

Our last stop in South Africa was Johannesburg, one of the country's other capitals (the last being Pretoria). Colloquially called Joburg, it's also known as the City of Gold as it began as a nineteenth-century mining settlement.

We headed first to take a guided tour of Constitution Hill, both a historical landmark and a symbol of justice and human rights. It's home to the Constitutional Court of South Africa, the highest court in the country on constitutional matters. The complex has a deep history, as it was previously a prison notorious for detaining political activists, including many apartheid-era freedom fighters. The tour gave us more insights into South Africa's troubled past, while also focusing on its transformation and commitment to the ideals of democracy and equality.

We walked around Number Four, the overcrowded section of the prison where Mahatma Gandhi, Nelson Mandela (in another period of imprisonment), and thousands of others served time in squalid and inhumane conditions.

That afternoon, Finn gave me his completed essay to read then trotted off to FaceTime friends, assignment checked off his list.

I struggled with how to respond to him after reviewing it. I thrust the paper at Randy. "This is a fiasco," I hissed, as though it were all his fault.

He raised an eyebrow and didn't say anything.

"OK, I know you warned me that it might be too much," I conceded.

"It feels like maybe—just maybe," he calmly began, "you may have had too high expectations for this. Like, a college-level term paper, which could take weeks to research, develop an outline, rough draft, then final, not something an eighth grader would do in two weeks in the few hours here and there he had to complete it. Did you give him a rubric to follow?"

"I told him to follow a CER structure, which is what his teachers said is a good model. Start with a *claim*, show *evidence*, explain *reasoning*."

"Well, he did pretty much do that," said Randy, fairly. "His essay's a tad convoluted as he talks about each of the three leaders and their philosophies, and he does use abysmal grammar, but it was a tough assignment, and he arrives at a reasonable—if not super polished—answer. Be easy on him and try to give clear, constructive feedback."

I tried to get my annoyance in check. It was possible Randy had a valid point.

"Maybe not a complete fiasco then," I grumbled, wondering which of us—Finn or I—was going to learn more from the incident. Mustering all my patience, I wandered into the living room to give Finn constructive feedback and vowed to give Aria a better thought-out essay when it was her turn.

On our last morning in Johannesburg, we faced a moral dilemma: should we tour a township? There are more than five hundred townships across South Africa. These originated during apartheid as segregated areas designated for nonwhite residents, characterized by limited resources and separation from city centers. The system enforced strict racial divisions and inequality.

Today, no longer defined by apartheid's segregation laws, townships are slightly more diverse and integrated. Challenges persist, though, including crime, violence, and hindered development due to inadequate infrastructure, economic constraints, and limited government support. One of the poorest urban areas in Joburg, Alexandra township—known locally as Alex—houses over a million people today in infrastructure meant for seventy thousand.

Tours of various townships were available, but we were torn between feeling that it might be exploitative and that it could be profound and educational, if done right, giving a deeper lens on the communities and cultures of the country. After talking to local friends and researching more, we decided to go, choosing a local guide known for ethical practices.

An Alex resident himself, Abby described the afternoon we would share together as an "experience" rather than a tour. We were joined by two of his friends from the neighborhood, who served as both bodyguards and assistant guides to share their perspectives and give added context to what we were seeing. Driving through the different neighborhoods, Abby answered Finn and Aria's questions honestly and openly, providing insights into township life.

Crossing the Jukskei River, tightly packed wooden houses rose pell-mell up the hill, their metal roofs weighed down by bricks. Electrical wires crisscrossed overhead, and torn tarps provided shade. By the side of the road, a woman waited while her little boy squatted in the dirt to defecate on a scrap of paper. Piles of garbage, car parts, and old tires lay in mounds along the bank, and plastic bags flew in the wind. A stench, as of rotten food and feces, filled the air.

We drove north, past the low wall dividing the Black township from the "colored" area, a remnant of apartheid divisions. "It's like the Berlin wall," Abby said, "only we left it up, in remembrance."

In the commercial center, goats rummaged through trash amid busy traffic, the cacophony of horns and shouting and bleating deafening. Men milled about or sat on stoops; women navigated the streets balancing loads on their heads, with babies strapped to their backs. Children played nearby, smiling, and waving as we passed.

Abby showed us his home, which he has lived in since childhood, in the residential area. He pointed out the communal toilet and water facilities shared by many families. Across the street, a river of dirty water flowed downhill, gushing up in little geysers from the ground.

"A sewage pipe burst," Abby explained. "We have been trying for months to get it fixed, working with our local representative. We will have to escalate soon."

Despite the hardships, he spoke of a deep sense of community.

"Why have you stayed?" Randy asked, noting Abby's qualifications and opportunities elsewhere.

He shrugged and said simply, "It's home."

As we walked around Alex, Abby showed us the fabric of the community beyond the facade—churches, schools, museums, parks—and introduced us to some of his other friends, including the new city council representative, a young local respected by the community.

"It's the first time ever that we have been able to vote for our own representative," Abby said. "Floyd is respected in the community. He's from Alex. He'll be good for us."

In the east bank of Alex, where nicer homes represented the promise of upward mobility, we climbed the steps of the newly constructed mall, which Abby told us is a real source of pride in the neighborhood. From there, we could see more of a bird's eye view of the sprawling township, lying in the shadow of the posh business district of Joburg, with its tall, gleaming towers, a stark contrast to the poor community below.

"Is there any bitterness among the people here?" I asked.

"Oh, yes," Abby replied matter-of-factly. "You hope for change for so long, and when you see the fat-cat politicians getting richer and richer and us continuing to live the way we do, not even able to get our sewage fixed, it's hard for people not to feel angry."

"How do you think things will play out?" Randy asked.

Abby shrugged. "We are at a turning point. There is no way to tell which way it'll go. It is easy to be mad at the party in power but another thing altogether to know how to fix the problems. I don't think it's something any one party can do alone."

We took a group selfie of all seven of us—Abby, our two bodyguards, and our family—together in front of a huge, canary-yellow picture frame that positioned Alex against the towers of the affluent neighborhood of Sandton rising just above it. A picture of two completely different worlds set side by side, a complicated juxtaposition of past and future, transience and permanence, wealth and poverty.

I guess, as they say, that's Africa for you.

ALMOND FAMILY REPORT CARD ON SOUTH AFRICA

- *Top Marks*: Consider a guided tour of a township for a more nuanced sense of communities and cultures across South Africa. Choose guides known for ethical practices for a respectful and enlightening experience.
- *Needs Work*: Familiarize yourself with local safety guidelines for nighttime activities in cities and prepare for issues like load shedding to manage potential disruptions effectively.
- *Learning Tips*: Enhance your grasp of South Africa's complex history by visiting sites like Robben Island and Constitution Hill, offering insights into the legacy of apartheid and the country's democratic journey.

8

TRAPPED BY A RHINO

Namibia

Excerpt from Aria's Journal
August 12, 2022 | We Kebi Safari Lodge, Namibia

This afternoon, we arrive at the We Kebi nature reserve in the Namibian desert. After settling into our rooms, we head out on a sunset game drive. I am wearing pants, a T-shirt, and my fleece. This turns out to be a mistake. As soon as the sun sets, the temperature drops so much. It's freezing! The safari jeep doesn't have doors or windows, so as we zoom along, the wind goes straight through my fleece. Finn and dad are cold too. For once, mom isn't. She has on all her layers and refuses to lend me any!! Luckily, we get distracted by the animals we see—oryx, zebra, giraffes, red hartebeest . . . and four rhinos! Incredible! Two are a mom and her baby!!!! It is an eventful evening in the desert.

"Three days until my birthday," Aria trilled in a sing-song voice from the backseat. "Not many kids can say they spent their golden birthday in Namibia, turning eleven on August 11!"

"That's true," Randy smiled. "Celebrating your big day here will be very special."

"Have you decided what you'd like?" I asked. We had told her she could have something little, and she had been pondering the decision.

"I'd love a small souvenir from Namibia—and candy," she said finally. "Also, can I drive the truck again, daddy? Not many kids can say they got to *drive* on their eleventh birthday, either!"

"We'll see," he laughed.

We had rented a white Toyota Hilux truck to drive from South Africa north overland into Namibia, across vast open plains that made the Mojave Desert in the southwest United States look bustling.

Africa's least densely populated nation, Namibia is nearly two and a half times the size of Germany, but home to only 2.5 million people. Situated on the Atlantic coast, it borders Angola, Zambia, Zimbabwe, Botswana, and South Africa. It is a land of extremes, from the rust-colored dunes of the Namib Desert to the cool Atlantic coastline, central highlands, and verdant shores along the Zambezi River in the northeastern Caprivi strip.

For miles after leaving the Namibian border town of Noordoewer, we saw more wildlife than cars or humans. Ostriches preened on the side of the road. Little dik-diks, gazelles, and zebras grazed in the grasses. At rest areas, warnings alerted visitors to "Beware of the Baboons." At one point, a herd of oryx with their long, spear-like horns thundered across the road in front of us, bounding up the rocky hillside, then galloping away across the plains.

Given how desolate it was, it hadn't come as a surprise when Finn asked if he could try driving shortly after crossing the border. He had been advocating for the idea since we road-tripped across the Cape, but the answer was always no; there were too many cars and people.

Besides seeing friends and family again, what Finn was most looking forward to when we returned home was getting his learner's permit. He would turn fifteen shortly after returning to Colorado, which was when he'd be able to begin driving in our state. He was keen to get a jump-start on lessons, if we would let him.

On a dusty stretch of open road in southern Namibia, Randy pulled over into a field to give Finn his chance.

"OK, buddy, are you ready to give driving a try?"

"Actually?" Finn asked, his eyes shining. "Definitely!"

"Oh, can I try also?" Aria jumped in, never one to be left out. "I want to drive, too!"

"One step at a time," Randy replied. "Let Finn give it a go, then we can see."

Finn smirked and climbed into the driver's seat. Aria managed to look mutinous and hopeful at the same time.

"Go ahead and adjust the mirrors," Randy instructed.

"Done," Finn said, putting one hand on the wheel and slinging the other suavely over the passenger seat, like he'd been driving his whole life. "I'm ready!"

"Both hands on the wheel," Randy said, hiding a smile. "Put it in drive, and don't go more than 60 kilometers per hour—that's your max."

"OK, I've got it," Finn replied. "Where should I go?"

"Drive straight through those two scrub brushes. Turn left at the acacia tree, then come back to a stop in front of the carcass."

"Can we please not say 'carcass?'" Aria asked. "It makes me nauseous."

"Fine, pull to a stop in front of the pile of bones and feathers, then," amended Randy.

"Got it," Finn said, easing the truck into drive. For the next twenty minutes, he practiced turns, shifting into reverse, and stopping smoothly.

"Nice job, Finn," Randy said, then turned to Aria. "All right, you want to give it a go?"

Aria's eyes lit up, and she scrambled out as Finn reclaimed his spot in the back. "Yay!"

"You need to sit on my lap, kiddo, and I'll work the pedals," Randy said. "But you can steer and put it in gear, OK?"

Knowing that was the best deal she was going to get, Aria had accepted, crawling onto Randy's lap. She steered us around for a bit and clearly logged the idea as a potential repeat activity for her birthday.

"All right, everyone, good stuff," Randy said as he readjusted mirrors and pulled onto the main road. "Let's get going; I want to arrive at Canyon Lodge before dark."

Located in southern Namibia's Gondwana Nature Park, Canyon Lodge was our home for the next few nights. Built in the shadow of rocky hills, the main building and its stone-and-thatch cottages blended seamlessly with the barren, bush-dotted landscape. A fuchsia bougainvillea draped over the roof, a lone splash of color against the parched desert backdrop.

Finn and Aria headed to the lobby for shaky Wi-Fi and texts with friends after we settled into our cottage. Randy and I opted to explore, climbing a towering rock formation to take in the panoramic views.

"It feels like we're on Mars," I remarked, mesmerized by the setting sun tinting the rocks in shades of reddish-orange, pumpkin, rust, and sienna. Endless sand, rock, and low bushes stretched before us.

Randy nodded, "Totally otherworldly."

We stayed there, our feet dangling over the outcropping, until the sun slipped behind distant hills, then made our way down in the lingering alpenglow.

FAMILY TRAVEL: BALANCING TOGETHERNESS AND PERSONAL SPACE

Extended family trips can be wonderful, but they can also be overwhelming with constant closeness. Here are a few tips we found helpful to our family to maintain everyone's mental health while enjoying the journey together:

- *Personal Time*: Carve out time for solo activities or quiet moments for everyone. This can be as simple as individual walks, reading, or listening to music.
- *Diverse Accommodations*: Opt to stay in places that offer separate spaces, like Airbnbs, which can provide slightly more room and privacy than standard hotels.
- *Scheduled One-on-One Time*: Plan activities where each parent spends time with one child at a time. It can be a short excursion,

cultural experience, or a simple coffee date, offering a chance to connect individually.
- *Group Activity Choices*: Give kids a say in the day's activities. This ensures that their interests are considered and helps avoid burn-out from activities that don't appeal to all.
- *Regular Check-Ins*: Have family meetings to discuss how everyone is feeling. This is an opportunity to adjust plans if needed and to address any concerns.

The key to a successful extended family trip is balancing group adventures with individual needs and preferences.

The Fish River Canyon, the world's second-largest canyon after Arizona's Grand Canyon, dramatically carves through southern Namibia's arid terrain. At a rest stop, we turned posters explaining the canyon's geology into an impromptu science lesson for Finn and Aria. We discussed the natural forces shaping the gorge while overlooking the winding, turquoise river far below.

"Think of how water, wind, ice, and gravity worked over millennia to shape this gorge," Randy explained. "Like how plate tectonics split Pangea, lifting Africa and steepening this canyon's gradient. A steeper gradient means more powerful water erosion."

"Making the river carve deeper into the canyon," Finn added.

With no guard rails or crowds, the canyon's vastness felt both immense and intimate, and we lingered for hours along the rim, watching the lengthening shadows across the rock layers, hundreds of millions of years old.

Before the sun dipped too low in the sky, we continued north toward Keetmanshoop. When, hours later, we slid open the heavy wooden gate to the remote Alte Kalkoefen hotel, I wondered what we had gotten ourselves into—not that there were many other lodging options. There was little but rock, brush, and sand for miles.

The name of the lodge derived from two limestone ovens (*kalkoefens*) from the 1800s, which were still visible. The rusted shell of a wheel-less, turquoise Ford pickup stood beside a derelict gas pump, just outside the reception building. A couple of cacti and hardy camel thorn trees mocked us with wisps of greenery.

CHAPTER 8

"Is this really it?" I whispered to Randy, stepping out into a cloud of dust.

He assured me, "It got good reviews."

But I was already thinking about how we were going to make Aria's birthday the following day feel special in a place so barren and lonely.

Inside, the lodge had a charming, almost kitschy feel. Quaint signs and decorations, like a vintage Great Western Cooler Beer poster, added character. A framed print caught my eye: "Life is like a cake . . . If you put in stress and long hours and not enough fun, you get something that is flat and hard and bitter. But if you put in care and good work and food that you love, you will get something beautiful." I smiled despite my reservations.

Vivian, the manager, welcomed us with refreshing iced tea. She told us she had put us in the largest cabin and pointed the way toward it down a dirt path, past a "reading nook" overlooking the plains, a cacti garden, and a jackalberry tree that was home to two owls.

"Do you want to see them?" She asked. "I spotted them earlier today."

"Oh, yes, please!" Finn and Aria replied. We followed her outside, past dozens of guinea fowl, who clucked at our heels, and the resident donkey named *Soet Suen*, which Vivian said means "sweet thanks," in the local Nama language.

We peered into the high branches, finally spotting a tiny gray owl, who gazed at us through heavily slit eyes. Vivian said his mate must be out and told the kids to keep a lookout.

She invited us to settle in and take a sundowner walk on the property before dinner, cautioning us to stick near the train tracks and return before dark. The open land teemed with wildlife, including oryx and kudu, but also posed risks.

"Snakes?" Aria asked.

"You never know," Vivian said. "Namibia has more than eighty types of snakes—Cape cobra, black mambas, adders. We haven't seen many here recently, but it is possible. Keep your eyes open and step carefully. Have fun!"

After thanking her, we made our way to our cabin at the property's edge, being hyper vigilant of where we stepped. The cabin, like the lodge, was modest yet inviting, boasting a wraparound porch with expansive views of the flatlands. During our walk, an ostrich dashed away at our approach, and a herd of springbok eyed us warily from a distance. Randy and Aria strolled along the tracks, captivated by the sunset to the west and moonrise in the east.

Suddenly, Aria leaped backward, exclaiming, "Oh my gosh!" She had been looking down, on the alert for slithering movements. "Check this out! It's a stick insect! How cool!"

We looked down but saw nothing but dirt. "What are you looking at?"

"Watch! I wouldn't have spotted it, but it grazed against my leg!" She bent down, waving her hand at what looked like a twig. Then, the "twig" hopped forward.

"Oh, wow! That's crazy!" We laughed as the stick insect jumped to another resting spot, indistinguishable from a tiny branch even once we knew what to look for. "Great find, Aria!"

"I like this place," she announced as we walked back, bushwacking through the tall grasses toward the back patio of our cabin. "It'll be a neat place to have my birthday tomorrow."

"I agree, honey," I replied, hugging her. "Not many kids can say they've celebrated birthdays with stick insects, oryx, owls, and donkeys named Sweet Thanks, right?"

The next morning, Randy and I sought Vivian's help. We wanted to get Aria a birthday cake; but given there was nothing around for hours, we weren't sure where to go. We planned to take a day trip to the coastal town of Luderitz but were unsure of our chances of finding a bakery there. Vivian instantly offered to bake one herself.

"What flavor does she like?"

"She loves chocolate, but really, anything you make will be so appreciated," I responded.

At breakfast, we gave Aria her gifts: a wooden bead bracelet and colorful cloth hair scrunchy from a local women's cooperative, and a bag of candy.

"Thank you," she beamed, trying on the bracelet. "These will always remind me of Namibia."

As we set off for Luderitz, Vivian mentioned keeping an eye out for Namibia's unique wild horses.

"It's the only feral herd of horses in Africa," she said.

Finn, allergic to horses, frowned, but Aria eagerly embraced the challenge. The drive to the coast took several hours, and we didn't see any horses. We did see a lone zebra and, as we neared the coast, more rust-colored dunes streaked with black.

"I wonder what makes the dunes red," Finn wondered aloud. "It's so different from the Sahara. Also, why do they have those black smudges? Do you think that's soot from the trains?"

"Not sure," Randy replied. "It is different."

In Luderitz, we ate at a seaside restaurant, steeling ourselves against the chilly Atlantic breeze. Randy and Aria braved the ocean, wading ankle-deep, while Finn and I skipped stones.

On our return, Aria spotted some wild horses in the distance. They were far enough away to make Finn happy but near enough to count as a cool wildlife sighting for Aria. Back at the lodge, we refreshed quickly, then dressed for dinner.

The dining room had a lively energy with a handful of other guests. At our table, a vase of flowers and chocolates awaited Aria.

"That's so thoughtful," she said, knowing she had Vivian to thank for the surprise. "Can I eat the chocolates now?"

"Go ahead," I smiled. "Birthday privilege."

At the end of dinner, Vivian, along with the other staff members, came out carrying a chocolate cake. Adorned with eleven candles, it was slightly lopsided, with glistening chocolate frosting that only partially covered the sides. It looked like the cakes my grandmother used to bake—simple, unpretentious, and made with love. Aria's eyes lit up as she spotted Vivian coming out of the kitchen with it.

They sang happy birthday to her, first in Nama, then in English. She closed her eyes, made a wish, then blew out the candles only to find them still lit a few seconds later. She inhaled and blew again. And again, they relit.

"Trick candles?" She let out a giggle. "That is hilarious."

We all laughed as she tried in vain to blow them out, eventually getting an assist from Randy and Finn who snuffed them out with wet fingers.

"Thank you," Aria told Vivian, still laughing, and gave her a hug. All the staff followed, giving Aria a kiss on each cheek. In a small way, it felt like home for the first time since leaving Colorado.

As we tucked her into bed that night, Aria snuggled up with her mini koala stuffie, Kaleb, and said, "That was the best birthday ever."

We said goodbye to our friends at Alte Kalkoefen the following day to continue our overland journey north. We again passed the rusty Ford pickup and gas station, which we had learned were remnants from the time when the farm and kilns were functional, left to preserve the history of the land.

It wasn't the fanciest or nicest place on our trip thus far, but it had been homey and friendly, and utterly perfect.

Over the next few days, as we made our way toward the capital, Windhoek, we explored more of southern and central Namibia, which slowly revealed more of its facets to us, like layers of rock chipped away and exposed over time.

After one particularly long driving day, tensions peaked with the kids arguing, leading to a shouting match in a cramped hotel room in the middle of nowhere. Randy, frustrated, raised his voice; Aria ended up in tears, and Finn angrily retreated to his bed. I went and sat in the bathroom, needing alone time but finding space at a premium.

Once we'd all cooled down, Randy and I separately spoke with each kid, giving them time to reflect. We asked them to write about what the trip meant to them, their feelings, and ideas to improve our travel experience.

Then, we convened a family meeting that evening. We discussed our journey so far—what was working and what wasn't. While we all were loving the trip, the nonstop togetherness of our two-week Namibian road trip had left us craving personal space and downtime. Finn and Aria suggested occasional sleep-ins, a bit more alone time or one-on-one parent time, and days where they could plan activities.

The discussion felt cathartic, and we went to bed feeling lighter and ready for more exploration.

In the language of the San Bushmen, the people of the desert, *We Kebi* means invitation. When we checked into the desert lodge, dusty from another day of bouncing over rocky roads and barren plains—but one in which we let everyone sleep in—the receptionist greeted us with fruit juice and welcomed us to enjoy the beauty of the surrounding savanna.

"Come," he said. "There were Kudu by the watering hole. Shall we see if they're still there?"

Yes," Finn cried, already charging outside.

"We're on a large piece of land with many wild animals," he continued.

Finn's curiosity peaked. "Rhinos?"

"Yes, a few white rhinos. Maybe you'll spot them," he said. Finn's face lit up with the prospect of seeing the rhino that eluded us in Tanzania.

The lodge's reception area led to a wooden deck, overlooking two watering holes and grasslands beyond. Couches and chairs were arranged around a large camel thorn tree, perfect for animal watching at dawn and dusk.

"There, look! Kudu drinking right now!" Aria pointed excitedly at the watering hole.

Our gaze strayed to a large, bulbous nest high in the tree. "That's a communal nest," our host explained. "The weaver birds construct it, with entrances facing downward to protect against snakes. They even build fake entrances to trick predators like Cape cobras."

"Smart," Aria remarked, impressed by the birds' ingenuity.

Our host added, "But don't stand directly underneath—bird droppings, and you wouldn't want a snake falling on you."

We sidestepped quickly.

"Let me show you to your rooms," he said, guiding us along a stone pathway. Our hut had some unique features. "Signs you're in remote Namibia," I noted wryly, calling out the emergency horn for wild animal encounters, mosquito spray, and a genuine zebra pelt on the floor.

"Certainly not your everyday hotel amenities," Randy agreed. He and Aria chose to remain to read and rest until dinner, while Finn and I ventured out to the main lodge.

Later, as the sun set, a stir arose near the common room. Finn and I hurried outside to see what the commotion was about.

"Mom! Look, two rhinos!" Finn whispered excitedly.

We watched the pair shuffle toward the watering hole, drink, then graze. One lumbered along the stone path, headed directly toward the cottages.

In the same instant, Finn and I spotted Randy and Aria, who were crouched behind some bushes, now trapped by the rhinos.

"Oh, no!" Finn cried. "They must have been on their way over here. What will they do?"

"I don't know. If they keep coming, they'll run right into that rhino by the hut. But if they go back the other will see them."

They seemed unsure of what to do. A nearby guide, noticing their predicament, motioned frantically for them to stay put. He waved and pointed to indicate he'd come guide them, telling us as he ran off about the rhinos' poor vision and tendency to charge if startled.

He circled the huts, reaching Randy and Aria in minutes. The rustling alerted the rhino, who jolted as if to charge but then relaxed, returning to the watering hole.

"That was close," Aria said, arriving breathless at the lodge.

"Were you scared?" I asked.

"A bit," Randy confessed. "I was figuring out an escape route. Thankfully, not needed."

"Well, that's an exciting way to start dinner," I said, slightly shaken.

By contrast, Finn seemed to think it had been a grand adventure. "We've seen all the Big Five now. Some closer than others!"

Driving northwest, the savanna gradually gave way to the rust-colored sand dunes of the Namib Desert, a region stretching along the Atlantic coast from South Africa to Angola. The Namib, the oldest and driest desert on earth, derives its name from the Nama language, translating, fittingly, to "an area where there is nothing."

Our destination was Sossusvlei, a valley within the Namib-Naukluft National Park. Here, some of the world's highest dunes rise to 1,300 feet (400 m) from a large salt and clay pan. Sossusvlei, meaning "dead-end marsh," is where the Tsauchab River meets its end among the dunes. The dry conditions allowed us to walk across Deadvlei, a cracked white clay pan dotted with ancient, dead camel thorn trees that created a surreal, otherworldly contrast against the red dunes and bright blue sky.

We set our sights on Big Daddy, one of the tallest dunes. From the base, hikers at the top appeared tiny.

"That looks intense," Finn remarked, eyeing the dune.

"We've got this," I encouraged. "Let's go."

With every step, we rose and sank in the soft sand. Randy and the kids opted to hike the steep dune barefoot; I quickly realized the folly of my choice of sandals, frequently stopping to tilt them upward, letting sand pour out.

Reaching the ridge line, we were rewarded with stunning views. The dunes spread out in shades of apricot and rust-orange, encircling the parched pan below.

"Race you down!" Finn called.

Aria had already started forward. "Bring it on!"

"Wait for the countdown!" I protested, joining them.

Randy became our referee. "Ready, set, go!"

We took off, sand flying as we sped downhill. Halfway through, I kicked off my sandals at last, dashing in earnest to the flat pan of Deadvlei. At the bottom, we strolled past the haunting black trees, enchanted by the light playing tricks on the dry salt bed.

On our last night in Namibia, we stayed near Sossusvlei at a desert lodge. Our guide, Sam, entertained Finn and Aria with tales of his bushman upbringing near the Caprivi strip. They laughed at stories of his antics as a mischievous boy in the bush and held their breath hearing about his encounter with a black mamba.

"You didn't run?" Aria asked, wide-eyed.

"I couldn't," Sam explained. "Running would have meant death. I just stared until the big snake slithered away."

Quad biking through the red dunes, we encountered two oryx standing sentry-like on both sides of the narrow trail. "Speed up the hill," Sam advised, already zooming off. We followed suit, feeling a rush of adrenaline as we revved the ATVs past them.

Afterward, Sam offered a mini-science lesson. "Ever wonder why the sand is red and sometimes streaked with black?" he asked.

We hadn't figured it out yet. Sam revealed the secret. He pulled a small magnet from his pocket, wrapped it in tissue, and ran it along the sand. We peered to look as it pulled up tiny black flecks from the sand.

"It's iron," he explained. "The red color comes from oxidized iron. The black streaks are where the iron hasn't rusted yet."

We all took turns running the magnet through the sand, intrigued by the coarse black grains hidden underneath.

"Come," Sam called as we maneuvered our ATVs back to the shelter and hopped into the truck. "Let's do a short hike to a cave before we return to the lodge.

"The Namib Desert is rich in archaeological sites," he continued. "Early man lived here seasonally, during wet cycles. Some permanent homes have been found in these hills. Nomadic San Bushmen passed through for hundreds of years. Look."

At the cave, Sam pointed to faded rock paintings. "What's this?" he prompted.

"A giraffe!" Aria exclaimed.

"And this one?"

Finn peered in closer. "A person!"

Sam nodded, then showed us relics found nearby - stone tools, ostrich egg shards, arrowheads, and ancient jewelry.

"Cool," said Finn.

That evening, after sunset, we gathered at an outdoor observatory for stargazing. With no light pollution, the desert's night sky was a spectacular display of stars and constellations.

Frank, a visiting astronomer, guided us through the cosmos. We wrapped ourselves in woolen blankets, taking turns at the telescope.

"That is Omega Centauri," Frank said, "the largest globular star cluster. It's more than seventeen thousand light years outside the Milky Way galaxy."

"Wow," Finn whispered. "Amazing."

Frank adjusted the telescope again, pointing out first the Eta Carinae Nebula, one of the Milky Way's largest stellar nurseries, and then the Jewel Box.

"What's that?" Aria asked.

"Another open star cluster—a collection of a few dozen brilliant stars that formed from a nebula. It's named for the colorful stars, which look like jewels," Frank explained.

He said there was time for one more; Finn and Aria eagerly requested Saturn. They hoped to see its rings up close. Frank told us that it had just reached opposition, meaning the earth was positioned in orbit between the sun and the huge planet, so we'd be able to see it well.

"Saturn it is," he said, swiveling the telescope and inviting us to take a look. "Its rings are brighter than usual because the ice particles are reflecting the sun's light back at earth, like a frosted mirror."

"Incredible," I breathed. It was like photos in textbooks, the rings and planet sharper than anything I had ever seen before, and I found myself getting a little teary-eyed.

As we stood together, huddled in the prickly wool blanket against the cool desert night, eyes trained upward toward the southern skies, I thought about a quote I had read once by Mary Ann Radmacher about travel. It had always resonated with me, but never more so than it did that night. "I am not the same, having seen the moon shine on the other side of the world."

I closed my eyes and breathed deeply.

"Look," I said softly a few minutes later, and pointed toward the horizon. "Moonrise."

Because, sure enough, the moon had begun its ascent and already the stars were starting to fade away in its soft, white glow.

ALMOND FAMILY REPORT CARD ON NAMIBIA

- *Top Marks*: Rent a truck or camper van for a self-guided tour across Namibia's expansive landscapes. Book early during the summer months as availability is limited.
- *Needs Work*: Dress appropriately for the desert climate, which can be misleading. Temperatures drop drastically after sunset, so carry extra layers for evening game drives to stay comfortable throughout the experience.
- *Learning Tips*: Use Namibia's diverse environments for educational experiences. Discuss geological formations at Fish River Canyon, observe wildlife behavior across the plains, and research why the Namib sand dunes have their distinctive rust-colored hues.

II

SECOND-QUARTER WORLDSCHOOLING GOALS
(September–December)

September 2022
Dear Finn and Aria,

What a summer we have had! We loved backpacking with you over the last three months, and we're proud of how much you have grown on our travels across Morocco, France, the Netherlands, Tanzania, South Africa, Namibia, Zimbabwe, and Botswana. And we're not even a third of the way through our family gap year. There's so much more to come.

You have learned more than you probably realize since leaving home. You now know how to say "hello" and "thank you" in Arabic, French, Dutch, and Swahili. You've expanded your palate to appreciate (or at least try) new flavors, sampling tagines and shakshukas, oryx and ostrich. You navigated the metro system in Paris and began to better appreciate great works of art at the Louvre. You studied the physics of diving and earned your PADI scuba certification. You learned about injustices under apartheid in South Africa and its lasting effects to today. You can identify the tracks of a range of wild animals and constellations in the southern skies, and you seem more comfortable in a range of places in the world, from the wide-open deserts and the Okavango Delta to cosmopolitan European cities.

Back home, your friends have started school again. So, we will be doing the same and layering onto our travels more of your worldschooling curriculum. The primary focus will continue to be on learning through immersive travel and our day-to-day experiences. We'll ramp up other lessons, as well, namely in math and structured writing assignments. We want to make sure you have the tools to be successful when you return and rejoin your classes next fall—and to ensure that you don't fall behind in any subjects.

These are the goals we have for you for our next quarter (September–December):

1. *Continue to read the guidebooks in each country we're in.* This has been helpful to ground us all in each area and give context for our travels. It has worked well to alternate reading on our own and reading aloud to each other in cafes or on car trips, so we can continue doing that. Focus on the history and culture sections, in addition to chapters with general insights and suggestions for places we're visiting.
2. *Continue reading fiction and nonfiction texts tied to where we are in the world.* Some of the books we read in our first three months you loved and others you found tougher. That's natural—and akin to what you'll find in school. Not every book assigned will be one you'd choose to read for pleasure, but they all enriched your understanding of the countries we're exploring.

    In the fall quarter, we'll focus on reading a mix of classics—like Homer's *Iliad*, which may be a little heavy, but we will listen to it as an audio book and can talk through it together and explain anything that's challenging to follow—as well as memoirs and fiction.

    Here's our starter literature list for this quarter:

    - Greece: The *Iliad* by Homer
    - Jordan / Egypt: *The Language of Baklava* by Diana Abu-Jaber
    - Brazil: *My Sweet Orange Tree* by José Mauro de Vasconcelos; *The Alchemist* by Paolo Coelho
    - Argentina: *The End of Ice: Bearing Witness and Finding Meaning in the Path of Climate Disruption* by Dahr Jamail

3. *Watch films or TV series to enrich our on-the-ground experience.* It has been helpful to watch documentaries and movies that offer

deeper insights into a country. So, we'll continue to find opportunities to do that. Here is our target list:

- Greece: *The Greeks* (three-part series from *National Geographic* and PBS)
- Egypt: *The Square* (Emmy-award-winning documentary about the 2011 Egyptian Revolution and Arab Spring) and *Lost Treasures of Egypt* (*National Geographic* documentary series)
- Brazil: *The Edge of Democracy* (2019 Brazilian documentary film exploring the first term of President Lula and the events leading up to the impeachment of Dilma Rousseff—this will be particularly relevant as we will be in Brazil during the 2022 presidential run-off between Lula and incumbent Jair Bolsonaro, so the film will provide us all with helpful context)
- Argentina: *Evita* (musical about the life of Eva Duarte Perón and her rise from poverty to First Lady of Argentina)
- Relevant to anywhere: *The Last Tourist* (documentary about the dangerous effects of over-tourism and the potential of responsible tourism)

4. *Continue the daily practice of writing in your journal.* You have gotten more disciplined about writing almost every day. Now, we'll focus on the *quality* of your entries. I (Mom) have outlined a rubric that will help guide you in thinking about what kinds of things to write:

- Start each entry with the date and location (city, country).
- Write three to four pages (Finn) and two to three pages (Aria) minimum daily.
- Use dialogue to bring part of the day to life.
- Avoid generic words and phrases that are meaningless to the reader (e.g., it was a fun day; our guide is nice; the animals were cool). Instead, make it concrete (e.g., today we did a six-hour hike in a narrow slot canyon; our guide, Sam, makes us laugh telling us funny stories from growing up near the Okavango Delta and the mischievous things he and his brothers would do; the zebras bop their heads as they walk, making us think they are dancing to their own music).
- Bring in specific sensory details (sight, sound, taste, smell, feel).

- Talk about things that surprised you, what made you laugh, what frustrated you, what you liked and what you did not.
- Talk about how you felt after whatever part of the day you focused on.
- Talk about anything that you learned that day or from the experience.

5. *Continue learning the language basics—and more in South America.* You have seen how much people's faces light up when you speak to them in their local language. We'll continue to learn the pleasantries everywhere we go and seek to go deeper in a few countries. In Brazil, we'll spend a couple of weeks taking Portuguese lessons as a family. And in Argentina, you'll build on your already-solid Spanish by taking another two weeks of lessons in Buenos Aires.

We will use the Duolingo app, Google Translate, and lists of phrases to give us the basics everywhere else:

- Greece: Greek
- Jordan and Egypt: Arabic
- Brazil: Portuguese
- Argentina: Spanish

6. *Write one short entry to a children's travel magazine.* After our more serious nonfiction essays in your first quarter, we'll now turn to a more fun type of nonfiction writing—travel writing. You are to submit answers to a series of questions for a kids' travel magazine called *Wild Explorers*. You will select one experience from our travels and focus your answers on that story. We'll submit it to the magazine for publication so you can see your words in print!

7. *Start math curriculum.* This year, you'll be covering the same topics in math as your classmates in Colorado. Your teachers back home pointed me (Dad) to an online curriculum that covers everything you need, and I can help you if you get stuck.

- Finn, you'll be learning geometry this year. Given your intuitive feel for spatial relationships, I think you'll enjoy it. For this quarter, you'll cover the first four units:
  i. Geometry Basics
  ii. Logic and Proof

iii. Parallel and Perpendicular Lines
iv. Congruent Triangles

- Aria, you'll be covering sixth-grade math, which will provide you with the foundation for more specialized work in seventh grade and beyond. For this quarter, you'll cover the following:
  i. Decimals
  ii. Fractions and One-step Equations
  iii. Introduction to Geometry

8. *Be fully present in the experiences we are having.* As you have seen, you're learning so much just by being present and approaching all the new experiences we are having with a sense of wonder and curiosity. Keep doing what you are doing. Ask lots of questions. Talk to people we meet. Try new things. Push yourselves. Be safe and street smart. And enjoy the experience!

We're excited for the fall quarter and all the new adventures we'll have.
Love,
Your worldschooling teachers (Mom and Dad)

9

WISDOM BEGINS IN WONDER

Greece

Excerpt from Finn's Journal
September 13, 2022 | Delphi, Greece

As we wind our way up the cobbled path, we see the ruins of ancient Delphi. In all of Greece from what we've seen, this site, in my opinion, is the best restored. We walk past the ruins of the Temple of Apollo and the place where the oracle of Delphi gave her famous prophecies. Ancient Greeks would come from all over to ask the oracle for wisdom, bringing sacrifices to Apollo, the god of prophecy. They would bring these in the hope that he would give them a good prophecy, not one of death and destruction.

One ancient king didn't bring an offering and was told by the oracle that if he invaded Rome, a great empire would fall. Interpreting that to mean that he would be victorious, he charged into battle. Apollo, angered on Olympus, snickered because the oracle had not said which empire would fall. And in turn, the king's empire fell.

I really like Delphi because I think the stories are amazing, and it's very pretty. It has the best location. No towns in sight and it is in a valley full of trees and rivers. I love it so much.

CHAPTER 9

In the shade of a cypress grove on the site of ancient Olympia, Finn and Aria inserted headphones into their ears. They then lifted a set of bulky goggles to their eyes and swept their gaze across the ruins before us, as though looking through binoculars.

"Whoa! I just lit the Olympic flame!" Aria shouted, one hand firmly holding the goggles in place, the other stretched in front of her. She pawed the air, as if trying to grasp something in front of her.

Nearby, Finn trained his gaze through his goggles toward an open field, gesticulating wildly into nothingness. "And I am training the Olympians! Look at them! C'mon boys, you can do better than that! Move it, move it, move it!"

Continuing to peer through the goggles, they spun their heads left and right, up and down, as if on a swivel, being careful to keep their feet firmly rooted to one spot. The virtual-reality (VR) goggles, which use geo-tags to identify location markers in the ruins, created three-dimensional illusions in front of their eyes, bringing to life the history of the ancient Greek civilization.

Walking across the expansive archaeological site, around remnants of once towering temples and statues, we shared the two VR sets we had rented among the four of us, alternating between projections of the past and the ruins at our feet.

Rather than trying to imagine a statue of Zeus on the now-empty plinth before us, we watched it being erected, seeing rather than simply reading how the Greeks managed the feat of engineering thousands of years ago. We heard the tinkle of water in the Nymphaeum, seeming so real we reached out to touch it but found only air. And as we ran under the archway into the stadium, we were deafened by the roar of forty thousand Greek spectators cheering on the athletes as they raced in the first-ever Olympic Games. Aria pumped her fist in the air as she watched the imaginary Olympians cross the finish line, feet from where we stood.

"Come on," Randy said, pulling off the goggles and removing the earbuds. He stepped onto the dirt on the long stadium field. "Let's race for real where the Olympians once ran! Who's with me?"

Finn sprinted up, grinning. "You're on!"

"I'm in, too," Aria called. "Mama, you can be the referee!"

"For the first race, I will. Then it's my turn to run," I agreed, jogging over to stand on the sidelines near the middle of the field.

"On your mark," I shouted. "Get set! Go!"

They took off. Finn crossed the finish line first; Randy, who had made the mistake of giving the kids a head start, came in second; and Aria pulled up the rear.

"You know, in the early Olympic days, there was no recognition for silver or bronze," I noted. "You either won gold or you got nothing. Well done, Finn! The victor! Randy, Aria, better luck in four years."

We laughed as Aria slouched in a defeated position, pretending to sulk, and headed back toward the entrance. On the way, she noticed an archaeologist working on one of the ruins. Hunched over a large stone base, the woman was sweeping the surface with a small brush and jotting down notes in a book.

"What do you think she's doing?" Aria asked me.

"I don't know, honey. Why don't you go and talk to her? You can ask."

"You think it's okay? I don't want to disturb her."

"I'm sure it's fine. Go on. We'll wait for you here."

Squaring her shoulders, Aria walked over and chatted with the woman for a while before trotting back.

"She was doing field work—taking measurements," Aria reported. "She's trying to figure out how the columns once connected to the bases. Super cool!"

"That's really interesting," I replied. "I'm glad you went and asked; I was curious too."

As we neared the exit, on our way to catch up with the guys, Aria turned and looked back at the ruins. "I feel like archaeology would be an interesting career," she mused. "You'd get to travel to far-away places, be outside, learn new things, and solve puzzles. Seems exciting."

I smiled. "I love that you're thinking about things like that and connecting what we see on our travels with possibilities in your own life. I'm sure we'll have many opportunities in upcoming weeks for you to learn more about archeology. It is fascinating."

She grabbed my hand, lost in thought, as we caught up to Randy and Finn and headed back to our rental car to continue our explorations of the Peloponnese.

❖ ❖ ❖

Greece is a worldschooling godsend for a teen and tween, and not just because it's the home of Zeus and the Olympians. Though, in Finn's eyes, that automatically endowed it with endless mystique and created a unique bridge from myth and legend to history and present day.

By virtue of the fact that you are literally walking on history almost everywhere you go, each day offered endless immersive lessons in philosophy, history, government and civics, art, mathematics, science, and more. So, it was the perfect place to shift out of summer break mode into a more focused fall quarter. Coupled with plans for subsequent travels through Jordan and Egypt, our time in Greece shaped an ideal Worldschooling 101 course in the cradles of Western civilization. Randy, the history buff, had been eagerly awaiting this portion of our trip. And I had been pleased to find a fitting choice for the kids' literature assignment for Greece, one that would complement our real-world experiences.

"When we start our road trip tomorrow, we'll begin Homer's classic the *Iliad*," I told the kids upon arriving in Athens. "We can listen to it as an audiobook in the car."

"What's it about?" Finn asked.

"It is a poem that tells the story of the last year of the Trojan War and the clash between King Agamemnon and the Greek hero Achilles."

"A poem?" Aria asked. "Will it be short?"

"No. Not all poems are short. And this one is definitely not! Homer wrote two epic poems, the *Iliad* and the *Odyssey*. The *Iliad* is around seven hundred pages, and it's something like four hundred pages for the *Odyssey*. So, it'll take us a while to get through the *Iliad*."

Luckily, we were used to listening to long audiobooks. One of the last ones we had tackled back home, *The Count of Monte Cristo*, took us almost two years of road trips across Colorado to finish. (Incidentally, I felt that Alexandre Dumas could have used a better editor to tighten it up.)

"Doesn't odyssey mean a long journey?" Finn asked.

"Yep," I said.

Aria nodded wisely. "Like us. We're on an odyssey, too."

Randy smiled and jumped in, "True. Though sometimes an odyssey is defined as a long and complicated journey, filled with obstacles. Let's hope ours is just one that's full of adventure."

MATH IN THE REAL WORLD: INTERACTIVE CALCULATIONS FOR KIDS

Turning everyday experiences into math lessons is a fantastic way to engage kids with numbers and concepts in a real-world context. On travel of any length, there are countless opportunities to make math fun and practical. Here are some ideas:

- *Calculate Distances and Heights*: If you're hiking or cliff jumping, use simple formulas to estimate the height of a rock wall or the distance of a trail. This helps kids understand measurement and basic geometry. (Pro tip—Google can remind you of the formulas if math isn't your forte!)
- *Budgeting for a Trip*: Involve your kids in planning the budget for a family outing or vacation. Let them handle money, compare prices, and calculate expenses to understand the value of money and basic arithmetic.
- *Cooking and Baking Measurements*: Involve kids in cooking by asking them to measure ingredients, teaching fractions, conversions, and basic algebra in a tasty way.
- *Nature Patterns and Counting*: Identify and count patterns in nature, like the number of petals on flowers or the arrangement of leaves on a stem. This helps kids see the connection between math and the natural world.
- *Shopping for Deals*: When shopping, ask them to calculate discounts and final prices. It's a real-world application of percentages and mental math.

Our plan for our time in Greece was to rent a car and spend time exploring the mainland, starting in the eastern Peloponnese, and making our way west, then traveling as far north as Meteora before looping back through Delphi and returning briefly to Athens. From there, we would take a ferry to one or two of the Greek islands.

Before we set off, our deep dive into history began with a full day in the capital. We started with a morning at the Acropolis Museum, learning about the artifacts and sculptures created two thousand years earlier. In the afternoon, we met up with George Kokkos, an archaeologist and author of a young adult book on influential philosophers, who had been recommended by a friend as a great local guide. He gave us a tour of Athens focused primarily on Greek mythology and its lasting influence up to present day.

We met George at a coffee shop. He ordered an *espresso freddo* to go, and we set off on foot toward the iconic Academy of Athens. We took refuge from the sweltering summer heat by standing in the shade of two olive trees while he talked about the statues around the landmark building.

"See that statue of the goddess in armor? Do you know who she is?" he asked.

"Athena," Finn replied immediately. "And that's Apollo with his lyre on the other side!"

"Correct," George said. "You can always recognize Athena by her helmet and spear. She is the patron and protectress of Athens. The goddess of wisdom and warfare. But different from her brother, Ares, who is also the god of war. Athena is about strategy and generalship; Ares, brute strength and bloodlust."

Finn nodded, grinning. He knew a lot already about mythology from reading Rick Riordan's *Percy Jackson* books as well as other books on Greek, Roman, and Egyptian mythology. Being in Greece made all the myths he loved tangible, their legacies and lessons clearer.

As we got up to walk on, George drew our attention to the seated marble figures of Plato and Socrates.

"Socrates was a Greek philosopher," he told the kids. "Arguably the most influential thinker ever. He was one of the first moral philosophers who investigated the field of ethics—what's right and wrong. He was Plato's teacher. He was accused of corrupting the youth and was sentenced to death for his constant questioning about truth and justice."

"That's harsh," Finn said.

"Yes," George agreed. "He spent his life asking questions and challenging social norms, always in search of truth. One of his legacies is devising a system of free speech, which is one of the most important pillars of democracy today."

We continued, winding our way through the streets of the city, stopping by the train tracks to gaze up at the Acropolis and Parthenon, through Monastriaki, past the ancient *agora*, or marketplace, and ultimately stopped at the brass statue of Theseus.

"Now, why did I choose to end our tour with Theseus? Do you know who he is?"

On cue, Finn jumped in. "He was the hero who slayed the minotaur on the island of Crete."

"Right again," George said. "But do you know what happened after that?"

"He lived happily ever after?" Finn guessed.

George grinned. "Not so much. His father, Aegeus, the King of Athens, had told him to put up white sails if he succeeded in slaying the minotaur, something no one thought possible. Aegeus stood every day on a promontory overlooking the sea, keeping watch for his son's ship. When Theseus returned, so excited about his victory over the beast, he forgot his father's instructions. As his ship approached the mainland still flying black sails—a sign of mourning—his father, thinking his son dead, killed himself by jumping off the cliffs into the water below, which would later be known as the Aegean Sea."

"Why didn't Aegeus wait to see if it was true that Theseus died?" Aria asked, indignantly. "That would have been a better idea."

George shrugged. "True, but he did not. Theseus was so consumed with grief when he learned about his father's death that he resigned the throne and placed power in the hands of the people. He established a government by the people, where all were equal . . . the birth of democracy. So, Theseus is a really important figure for us. Myth and legend, you see, are always tied together with history."

The kids nodded, thinking that through.

As we said our goodbyes, George gave Finn and Aria copies of his recently published book, *Heroes of Philosophy*.

"Oh, that's so nice," I said. "Would you autograph them?"

Nodding, he thought for a moment before signing his name on the cover and adding, fittingly, a quote from Socrates, "To Finn and Aria—Wisdom begins in wonder."

I loved that. What a perfect summary of exactly what we hoped to accomplish on our travels and through worldschooling the kids.

"Wisdom begins in wonder," I read aloud. "It's perfect, George. Thank you."

The following day, we picked up our rental car, eager to leave the crowds of Athens behind. While it was past peak summer tourist season, and children across Europe had recently returned to school, there were still heavy throngs of visitors in the capital. We'd made the mistake of visiting the Parthenon when all the cruise ships disembarked, and thousands of people funneled into the site at once.

"Ugh, this is insane," I mumbled to Randy as I held Aria's hand in a death grip. "Can you imagine what this place must have been like in July and August?"

He was smushed in the mass of humanity and replied something that sounded like mumble wumble mumble.

"What?" I called.

"Just keep walking," he said, peering around a large shoulder. "At least we're good at avoiding crowds most of the time."

We kept walking, swept toward the Parthenon by the tidal wave of people, trying to keep Finn and Randy in our sights. And while it was impressive when we finally arrived at the top of the steps, we were thankful to have the rental car thereafter, giving us the opportunity to exit the main tourist track. As soon as we drove across the Corinth Canal to the Peloponnese peninsula, we noticed a marked decrease in the number of tourists. Restaurants had ample seating. We could roll up to a small hotel and book a room for the same night without a problem. Shopkeepers and guesthouse owners spoke more limited English, leaving us to communicate with the help of our basic Greek, translator apps, and sign language.

One particularly memorable exchange happened as we checked into a B&B (bed and breakfast) in a small town and tried to converse with the gregarious elderly owner. The woman misunderstood Aria's name and took to calling her "Oreo" as she talked at us in rapid-fire Greek. We finally understood that she was very excited to learn we had named our daughter after a popular sandwich cookie. She was so enthused about our sweet name choices—pun intended—that she took to calling both kids "cookies," and showered them with local candy when we left.

Over the next two weeks, we road tripped across the Greek mainland, staying a range of one to four nights in any given place. We rented a mix of Airbnb apartments and rooms in guesthouses and small hotels with names like Hotel Hercules, Olympic Hotel, and Apollo Inn. Our days fell into a familiar rhythm, with a natural balance to them.

In the mornings, we were students of history, touring ancient ruins and temples at Mycenae, Sparta, Epidavros, and more. Walking through the remnants of civilizations we were hearing about at their apex in the *Iliad*. Exploring the medieval castle city of Mystras surrounded by orange and olive groves on the slope of Mount Taygetos. And, on the three-month anniversary of the start of our year-long odyssey, as Aria had taken to calling it, lighting candles at the monastery of Varlaan perched atop a towering rock spire in Meteora.

In the afternoons, we found adventure—cliff jumping and swimming in the clear waters of the Argolic and Ionic seas; gliding in a rowboat through the vast subterranean lake caves of Diros, gazing up at thousands of tiny stalactites hanging like icicles from the low-lying ceiling; white water rafting on the Arachthos River; and hiking, rock climbing, and mushroom foraging with local guides in the hills.

In the evenings, we carved out time for math, reading, journaling, and working on essay assignments, as well as simply relaxing. When we stayed at an Airbnb with living space and a kitchen, Finn and Aria not-so-subtly encouraged us to go out for a date night. They looked forward to those quieter nights where they could stay in and have alone time to finish their work then play video games, watch TV, and catch up with friends. And we were only too happy to comply with their plan.

"How's the research going for your essay?" I asked Aria before Randy and I headed out on our last evening in Meteora, in northwestern Greece. The kids were having *gyros* for dinner, a popular Greek sandwich consisting of slow-cooked meat stuffed in a pita bread and topped with tomato, onion, french fries, and creamy tzatziki.

"Good," Aria said, flipping through her notes on a tiny spiral bound notepad. "I want to talk to you about four possible solutions I found to the elephant overpopulation problem in Africa. I can see why nothing has been done for a while. All the solutions have really serious downsides to them!"

"Awesome," I said. "Let's talk through them tomorrow. I can help you think about an outline for your essay. Then you'll be close to starting on your rough draft."

I turned to Finn. "And how about you, buddy? How is your entry going for the travel magazine?"

"Pretty good," he said. "I'm trying to figure out what story I want to tell—it'll probably be when we saw the cheetah take down the gnu in Tanzania."

I gave him a quick hug. "Good, make sure to work on it before TV." They both nodded. "We know, we know . . . bye!"

Randy and I drove a short distance down a path we had spotted earlier in the day. We hiked to the top of a rock pillar, far from the spot where we had seen all the tourists go, to watch the sun set over the majestic rock formations all around us.

Derived from the ancient Greek word *meteoros*, the name Meteora means, "raised from the ground, hanging, lofty." It was a fitting name for this place that's home to the largest and most precipitously built complexes of Eastern Orthodox monasteries in the world, I thought. We sat in silence for about an hour watching the last rays of light cast ever-longer shadows on the rocks before night fell.

While we had settled into a good rhythm of travel, we recognized the need to carve out time here and there to reflect, regroup, and decompress as well. Since our blow up and subsequent family meeting in Namibia, we were consciously trying to vary our pace of travel more, interspersing stretches of slower travel and creating opportunities for solitude or one-on-one time together in different combinations.

Retreating to the Greek islands for a week after our stint of 24/7 togetherness while driving across the mainland offered us the chance for space and downtime. The kids also needed time to finish their essays and stories and complete math assignments. After talking to locals and poring over guidebooks and ferry schedules, we settled on visiting two of the lesser-known Cycladic islands, Paros and Amorgos.

We spent lazy mornings driving to secluded coves and swimming in the turquoise waters. Aria and I carved out mother-daughter time by taking a watercolor class one afternoon, learning how to paint traditional Greek scenes, while Randy and Finn rented a motor scooter and whizzed around the island.

Aria and Finn completed their essay and story, respectively, which I reviewed. We discussed my suggested edits, then they had time to wrap up final drafts. Having learned from my past missteps, I graded them on a rubric I had outlined in advance, drawing on ones I'd found online. We also finished the *Iliad*, which Finn gave five stars out of five and Aria zero. And, occasionally, we found opportunities to sneak in practical worldschooling into our adventuring.

With their rocky shorelines, both Paros and Amorgos offered ample opportunities for cliff jumping, one of Randy's and the kids' favorite pastimes. Less of a fan, I would hang out on the nearby rocks, taking photos or napping in the sun. The three of them would scout locations, checking out the depth of the water with their goggles, then scramble up the cliffs above deep pools. They would gradually work their way to higher and higher spots. Then they leaped into the crystal-clear waters, Finn often doing a backflip, just because he could.

"How high do you think that last cliff was that we jumped off?" Finn asked Randy as we had a late lunch at an open-air restaurant on the beach.

"Well, the good news is, we can calculate that," Randy answered. He grabbed a pen and started scribbling formulas on the paper tablecloth, showing the kids how to solve the problem. Finn and Aria crowded around to work on it with him.

"We can also calculate how fast we were going when we hit the water. Math and physics can give us all those answers."

Finn, who loves math, hunched over the table, making calculations.

After a few moments, he had his answer. "The cliffs were thirty feet high! Is that right?"

Randy double checked his math. "Yep, that's right."

"And we were going thirty miles per hour," Finn continued. "That's so cool! I can't wait to tell my friends."

"Mom, can we get ice cream?" Aria asked after working on the problems.

"Sure, why not," I said. "Why don't you go check out what the flavor options are and ask how much it costs. We're not in a rush. After all, we've got nothing but time on our odyssey."

ALMOND FAMILY REPORT CARD ON GREECE

- *Top Marks*: Rent a car for an immersive road trip through Greece, starting in the Peloponnese, continuing north to Meteora's clifftop monasteries, through historic Delphi, and concluding in Athens. This route offers a fascinating, beautiful, and educational loop through some of Greece's rich landscapes and heritage.
- *Needs Work*: Choosing among Greece's six thousand islands can be overwhelming. Visit lesser-known islands for more cost-effective and authentic—but no less stunning—experiences.
- *Learning Tips*: Make history come alive with virtual reality goggles at sites like ancient Olympia and explore geological features to tie science into your travels.

10

THE DEATHSTALKER

Jordan

Excerpt from Aria's Journal
September 25, 2022 | Umm Qais, Jordan

Today we have a chill breakfast at the B&B. Finn and Mom take a stone masonry class where they learn how to carve beautiful designs in stone. I work on math with dad. After finishing chapter 2, I take a quiz. In the afternoon, we all take a cooking class and learn how to make Jordanian dishes at the house of a local woman. We make chicken, a lamb-milk yogurt dish, and salad. We stuff the chicken and put it in the oven. For the salad, we chop onions, which make me cry. We also cut up cucumbers and tomatoes and mix them with olive oil. We roll meatballs, which we put in the lamb-milk yogurt that is boiling on the stove. The milk is super tangy, so that turns out to be my least favorite dish. My favorite is a wheat side dish with slivered almonds. When the food is ready, we sit cross-legged on the floor around the low table in the living room and eat the feast we made. It is amazing!!! We are very good cooks.

THE DEATHSTALKER: JORDAN

CHAPTER 10

"Do you play sports?" Aria typed into my Google translate app. It was set to an English-to-Arabic translation. She looked at the eleven-year-old girl with long, brown hair in a pink T-shirt that read, "Dance, Dance, Dance," sitting across from her, held out the phone, and clicked the audio button.

Instantly translating Aria's question into Arabic, the app narrated it aloud on speaker. The girl nodded excitedly at the question, then replied in Arabic. Her mother, Umm Mohamed, typed the response into her phone, clicked to translate it into English, and held it out for us to see.

"Oh! Nice!" Aria exclaimed. "She likes gymnastics and dance."

The girl, her brown eyes shining, asked something else. Umm Mohamed typed again.

"Do you dance, too?" The app translated. Aria rotated her hand back and forth. "Kinda."

She tried to figure out how to convey in a short text a more complex answer. She settled on simply, "I do dance but prefer soccer."

After the app voiced the Arabic reply, the girl motioned for Aria to follow her, and they ran off to play. Language barriers didn't prohibit them from petting cats, doing cartwheels, kicking a soccer ball, and running around together in the warm Jordanian night.

We were at the home of a Syrian family who was hosting us for dinner in the northwestern town of Umm Qais, near Jordan's border with Syria and Israel. The father had picked us up from our guesthouse to escort us down dirt roads, past olive, lemon, and kumquat trees, to his home just down the hill.

"Abu Mohamed." He introduced himself as he picked us up from the Beit Al Baraka guesthouse where we were staying. He took a long drag from his cigarette, patted his chest, and repeated, "Abu Mohamed."

In Arab countries, Abu means "father of" and "Umm" means "mother of." We had learned that using the *kunyas*, or nicknames, of Abu or Umm is a sign of respect.

"Randy," Randy said, pointing to himself. The rest of us followed suit. It was hot, even after sundown, as we headed to Abu Mohamed's home.

Randy tried to engage our host in conversation as we walked through the winding streets. "Kids?" he asked, pointing to Finn and Aria, then gesturing questioningly.

"*Naeam*," said Abu Mohamed, understanding. Yes. He held up seven fingers.

Randy gave him a thumbs up. "Seven! Wow! How old are they?"

Abu Mohamed used his fingers to tell us that his kids ranged in age from twenty-two to eleven. I did the same to indicate that Finn was thirteen and Aria eleven. He nodded and gave a thumbs up.

As we arrived at the house, we shed our shoes beside an array of scattered sandals. The tile floor inside felt pleasantly cool beneath our bare feet. Inside, a large, carpeted room greeted us, traditional cushions lining the walls, surrounding a long, low table set for dinner.

Umm Mohamed welcomed us at the doorway, emerging from the kitchen. Dressed in a black long-sleeved dress and an *esharb*, her head and neck modestly covered, her eyes sparkled with a warm, inviting smile. She gestured for us to sit before vanishing into the kitchen.

We settled cross-legged on the carpet, engaging in small talk with two Swiss women who were also staying at our guest house. Silence fell as our hosts served *manakish*, a Middle Eastern flatbread, its nutty aroma enveloping the room. I savored the scent with a deep breath.

The table soon overflowed with dishes: oven-roasted vegetables, saffron-infused chicken with rice, and a fresh tomato-cucumber salad seasoned with mint and coriander. Hummus, baba ghanoush, and sweet basil rounded out the feast.

I broke off a piece of *za'atar*-sprinkled flatbread, diving it into a caramelized eggplant dish. "Oh, wow," I murmured. "This is so delicious."

Aria, after finishing her plate, reached eagerly for seconds. We looked on, surprised.

"This food is alive with flavor!" she exclaimed, her mouth full of bread. "No offense to American food, but I'd eat a lot more if it were like this!"

Our laughter echoed her sentiment. Finn was already helping himself to thirds.

Abu and Umm Mohamed, eating modestly, watched us with broad smiles. Grateful, I gestured toward the dishes, "*Ladhidh*," I said, hoping the word (delicious) conveyed our appreciation.

Umm Mohamed's smile widened, her eyes reflecting her pleasure at the compliment.

After dinner, we shifted to the open-air deck for a light dessert of grapes, sliced pears, and mint tea. Abu Mohamed and the Swiss women lit cigarettes, while Umm Mohamed sweetened the tea with sugar cubes. Using the translate app, we conversed with our hosts, learning about their decade-long life in Jordan since fleeing Syria.

Savoring the fruit, we relished the comfortable, if not fully articulate, companionship. As we rose to leave, Aria's new friend dashed to her room, returning with a teddy bear holding a red heart that read, "I love you." The girl spoke in Arabic, once again translated by her mother's app: "For you to have in your room in the United States to remember us."

Aria, visibly touched, said softly, "*Shukran*."

We said our goodbyes. Aria held her new stuffed animal tightly, lost in thought as we climbed the hill. "That was so nice of her," she said finally. "She doesn't have much, but she gave me her bear."

"It was incredibly sweet," I agreed. "What will you name her?"

Without hesitation, Aria replied, "Jordan."

The Kingdom of Jordan, a country in the heart of the Middle East and western Arab World, is a semi-arid land that takes its name from the Jordan river, which forms its northwestern border. Considered one of the cradles of civilization, it is a place in which many kingdoms and peoples once flourished, from the Nabateans—the builders of the city of Petra—the Persians, and the Babylonians to the Romans and the Ottomans. Coming on the heels of our explorations in Greece, our travels through Jordan would allow us to continue a worldschooling tour of ancient history and modernity at the crossroads of Asia, Africa, and Europe.

Before our trip, my perception of Jordan was vague, shaped by the Western media's portrayal of the Middle East and further colored by the desolate desert scenes from *Lawrence of Arabia*, a film I found tedious. Randy, with his interest in history, had a more nuanced understanding of the region. The kids were blank slates. I was excited for us all to learn more about it as we traveled the length of the small country, roughly the size of the state of Indiana.

Situated near the Mediterranean and Red Seas, Jordan is surrounded by Israel, Syria, Iraq, and Saudi Arabia. The big tourist attractions—the "Lost City" of Petra, the Dead Sea, Wadi Rum, and the seaside town of Aqaba—are clustered in the south. While we planned to visit them, we first wanted to get an authentic flavor of the country and its people.

After a late-night arrival in Amman, we rented a car and headed to our budget hotel. Hours later, we awoke to the Call to Prayer, a familiar sound from our time in Morocco. We spent our first afternoon in the city with family friends, Khaled, Tamara, and their children, who were introduced to us by Randy's aunt and uncle. They had lived in Amman, Cairo, and Manhattan, so they had lots of advice for us as we set off on our journey across Jordan. Their suggestions influenced our two-week itinerary, starting in the northern city of Umm Qais and ending in Aqaba. First though, we had to navigate out of Amman.

Driving in Jordan was no easy feat. Even with GPS, it was challenging to interpret the Arabic signage and local norms. Drivers didn't seem to consider lanes important. They zigzagged in a frenzied, free-for-all; right of way in traffic circles went to the most aggressive driver, regardless of who technically might have had it. And stop lights appeared to be mere suggestions. Randy learned to keep pace with the car ahead.

"Daddy, aren't you worried about getting a ticket?" Aria asked.

"Not really," he replied, driving through a red. "I'm taking my cue from the locals."

The city quickly receded into the distance as we headed north, past citrus orchards, rolling hills, and blooming jacaranda trees until arriving in Jerash. There, we spent hours exploring the sprawling Greco-Roman ruins of Gerasa, built by Alexander the Great. It was fascinating to walk along the stone walkways, feeling the grooves where carts rumbled along thousands of years ago, then look up to see the modern city all around.

Continuing our drive to the border town of Umm Qais, we checked into the three-bedroom Beit Al Baraka B&B. Best known for the ruins of the ancient Decapolis city of Gadara, dating back to the Ottoman Empire, Umm Qais was once a pass-through destination for visitors. In 2017, an Amman-based organization focused on sustainable tourism opened the B&B. It partnered with local community members to build businesses connecting tourists to the culture and history of the region, offering experiences like cooking classes, stone masonry, and basket weaving—and the dinner with our Syrian host family. These activities not only provided authentic experiences for tourists but also bolstered the regional economy, preserving traditional crafts and practices.

On our final night in Umm Qais, we took a guided tour of Gadara's ruins with Ahmed, a local man who grew up there before it was deemed a World Heritage site. As a child, he and his friends would play soccer amid the remains of ancient theaters and crumbling fountains.

At dusk, we had tea on a promontory overlooking the Sea of Galilee. The sun set over Nazareth and twinkling lights flickered on across the Golan Heights in the distance. Ahmed told us that his greatest wish was to have breakfast in Damascus, lunch in Beirut, tea in Haifa, and dinner in his hometown of Umm Qais. "It would be so easy if there were no borders, no tension between the countries," he said wistfully. "It is all so close. But also, so far."

The last rays of light cast longer and longer shadows on the ruins of Gadara before us and on the storied lands of Israel, Syria, and Lebanon beyond, stretching to the horizon. Smoke from neighboring hookah pipes—"hubbly bubbly," as they're called—swirled with lightly sweet scents on the breeze. We talked and sipped our tea, taking in this place in the northwestern corner of the kingdom, steeped in so much deep, complicated history.

A TASTE OF CULTURE: CULINARY EXPLORATIONS IN WORLDSCHOOLING

Exploring different culinary traditions can be a delicious and fascinating aspect of worldschooling. Food is a window into the culture, history, and people of a region, offering kids a unique perspective on their travels near or far from home. Here's how to incorporate food into your educational journey:

- *Local Cooking Classes*: Depending on your kids' ages, enroll in cooking classes designed for families or children. This hands-on experience is not just about cooking but learning about local ingredients, traditional techniques, and the history behind dishes.
- *Market Visits*: Take your kids to local markets. It's an inexpensive, vibrant learning opportunity about regional produce and a way

- *Try Street Food*: Encourage your kids to try new, local foods. It's an authentic way to experience traditional flavors.
- *Farm Visits or Agricultural Tours*: If possible, visit a farm or agricultural tour. This helps kids understand where food comes from, and the process involved in farm-to-table.
- *Food as a Learning Tool*: Use food to teach measurements, conversions, and basic math. Recipes can be a fun way to practice reading and following instructions or learning the words of different foods in the local language.
- *Cultural Stories through Food*: Encourage teens to learn and share stories about the dishes they try or cook. Most recipes have a history that's linked to the culture of a place.
- *Documenting Culinary Adventures*: If they get really into it, encourage kids to keep a food journal or blog, writing about or photographing different foods they try in different countries, what they liked or didn't like, and their cooking experiences.

to interact with locals. Children can learn about different fruits, vegetables, spices, and how they are used in local cuisine.

From Umm Qais we headed south, stopping for an afternoon to experience the crazy, weightless sensation of floating in the Dead Sea, before continuing to a remote tent camp near the village of Dana in central Jordan. It was nighttime when we arrived at Al Nawatef camp on the rim of a deep canyon in the middle of desert and scrubland.

One of the staff members met us with a flashlight and showed us to our tent-cabin. It was decorated simply, in Bedouin style, with one queen mattress and two twins shoved together in a stiflingly hot room. We threw open the window to let in a wisp of breeze.

"Family, welcome," our Bedouin host told us. "Come, dinner is served. It is a buffet, local food—what we eat, not tourist food. Delicious."

Picking our way in the dark, our headlamps lighting the way, we followed him across the sand to the dining cabin. Grabbing plates and silverware, we joined other travelers already in the buffet line.

We piled our plates high, trying a little of everything—falafel; baba ghanoush; tomato salad with a pomegranate reduction; yogurt with mushrooms and caramelized onions; tabbouleh; and syrup-soaked cake topped with coconut.

"OK, it's official," Aria said. "Jordanian food is incredible."

Finn simply patted his belly and nodded. "Cooking this at home is a must."

At daybreak, we headed into Wadi Ghuweir for a ten-mile hike. The rim's dry terrain transformed as we descended to a verdant valley, where pink oleanders and a mossy stream scented the air. Initially determined to keep our shoes dry, having few alternatives with us, we soon surrendered to the widening, crisscrossing stream.

"I can't get over how beautiful and lush this is," I remarked while we waded through the river. "This is not what I pictured when I thought of Jordan."

We followed the stream through shaded slot canyons, covered in ferns and moss. Bedouin shepherds keeping cool under overhangs offered us mint tea while their sheep grazed nearby. The trail led into a narrow valley, with palms sprouting from steep rock walls. A natural pool beneath a waterfall called to the kids as we clambered over huge boulders.

"Can we swim?" asked Finn.

"Go ahead," Randy said. The kids climbed down a rickety bamboo ladder into the pool, soaking themselves in the cascade.

Later that afternoon, back at camp, we carefully laid out our soaked hiking shoes and socks to dry, then slipped into flip flops to head to dinner. No sooner had we sat down when a camp manager excitedly called us all outside.

"Look, a desert fox; come see!"

We leaped back up, just in time to watch the fox snatch a piece of pita bread then vanish into the night.

Returning to the dining cabin, Randy suddenly yelled and clutched his foot, hopping in pain and cursing. At first, I thought he stubbed his toe, but then he shouted, "Something stung me!"

At the same time, a staff member stomped on something nearby. In the split second I had before he kicked the remnants into the sand, I caught sight of a pincer.

"Scorpion," the man said in a low voice, glancing anxiously at Randy. "Only a baby though, should be okay."

Despite the man's reassurance, within minutes, Randy turned pale; without a word, the camp manager whisked him off in his truck, presumably to a hospital, zooming off in a cloud of dust. The kids and I, shaken and no longer hungry, returned to our cabin, suddenly hyper aware of wearing flip flops across the sand. On the deck, we nervously checked our damp shoes and socks before bringing them inside to dry.

"Will Daddy be okay?" Aria asked tearfully.

"He should be fine," I said, putting on a brave face. "They'll know how to treat it."

"What if it's poisonous?" Finn added. I could tell he was about to launch into a litany of questions I'd have no answers to.

"Let's watch a TV show," I suggested, already turning on my iPad.

We watched a few downloaded episodes of *Friends* while waiting for news. The Wi-Fi was terrible, but a few texts managed to trickle in. Randy was in excruciating pain. He had been taken to a rural hospital, but no one had done much to or for him. He asked whether any of the staff at the camp could identify the scorpion that stung him, as the doctors said it could be helpful.

I hadn't gotten a good look at it, but I figured the guy who smushed it might know more. Finn and I pulled clothes over our pajamas, put on headlamps and damp sneakers, and told Aria to stay put. We headed out into the inky black night. At the reception cabin, we found the man we were looking for. We followed him outside, casting the beams of our headlamps in the sand. After about ten minutes, we found the dead scorpion in the low branches of a juniper tree. It was partly mangled and missing a pincer but still identifiable. I took a photo and sent it to Randy.

"Try to sleep," I urged Finn and Aria. "We can't do more tonight."

After midnight, Randy returned, looking unwell. He had vomited on the way back and was in acute pain. He had been given an antihistamine and Tylenol, which didn't stay down.

Outside, the warm desert wind howled, rattling the windows as we tried to rest. Randy, shivering despite the heat, bundled under the blankets, enduring severe spasms all over his body. We settled uneasily into the night, hoping for improvement by morning.

CHAPTER 10

As dawn broke, light filtered through the window, rousing us early. Randy, having spent a sleepless night, looked alarmingly listless.

"I need to go back to Amman," he said weakly. "The pain's not going away. I need a proper hospital."

We quickly started packing, the urgency palpable. Randy messaged Khaled, seeking advice. Khaled texted back at once. He asked to see a photo of the scorpion, which he forwarded to a friend of his, a specialist in poisonous desert creatures.

Khaled's next reply sent a jolt of added concern through us: "Hurry to hospital in Amman. Likely a Deathstalker sting—*Leiurus quinquestriatus*. Very dangerous. Take the fastest route. I'll text you the address and meet you there."

He directed us to the sting-and-bite clinic at Jordan University Hospital. There, he acted as interpreter, speaking in rapid Arabic with the medical team. The doctors, after hours of observation and administering more antihistamines and anti-inflammatories, decided against an antivenom treatment, saying the potential side effects outweighed its benefits at this point. They said the best we could do now was wait, assuring us that the worst was likely over.

Randy was discharged later that day, still frail but stable. Khaled, Tamara, and their three kids welcomed us into their home, and Randy fell fast asleep on the couch. Finn and Aria, comforted by the knowledge that their dad would be okay, relished the chance to play with children their own age, enjoying a sense of normalcy over video games and art projects.

To ensure Randy's full recovery, we booked an Airbnb in downtown Amman near the bustling Rainbow Street. After another day of rest, his condition markedly improved.

Though still a bit pale, his relief was evident. "Lesson learned," Randy said with a weak smile. "No more flip flops in the desert."

After taking it easy for a few more days, Randy felt healthy enough to continue to the place that had drawn us to Jordan in the first place—the famous archaeological site of Petra. Nicknamed the "Rose-Colored City," Petra is considered one of the Seven Wonders of the World. It was once the capital of the Nabatean Empire, an ancient Arab civilization that prospered due to its control of the Spice Route between Arabia, Africa, India, and the West.

We spent two days exploring the vast ruins. Starting at the *siq*, the road that formed the ancient entrance to Petra, we wound our way into the narrow rock valley, its steep walls rising almost 250 feet on either side. At the end of a long, winding canyon, we caught a glimpse of the intricately carved facade of the Treasury.

"Just like in *Indiana Jones and the Last Crusade*," Finn said. We had watched the movie in anticipation of our time there. "But better."

He and Aria walked up to the beautiful building, lost in thought. We had been told of the legends of gold and treasures hidden within, but never found. It was captivating to imagine. As the park neared its closing at sunset, the dwindling crowds allowed us a more intimate experience than we'd anticipated. We paid a local Bedouin man a few dollars to take us to a vantage point opposite the treasury. The man, his eyes lined with black kohl, bore a striking resemblance to Captain Jack Sparrow, a comparison the kids excitedly whispered about. I gently reminded them that the Bedouin culture predated Hollywood's pirates, suggesting Johnny Depp might have drawn inspiration from such authentic figures. The man brewed tea for us over a small fire, the metallic pot gleaming in the fading light. Settled on vibrantly colored carpets and pillows, we sipped our tea and watched camel caravans traverse the *siq*, much like they did millennia ago.

"Imagine being a trader way back when," Randy said, "your bags laden with spices and incense, and suddenly coming upon these monumental carvings. Must've been awe-inspiring."

Aria chimed in with her newfound career interest. "I bet the archaeologists who discovered Petra felt the same thrill. And there's probably so much more to discover."

"Who knows? Anything's possible."

Our journey in Jordan culminated with a visit to Wadi Rum, known as the Valley of the Moon, a sprawling desert in the south. We met Suleiman, our guide, at his house on the desert's edge. Dressed in a simple *thoab*—a long, light dress-like cloth—and *keffiyeh*, the red and white headscarf traditional for Arab men, he gestured us into his sandy courtyard ringed by a circular brick wall.

"Park next to my camel," he instructed with a smile.

Exiting our car, we noticed the camel, her coat speckled with red sand. Suleiman chuckled, explaining her recent "shower" and subsequent sand bath.

"Does she have a name?" Aria inquired curiously.

"Shaylan," Suleiman said. "Welcome, friends. Let's have tea before heading into the desert."

We settled our bags in his Toyota pickup and joined him, sitting cross-legged on faded mattresses on the ground. Suleiman served us mint tea in the shade.

The kids were captivated by Shaylan, who was nosing around our bags near the truck.

"Will she eat my backpack?" Aria asked.

Randy laughed. "Only if she finds candy in there."

Aria's mix of horror and amusement was evident.

"Friends," Suleiman said. "We will drive out to the camp soon. No worry, no hurry, no chicken to curry."

After finishing our tea, we loaded into the pickup, its open flatbed fitted with wooden benches. We held on tight as Suleiman drove us, bumping along the sand, into the heart of Wadi Rum. We marveled at the alien landscape of red dunes, towering sandstone cliffs, and narrow *siqs*. Windswept and exhilarated, we arrived a short while later at Moon Camp, its tent-cabins sheltered by a massive rock wall.

Our time in Wadi Rum was filled with adventure. We explored the desert in Suleiman's pickup, scaling hills, sandboarding down dunes, cooking out over open fires, and watching the sunset from Jebel Abu Khsheibah's rocks. In the evening, Moon Camp came alive around a bonfire under a starlit sky. Guests passed around hubbly bubbly, and we enjoyed mint tea, heated in a copper pot beside the coals, while our Bedouin hosts' songs echoed into the night, complemented by the soft crackle of the fire.

On our last morning, as we prepared to depart for Aqaba, Suleiman escorted us through the desert back to his home. Shaylan, now a familiar presence in his courtyard, nonchalantly continued her grazing.

In the truck's shade, Suleiman squatted, casually rolling a cigarette. He inquired about our journey.

"We've been traveling for almost four months," Randy shared. "We're on a year-long adventure, worldschooling the kids on the road."

"Very good," Suleiman responded, sealing the cigarette. "Children learn a lot from their parents."

I laughed, agreeing. "It's challenging but rewarding."

"Definitely rewarding. We are all rich in this life, my friends." With that, he lit his cigarette, and sat back thoughtfully on his heels, the smoke curling around him. "There is so much to see in this world. And in everything, there is beauty."

ALMOND FAMILY REPORT CARD ON JORDAN

- *Top Marks*: Explore beyond Petra and the Dead Sea. Meander Umm Qais' historical sites, venture into Wadi Rum's deserts, and hike Dana's valleys for a rich Jordanian experience.
- *Needs Work*: Navigation can be tricky due to unfamiliar road signs and driving customs. Use reliable GPS and a translator app with downloaded Arabic (in case of Wi-Fi challenges) to facilitate communication, especially in rural areas. And always wear close-toed shoes in the desert!
- *Learning Tips*: Try activities like cooking classes and archaeological tours or stay in a guesthouse to interact with locals, enriching cultural understanding.

ARE WE RESPONSIBLE TOURISTS?

Egypt

Excerpt from Finn's Journal
October 10, 2022 | Giza, Egypt

I'm gazing out the Uber window when, out of the haze, I see a pyramid in the distance. We pull up and see the huge structure made of large blocks of stone. We get out of the car, and now I realize how tall it really is. "Wow, I've always wanted to see Giza's pyramids," I say. While we are admiring this ancient wonder, I see a little boy drawing his name on the bricks while his mother is just watching. I can only think, "What is this boy's mother doing? This is the last standing wonder of the world!"

We continue to a cafe with a great view of the pyramids. I order a kofta, which is a traditional sausage of spiced meat with rice. Then we head to see the sphinx. I am a little disappointed because it is smaller than I imagined and looks like a woman's head on a coffin.

Today I learned that there are some people who seem to go to ancient sites just for photos and don't care how they leave the place. I really enjoyed the experience and hope to go back in the future and not see it ruined.

"Are we responsible tourists?" Finn asked, turning to Randy and me.

I looked at him. "That's a good question. What do you think?"

He hesitated, contemplating it for a second. "I think we mostly are."

"I do, too," I answered. "But it's worth reflecting on it more. I'm sure there are things we do well and things we could improve as we continue our travels. Why don't we all think about it for a day or two, then we'll talk as a family?"

The four of us were cuddled on the couch in our Airbnb in Cairo, Egypt. We were watching a documentary called *The Last Tourist*, which posits that tourism—one of the largest industries in the world—is at a tipping point. The film argues that tourists are, often unintentionally, destroying the very things they travel to see. The effect of over-tourism on the environment, wildlife, and vulnerable communities is immense. On a more hopeful note, it also explores our ability to harness the power of tourism in a positive way, one that benefits both travelers and host community—a concept we found compelling.

Four months into our family's gap year, it was a good time to take stock and consider the impact of our travels. Randy and I had always valued ethical, sustainable tourism and hoped to impart this philosophy to Finn and Aria. We wanted them to travel thoughtfully, to be aware of their footprint.

That summer, news headlines were filled with stories of tourists gone wild. And almost everywhere we went, we saw disappointing behavior from fellow travelers: littering, graffiti, and disruptive behavior by those seeking the perfect, staged social media photo.

But the most egregious incident came the day before, when we saw a boy carving his name into the Great Pyramid and a tourist later climbing it, ignoring the signs prohibiting it, and the guards yelling at him to come down.

"I don't get it," Finn said, distraught. "It's the last of the Ancient Wonders. Why risk destroying it?"

"You'd think people would be more respectful," Aria added, incensed.

"It's upsetting," I admitted. "But what we can control is our own actions. Let's focus on being responsible visitors."

Finn agreed: "Leave only footprints, take only memories."

Arriving in Cairo, the sheer size and energy of the Middle East's largest city immediately captivated us. The constant honking, eclipsing anything we'd experienced in Amman, Marrakesh, or even Manhattan, created a unique symphony of urban chaos.

One afternoon, Aria and I were hanging out at a downtown café, reading the culinary memoir *The Language of Baklava*, while Randy and Finn satisfied a sushi craving nearby. I tried focusing on the book, but the vibrant street scene drew me in. The honking in Cairo seemed like a language in itself, each pattern conveying a distinct message: from friendly greetings to cautious tuk tuk alerts. As I watched and listened, the cacophony blended with other city sounds: vendors hawking street food, children's laughter, and the resonant call to prayer.

"I love this energy," I said to Aria. She looked up, momentarily pulled from her book.

"What energy?" she asked, oblivious.

I looked at her, bemused. "The sounds, the liveliness of Cairo."

She shrugged, her ability to tune out distractions while reading a point of pride.

We then set off to regroup with Randy and Finn, eager to delve deeper into Egypt's rich history. Our preparations had included watching documentaries like *Lost Treasures of Egypt* and *The Square*, giving us insights into ancient wonders and contemporary struggles.

"Is Egypt safe now?" Finn asked after watching *The Square*, a film that explored the series of uprisings in Egypt, starting with the 2011 Revolution at Tahrir Square.

"Yes, it is pretty safe overall," Randy answered. "The underlying issues the protesters were fighting for are far from resolved, though."

"We'll go see Tahrir Square tomorrow when we explore Cairo more," I said.

Our tour of the capital included the Citadel of Saladin, a medieval Islamic-era fortress perched atop the Mokattam hills. Once the seat of government, the Citadel is now a historic site featuring grand mosques and museums. Its elevated position offers a sweeping 360-degree view of Cairo, including the faint outlines of the pyramids in the distance. A highlight of our visit was the stunning Alabaster Mosque, visible from various points in the city. Known formally as the Mosque of Muhammad Ali, it's an architectural masterpiece with its gleaming white walls and

Ottoman design. In the late afternoon, we returned downtown to see Tahrir Square.

As we stood across a busy street from the square, now dominated by a tall obelisk of Ramses II, Randy explained its significance to Finn and Aria. "This is where the Egyptian Revolution and many other protests took place," he said. He delved more into history, talking about events like the 1977 Egyptian Bread Riots and the 2003 protests against the war in Iraq.

"Were they protesting against America?" Finn asked, trying to understand.

Randy clarified, "They were opposing the U.S.-led invasion in Iraq. It's less about hating America so much as a response to specific policies and actions."

"So, they don't hate us now?" Finn pressed.

Randy tried to explain the complexity of the U.S.-Egypt relationship, touching on Egypt's political history and its strategic alliance with the United States. "Egypt is an important ally, but the dynamics are intricate," he said.

"Dad," Finn said as we wound our way through downtown Cairo, "Do you think there will ever be peace in the Middle East?" We held hands to sprint across a busy street.

After making it to the other side, Randy turned to Finn. "I don't know, buddy. The issues are so deep and complicated, but I hope so. Maybe someday."

The next morning, we flew from Cairo to Luxor. Randy had found us a budget deal at a guesthouse on the West Bank of the Nile for four nights, but we hadn't planned anything else in advance. As was often our approach, we intended to figure out the details after settling in.

Ryan picked us up from the airport. He and his brother, Ahmed, ran the homestay where we would be staying. A Swiss man who had studied archaeology and ancient Egyptian history, Ryan had converted to Islam and moved to Luxor from Geneva five years earlier. We clicked with him instantly and arranged for him to be our guide during our stay.

"We're completely in your hands," Randy told him after explaining that, while we'd want to see some of the "can't miss" sights—like the tombs in the Valley of the Kings and the Temple of Karnak—we preferred exploring places that are more off-the-beaten-path.

"Excellent!" Ryan said. "I will map out a plan. Most tourists go to the same, big-name places. Meh! You can get a more intimate experience if you know where—and how—to go."

Ryan swiveled to look at Finn and Aria. "Do you like Indiana Jones? I will take you somewhere special where you can climb through tombs like Dr. Jones."

"As long as there are no snakes, great!" Finn replied.

"No snakes. No worries!" Ryan assured him, grinning. He talked a mile a minute, changing topics quickly as we bounced across the dirt roads on the way to the guest house. "You will like the West Bank of Luxor. It has a nice, slow pace of life. I didn't like Switzerland. It was too regimented. This—" he swept his hand out the truck window at the wide open fields. "This is different. People just let you be you."

Later that night, after we met our host, Ahmed, and settled into our comfortable room in the house we'd be sharing with his family, Ryan proposed an itinerary for the next few days. He planned to steer us away from many of the iconic sites we had read about, which he said weren't as worth visiting in the time we had (these included the temple of Hatshepsut, the tomb of Tutankhamun, the Ramesseum, and the Luxor museum). He said he'd take us instead to places with lower name recognition but no shortage of wonder—and no busloads of tourists.

In short: the kind of plan we love.

TRAVELING WITH PURPOSE: RAISING RESPONSIBLE AND ETHICAL YOUNG TRAVELERS

Family trips offer a unique chance to teach kids about responsible and ethical traveling. These journeys are not just about seeing new places, but also about understanding and respecting different cultures and environments.

- *Cultural Sensitivity*: Help kids learn about and respect local customs by trying local foods, learning basic phrases in the local language, and participating in cultural activities.
- *Environmental Awareness*: Engage in nature-friendly activities like wildlife watching and hiking, emphasizing the importance of preserving natural habitats.
- *Support Local Communities*: Choose local businesses and guides for accommodations and tours, teaching the value of supporting local economies.
- *Volunteering Opportunities*: Participate in family-friendly community or environmental projects to demonstrate the importance of giving back.
- *Responsible Souvenirs*: Guide children in choosing ethical souvenirs that support local artisans and avoid exploiting wildlife or cultural artifacts.
- *Leave No Trace*: Instill principles like proper trash disposal, staying on trails, and respecting wildlife to minimize environmental impact.
- *Discuss Global Issues*: Use travel experiences to talk about broader global concerns like sustainability and conservation, fostering a global perspective.
- *Lead by Example*: Show responsible and ethical behavior during travels and explain its significance, encouraging kids to follow suit.

Early the next morning, Ryan picked us up at our homestay and drove us to the Deir el-Medina necropolis, an ancient Egyptian workmen's village.

"This is where the craftsmen and artisans who created and decorated the royal tombs lived thousands of years ago," Ryan explained. "The village was called the 'The Place of Truth,' and it was deliberately remote—only accessible through narrow paths to protect the tombs' secrets. Few tourists come here; maybe they think the tombs of the workmen of ancient Thebes aren't as impressive as those of the kings. But come. Come inside the tomb of Pashedu, and see what you think."

We nodded to a guard standing beside a small pyramid jutting from the cliff face. He unlocked a padlock on the low-hanging doorway, and we descended into the darkness deep in the bedrock, then entered an antechamber.

I gasped as we took in the detailed, colorful decorations all around us and across the vaulted ceiling of the tomb. Against a yellow ocher background were scenes from the Book of the Dead. Ryan pointed out the Anubis jackal and different deities on both sides of the walls in the tight passage.

"Were the colors in the paintings here restored?" I asked Ryan, amazed at their vibrance.

"No, no," he said, looking surprised at the question. "This is all original."

"Wow, that's incredible."

"Who was Pashedu?" Aria wanted to know.

"He was thought to be the first member of his family to work at Deir el-Medina. Pashedu was believed to be a stonemason and later promoted to foreman. His tomb is beautiful, no?"

We nodded, continuing to gape at the incredible paintings in the small burial chamber. "The craftsmen who lived here three thousand years ago formed different groups specializing in specific trades, like stonemasonry, painting, and sculpting," Ryan explained. "Deir el-Medina is unique in providing a window into the historical life of the ancient Egyptians, from the intact dwellings and tombs with their intricate artwork. It's really a hidden gem."

Later that day, Ryan led us to El-Assasif's tombs, a necropolis for nobles under the Nubian pharaohs. While tour buses swarmed the Temple of Hatshepsut just up the hill, we had El-Assasif to ourselves.

"This area is under excavation by archaeologists," Ryan explained. "They discovered a new tomb here a few years ago, so only some parts are open to the public, and most people don't know about them. Come, ready to adventure like Indiana Jones?"

The kids nodded, eyes shining.

We followed two guards through a labyrinth of narrow tunnels and low ceilings. We crouched and crawled through the tight, winding passageways. In the dim light of our phones, one tomb revealed a trove of history—a basket holding bone fragments.

Aria leaned forward. "Is that a mummy?"

"Yes, spectacular, no? This is real-world learning," Ryan said, his voice echoing slightly in the caverns. "It's not just about history; it's about adventure and discovery."

We carefully retraced our steps, ducking under ancient structures and stepping over an ominous shaft until we emerged into the bright sunlight.

"That was epic," declared Finn, and Ryan beamed.

The next few days with Ryan continued a deep dive into Luxor's wonders, blending adventure with educational insights. We rose early each morning, before the heat of day, to explore sites like the Valley of the Kings and the grand Temple of Karnak. At Karnak, Ryan led us through a walkway of towering sandstone columns in the Hypostyle Hall, each intricately inscribed with the stories of gods and pharaohs.

Veering off the main path, he steered us to the quieter Temple of Khonsu, standing at the end of the avenue of sphinxes. The temple appeared to be roped off. Undeterred, Ryan wandered over to talk to the guards, who returned and dropped the rope. Leading us inside a courtyard, Ryan told us about the edifice, pointing out its painted reliefs and chapel. "It's a complete New Kingdom temple that was started under Ramses III. It was completed by later rulers, including Libyan generals who were kings of Upper Egypt." Post-exploration, we relaxed under the shade of a palm, sipping *shay koshari*, Egyptian tea with mint, with the guards.

Our evenings in the quiet West Bank of Luxor provided a serene counterpoint to our daytime adventures. On our nightly walk home, we passed corner shops and food carts, *tuk tuks* and motorbikes carrying entire families, and children playing in the sand. Veering onto a dirt side street, we strolled past donkeys and camels, irrigation canals, and houses lined with date palms and hibiscus bushes before crossing into the courtyard of our homestay, ringed by mango trees.

From our balcony, we gazed at the contrasting landscapes—verdant fields and barren hills, which we knew hid secret tombs. The sounds of nature enveloped us, a peaceful end to days filled with exploration and learning.

On our final morning in the valley, we rose at 3 a.m. for a hot air balloon ride. It was something we had dreamed of doing for years but passed on as it always felt too expensive. The German women we had met months earlier in Zanzibar told us that balloon rides in Egypt were reasonably priced, though, and we had been excited to find that to be the case.

In the hush of pre-dawn, we gathered in an open field, watching as dozens of flickering flames ignited balloons against the dark sky. We huddled close for their heat, the morning cool and crisp. As dawn broke, the balloons, like gentle giants, began their ascent. We climbed into a large basket with other eager guests, our hearts racing as we lifted off the ground.

Aria's giggles filled the air as we soared higher, watching the fields recede beneath us.

Two thousand feet up, we watched the sun rise over the Valley of the Kings, Theban necropolis, and the Nile's lush valleys. The poem "High Flight" by John Magee popped into my mind: "Oh! I have slipped the surly bonds of Earth . . . wheeled and soared and swung high in the sunlit silence."

Floating in the golden dawn, we sailed in a silent parade of balloons over Luxor and watched the world slowly awaken far below.

On our final day in Egypt, we again woke early, at 3:45 a.m., to Finn's chagrin, for a four-hour bus ride from Aswan to Abu Simbel, near the Sudanese border. This historical site is famous for its massive ancient rock-cut temples, which were recently moved to higher ground above Lake Nasser to escape the rising waters from the Aswan High Dam.

Inside Ramesses II's temple, we were struck by the grandeur of the huge statues guarding the entrance and the intricate reliefs depicting fierce battles and divine encounters. The interior, a labyrinth of chambers and hallways, was adorned with vibrant hieroglyphs, telling tales of gods, pharaohs, and the afterlife.

Outside, two women in flowing dresses, looking out of place in the desert, focused on their selfie photo shoot. They frowned visibly every time someone accidentally stepped into their shot.

"Do they even appreciate what's in the temples?" Aria asked, eyeing them.

"Maybe, maybe not," I replied with a shrug. "Their loss—this place is amazing."

Later that afternoon, after relaxing from the return to Aswan, we circled back to a topic we'd touched on a few days earlier. "So, what do you guys think about being responsible tourists, especially after watching *The Last Tourist*?" I asked.

Finn responded first, "I think we're pretty considerate. We use local guides, try to have authentic experiences, and leave places like we found them."

Randy probed further, "How could we do better?"

"Using fewer plastic water bottles by purifying then refilling our water bottles more. Using reef-safe sunscreen and protecting coral during dives. And maybe using public transport more often could help," he said.

Aria, pulling up her notes, added her perspective. "We're doing okay, but I agree, we can reduce our plastic bottle use because it's terrible in so many of these countries. We should always say no to plastic straws when offered at restaurants. And we should carry trash bags to pick up litter on our hikes, like we used to do at home in Colorado. We should keep avoiding shows with animals and stay in more homestays."

Randy and I nodded in agreement, and I shared a few thoughts about the ethics of travel photography and social media sharing. I had been reflecting on my own practices and distinguished between capturing genuine moments and creating content simply for social posting. "I've been trying to keep in mind whether my photos and posts could harm or help the places and people we visit. It's something I want to continue to be mindful of."

Randy added, "I think it's about striking the right balance as travelers, benefiting places and people we visit without exploiting them."

That evening, our last in Africa, we sailed in a *felucca*, a traditional wooden sailboat, along the Nile. Sitting on the bow of the small boat, our feet swinging over the edge, Finn asked, "Are you excited for South America, Mom?"

I smiled, gazing over the Nile, my thoughts turning from the present to where we were headed next. "For sure. Having grown up in Puerto Rico, speaking Spanish, South America has always held a deep kinship for me. Feels like going home. I'm excited to explore more of it."

He considered this. "What about the Middle East? Did you like it?"

I thought for a moment. "It pushed me out of my comfort zone, being so different from what we're used to. But I loved the hospitality and kindness we've found here, the history is fascinating, and the food—yum! So yes, I liked it. How about you? What do you think?"

"Same. Not a fan of scorpions and I'd never want to live in a desert, but I really enjoyed our time here, and I learned a lot," he replied.

"What are you looking forward to most in South America?" I asked.

Without missing a beat, he said, "Greenery and mountains."

I nodded in agreement. The endless deserts were captivating, but the allure of lush landscapes, cooler climes, and soaring peaks was undeniable. We fell into a comfortable silence, letting the soft breeze sweep our *felucca* along. The Nile's banks sparkled with lights, a beautiful farewell as we prepared to leave Africa and the Middle East, ready for our next chapter.

ALMOND FAMILY REPORT CARD ON EGYPT

- *Top Marks*: Discover Egypt's wealth of wonders beyond the iconic Pyramids of Giza. Explore Cairo's markets, sail a felucca along the Nile, and venture south to the far-flung temples of Abu Simbel.
- *Needs Work*: Be mindful of your impact when visiting historical sites. Avoid touching or climbing ancient structures and strictly adhere to local guidelines to help preserve these treasures for future generations.
- *Learning Tips*: Encourage learning through interactive experiences. Use educational apps to understand hieroglyphics and take guided tours with locals for off-the-tourist trail sites and insights into Egypt's history.

FOUND IN TRANSLATION
Brazil

Excerpt from Aria's Journal
November 6, 2022 | Rio de Janeiro, Brazil

I'm excited to visit the statue of Christ the Redeemer today. It is one of the Wonders of the World, and I have to say, it is easy to see why! It's built on a hill overlooking Rio de Janeiro, and easy to spot, even from miles away. It is HUGE! The views from the top of the mountain are beautiful too. We ride up in a tram from the city and, in minutes, are in a thick rainforest. It's like another world. It's really crowded around the massive statue. We have fun watching the monkeys, who are curious about the tourists and come close to check us out.

CHAPTER 12

Svetlana, the manager of the language school where we were studying in rural Brazil, invited us to pick papayas. "The yellow ones are ripe," she said. "We call them *mamão*."

Aria leaned over the balcony to pluck a couple of papayas from a cluster near the top of the spindly trunk. We were living and taking Portuguese lessons at the school in Maceió, on Brazil's northeast coast, immersing ourselves in the language, culture, and cuisine for a fortnight. The school's courtyard was a bounty of tropical fruits. We'd already gathered star fruit, bananas, sour cherries, *caju* (cashew) fruit, and added the freshly picked papaya to our haul. As we entered the common room, morning sun streaming through the sliding glass door, Randy looked up from his workbook.

"Ooh, what've you got there?" he asked. Svetlana, seizing the moment to teach, replied in Portuguese, nudging us to try our new skills too.

"*Temos frutas do jardim*," she said. We have fruits from the garden.

Finn grinned, ready for breakfast. "*Muito bom*."

We added the fruit to the kitchen counter, where Svetlana had laid out homemade sourdough bread, butter, and jam. Over weak Nescafé, buttered toast and tropical fruits, I opened my book and joined Randy, Finn, and Aria at the table, where we completed our homework before the day's lessons began.

In Maceió, our days were a mix of language classes and cultural immersion, all against the backdrop of Brazil's tense upcoming presidential election. The race between Jair Bolsonaro and Luiz Inácio Lula da Silva, or Lula, was a constant topic of discussion, creating an undercurrent of anticipation and anxiety. This wasn't just an election; it was a choice between two starkly different visions for Brazil's future. Everyone, from our language teachers to Uber drivers and beachgoers, had an opinion, enriching our understanding with their perspectives, as we grasped more Portuguese each day.

Besides absorbing the political landscape, we filled our afternoons with *capoeira* classes—a traditional Brazilian martial art mixing music, dance, and spirituality—beach outings, and explorations along the coast.

On the morning of Election Day, a Sunday, we sailed in a traditional boat, called a *jangada*, to Pajuçara's natural pools. These calm sandbanks teemed with people hanging out, chest deep, in the shallow water, surrounded by colorful fish. A bar boat served drinks in pineapples, delivered to swimmers on Styrofoam floats. We ate fresh seafood while standing in the warm water, watching fish swarm around us, munching on discarded shrimp shells. The atmosphere was festive, with music, dancing, and people hopping between *jangadas* under a cloudless sky. Red-hatted Lula supporters good naturedly ribbed those decked out in yellow, blue, and green, showing their allegiance to Bolsonaro. The mood was cordial and lively despite differences in ideology.

By late afternoon, we returned to Ponta Verde. Long shadows stretched across the shore. We bought *açaí* bowls from a street vendor and watched the sun set across the water. Election-night rallies for Bolsonaro and Lula created a buzz of anticipation as the polls neared closing.

Back at school, we crowded into our bedroom to watch the documentary *The Edge of Democracy*, which gave us the backstory on Lula's former presidency, adding context to the current showdown. Throughout the evening, Svetlana and our teacher, Kátia, updated us on WhatsApp with election developments. Around 8 p.m., we heard fireworks and chanting outside.

We caught bits of the tune and understood: Lula had won.

The vibrant cheers, the singing in the streets, the nuances of the race—it was a firsthand lesson in democracy and culture, and an unforgettable part of our Brazilian classroom.

Halloween wasn't widely celebrated in Brazil. Finn and Aria were a bit disappointed to miss the hoopla but understood the trade-offs of our year abroad. They had all but forgotten the day until Randy and I asked them to knock on our bedroom door before class.

"Um, hello?" Finn called skeptically.

I urged from the window, "That's not what you say on October 31. Try again!"

"Okayyy . . . Trick or treat?" Aria ventured.

"Treat!" I opened the door, showering them with local candies. Randy had found fake mustaches at the mall, so we each chose one—I had donned a pencil-thin mustache, Aria a handlebar, Randy a bushy thing that looked like a caterpillar, and Finn a ridiculous Fu Manchu.

"So, I must-achio a question," Randy began with a grin.

"Don't. That's the worst dad joke ever," sighed Finn.

Randy ignored him. "How dapper does Mommy look with a pencil-thin mustache?"

Aria giggled and Finn rolled his eyes spectacularly. Still chuckling, we went downstairs to class, our costumes the hit of the common room.

Our lessons that week were interactive. Kátia planned a practical class one day—visiting a market, pharmacy, and store nearby. We practiced our Portuguese with the clerks, feeling more engaged with the hands-on approach. The following day, in the small open-air kitchen of the schoolhouse, we learned how to make *brigadeiro*, a creamy local sweet made from condensed milk, cocoa powder, and sugar. And, on our last afternoon, we played a heated game of team Trivial Pursuit, all in Portuguese.

All too quickly, our two weeks in Maceió came to an end. When we hugged her goodbye, Kátia said, *"Vou ficar com saudade."* We looked at her blankly; not quite advanced enough students to know what that meant yet.

"*Saudade is* a word that doesn't have a direct translation," she explained. "It's a Portuguese word that means to miss or to express longing. You say *saudade* for a person or a thing or even a longing for a country. You have been some of my favorite students ever. I will miss you all."

"Oh, I love that. We'll miss you too," I said. "*Saudade.*"

Our first glimpse of Rio de Janeiro was from the sky, as we flew over its lush mountains, which seemed to plunge into the sea. Randy, charmed by the huge seaside city on a work trip years earlier, had set Brazil on his wish list of must-visit places, and we were all excited to explore.

As we walked along the boardwalk beside the sun-drenched sands of Ipanema beach in the south zone of Rio, we joined cyclists, skateboarders, roller skaters, and fellow pedestrians unhurriedly taking in the scene. Dotted with colorful umbrellas, the beautiful beach sits in the shadow of the Dois Irmãos (Two Brothers) mountains on its western end.

Finn was enthralled by the footvolley players in the throes of ferocious matches on the sand. We watched, fascinated by the blend of beach volleyball and soccer. First created in Brazil in the 1960s, it's known locally as *"pevoley."*

"Sweet!" Aria said as one of the players did a high kick to launch the ball over the net.

I nodded, then added, "Is anyone else hearing *The Girl from Ipanema* in their head?"

Aria shot me a look. "Nope."

"Just me then," I replied, happily humming the tune.

From Ipanema, we climbed up Pedra do Arpoador, taking in views of the surfers and landmarks like Sugarloaf Mountain, before continuing to neighboring Copacabana, one of the most famous beaches in the world. Sweeping along a crescent-shaped bay, the wide, white-sand beach is lined by rock formations and palms. From daybreak to night, it pulses with a contagious energy and *joie-de-vivre* vibe. As we walked along the shore, I couldn't resist singing another iconic tune, "Her name was Lola, she was a showgirl . . . "

Finn accelerated ahead, creating distance from me and my singing, and went to check out another intense footvolley match.

Continuing our adventures in Rio, the following day we took a tram from Cosme Velho to the top of Corcovado mountain, at 2,329 feet (710 m). The summit is renowned for its massive art deco statue of Christ the Redeemer. Standing nearly a hundred feet (30 m) high, the statue was impressive, but the monkeys around the base stole the show.

Randy struggled—and failed—to hold the kids' attention in the face of the monkeys' antics as he tried to tell them about the statue's history. Worldschooling 0: Capuchin monkeys 1.

"Haha, check this guy out!" Finn shouted, pointing to a monkey snatching a cap from a tourist's water bottle then pelting away into the treetops.

In the afternoon, we visited the *Museu do Amanhã*, or the Museum of Tomorrow. A futuristic science museum, it's designed to explore the possibilities of a sustainable future. Its modern architecture, with sweeping curves and sustainable design, beautifully juxtaposes against the historic backdrop of Rio. We spent several hours wandering the interactive exhibits and installations offering glimpses into the potential futures of our planet, furthering reflection on our impact on the earth and the legacy we leave for future generations.

Walking back to our Airbnb, we passed Olympic Boulevard, home to a mammoth mural painted by Eduardo Kobra for the Rio Olympics. Standing fifty feet tall and measuring over 32,000 square feet, *Las Etnias* (The Ethnicities) depicts faces from five continents, mirroring the Olympic rings and symbolizing global unity. We stopped to admire the vibrant colors and geometric patterns portraying Indigenous people from around the world. Moving and soulful, it captures the spirit of Rio, a seamless urban blend of art, culture, and social commentary.

NAVIGATING LANGUAGE LEARNING CHOICES

Choosing a language school for your child—or your whole family!—can be a tremendously enriching part of an educational and cultural experience. Here are some key points to consider:

- *Accreditation and Reputation*: Research if the school seems credible or is accredited by a reputable educational authority. Check online reviews from other parents or students.
- *Curriculum and Teaching Approach*: Evaluate if the school's curriculum aligns with your child's learning style. Are the classes conversational, traditional, or immersive?
- *Class Size and Composition*: Consider the class size and the student-to-teacher ratio. Smaller classes can offer more personalized attention. Also, check the diversity in class—a mix of nationalities can enrich the experience.
- *Qualified Instructors*: Ensure that teachers are qualified to teach a second language. Native speakers or those with a teaching degree in the language can offer authentic learning experiences.
- *Cultural Immersion Opportunities*: Look for schools that provide cultural activities or excursions, which can enhance language learning through real-life experiences.
- *Safety and Location*: The school's location should be in a safe area, especially for younger learners. Proximity to cultural sites or ease of transportation can be a plus.

- *Age-Specific Programs*: Check if the school offers programs tailored for different age groups, ensuring age-appropriate content and learning methods.
- *Flexibility and Duration*: Consider schools that offer flexibility in terms of course duration and start dates that align with your travel plans.
- *Cost vs. Value*: Compare the cost of the program against what is offered. Cheaper doesn't always mean lower quality, and expensive doesn't guarantee the best experience.
- *Language Practice beyond Classroom*: Assess opportunities for practicing the language outside the classroom, such as homestays, language exchange programs, or interaction with local communities.

Soccer—or football, as it's called locally—is the number one sport in Brazil and ever-present in the life of its people. With a deification of its players, soccer there is like a second religion, after the official Catholicism, and a source of deep national pride.

No experience of Brazil would be fully complete without taking in a live game, so on our last night in Rio, we took the metro sixteen stops to Maracanã Stadium. As we neared the stadium, the train got more and more crowded with cheering Fluminense club fans in their Tricolor jerseys. We streamed out into the warm night with the throng, swept up in a lively march toward the stadium.

It was an evenly matched game at the start between home team Fluminense and Goiás until a red card gave the Rio team the upper hand. They seized the advantage, dominating the second half. Then it was all over. The final scoreboard read 3–0, and the crowd went wild. We cheered with the home team in a thunderous uproar until we felt hoarse, then let ourselves be swept away with the masses back to the metro for the long trek back to Ipanema.

For our final week in Brazil, we rented a car to explore the coast south of Rio. As we drove toward Paraty, a quaint, colonial town surrounded by steep, jungled mountains in the Costa Verde, mist enveloped us.

CHAPTER 12

"Feels like we're driving through a cloud," Aria commented. We reached our Airbnb under a steady drizzle and unpacked, settling for an easy dinner of yogurt and granola to skip another trip out in the rain for groceries.

By the following day, the rain had subsided, dark clouds swapped for bright sunshine. "Perfect timing, huh?" I said happily as we explored Paraty's historic town center, admiring its churches and elegant white buildings adorned with iron lanterns, colorful borders, and latticed windows.

In the evening, we took a cooking class at the home of a local couple, Yara and Richard Roberts. Their house, in the heart of Paraty, radiated a warm, inviting vibe.

Richard showed us how to concoct *caipirinhas*, a classic cocktail made with *cachaça* (a local liquor produced from sugarcane), lime, and sugar. We shared laughs and stories over drinks with our hosts and two other travelers from the United Kingdom before heading into the kitchen to learn to prepare a traditional Brazilian meal.

Chef Yara handed us aprons and put us to work. Together, we made *farofa*, a dish consisting of manioc flour sautéed with onion, peppers, and garlic; steamed sweet potatoes; delicate white fish layered with mango and baked in a banana leaf, Northeast style; and, for dessert, pineapple flambéed with *cachaça*, vanilla, cinnamon sticks, and cloves. As we cooked, a delicious aroma filled the kitchen, a savory and sweet scent mingling in the tropical night.

Dishes complete, we sat at a long, wooden table and shared the meal we had cooked together. As I looked around, it felt again—as it had a few times before on our trip—almost like being home in a room filled with warmth, easy conversation, and newfound friendships. Finn and Aria chatted effortlessly with everyone, sharing their thoughts on favorite places we had traveled, their best experiences so far, and why every traveler should try footvolley in Rio.

Maybe it was the *caipirinhas*, maybe something more, but my heart felt happy and full.

For almost a hundred years, Ilha Grande (literally translated to "Big Island") was closed to settlement as it first housed a leper colony then one of the most secure prisons in Brazil. By 2019, though, Ilha Grande, along with Paraty, was named a UNESCO World Heritage Site and opened to limited facilities. This rugged island with no roads was our last stop before we returned to Rio. After taking a ferry to Praia Vermelha (Red Beach), we stepped onto the lone wooden dock. Three restaurants lined the cove, and a small handful of wooden buildings trailed into the undergrowth.

Ezekiel, the manager of the rustic *pousada*, or small hotel, where we were staying, met us at the dock. We kicked off our shoes and followed, barefoot, on the sand to the opposite shore, where we climbed up into the dense rainforest on a narrow dirt path. We picked our way over gnarled roots to get to the remote property overlooking the sea. Ezekiel showed us to our cabins, each strung with a hammock out front. The tropical foliage compounded the feeling of being in a jungle hideaway, a sense enhanced by sightings of marmosets and lizards, tropical birds and armies of fire ants marching in formation across the floor beams.

Ezekiel and his wife put out chunks of fresh papaya nightly for the porcupines to eat, and we had fun sitting in the open-air common space watching as they lumbered down to munch on the fruit before disappearing into the foliage again.

"Everyone have headlamps?" Randy asked as we got ready to walk back down to the beach for dinner.

We all held up our lights. "Yep!"

"Lead the way, then!"

"Can I go first since it's my birthday?" Finn asked.

Randy smiled. "Be my guest."

Finn picked his way down the muddy trail, taking care to step over a spider as well as the highways of ants, whose bites we learned the hard way stung terribly.

We had celebrated Finn's fourteenth birthday that morning before leaving Paraty. We gave him a box of chocolates, an orange, and a handmade card. But, unbeknownst to him, we also had called ahead to see if *La Dolce Vita*, one of the two restaurants in our sleepy cove on Ilha Grande, could make him a cake. They told us they would try.

CHAPTER 12

At the bottom of the trail, we kicked off our flip flops and jumped over the little tributary of water flowing into the ocean and wandered to the restaurant. We rinsed off our feet under a spigot, then grabbed a table on the deck. A briny breeze blew into the open-air restaurant.

"Happy birthday, Finn," I said, raising a *caipirinha* to toast him.

"To Finn," Randy added, "A great traveler and fellow adventurer."

Aria grinned. "To Finn, a good brother and my favorite person in the world to annoy."

We laughed. "Well, that's certainly true," said Randy wryly.

Finn was debating what dessert to order when the lights went out, and the manager and staff came out singing "Happy Birthday" in Portuguese. They put a massive cake topped with Finn's name, soccer players and a ball, in front of him.

"Who did this?" Finn asked.

Aria bounced up and down excitedly. "We did! We called ahead of time."

"How did they know I like soccer?"

"We told them!"

"Oh, wow," he turned to the staff, beaming. "*Obrigado! Muito bom!*"

Randy handed Finn the knife, and he sliced the cake, with five layers of vanilla filled with creamy *brigadeiro* and topped with buttercream frosting. Finn cut large slices for the four of us then offered slices to the other restaurant guests.

"I did not expect this," he told us. "This is an awesome way to celebrate fourteen."

Winding our way through the airport in Rio to make our way to Argentina, I thought of all the people we had met and become friends with during our five weeks in Brazil. Kátia and Svetlana, Yara and Richard, Ezekiel and his family. I reflected on our Portuguese lessons and how they helped us get a deeper understanding of the culture and gain greater insights into the election and chat with locals about a range of topics from politics to football.

As we approached our gate, I noticed a neon sign on the wall with a single word in blue lettering set against a fuchsia background, "*Saudade.*"

It felt fitting as we prepared to say goodbye to a country in which we had so many meaningful experiences. Since Kátia had introduced us to the word, I had Googled it to learn more about its meaning. Brazilians often proudly say it's a word without direct translation but which connotes a deep feeling of missing a person, place, or thing. A melancholic sense of nostalgia. It's both happy and sad.

"I'm going to miss Brazil," I told Randy. "I can see why you loved it so much on your brief visit and wanted to come back. Did it live up to your expectations the second time?"

He nodded. "Definitely. And it's such a big country with so much more to explore. I'm sure someday, we'll be back."

"Agreed." I gave a last glance out the windows before heading to our gate. "*Saudade,* Brazil. Until next time."

ALMOND FAMILY REPORT CARD ON BRAZIL

- *Top Marks*: Embrace Brazil's sports culture by watching a football game at Rio's Maracanã Stadium and giving footvolley a try on Ipanema Beach. Don't miss the colonial charm of Paraty or the beauty of Iguazu falls.
- *Needs Work*: Prioritize safety by staying vigilant in urban areas, securing belongings, and following local advice on security. And recognize that Brazil is a massive country, so planning and prioritization are key.
- *Learning Tips*: Take Portuguese lessons for a fun and educational family experience. Using the language in daily activities helps deepen your connection with Brazilian culture.

NO BRAVERY WITHOUT MADNESS

Antarctica

Excerpt from Finn's Journal
November 23, 2022 | *Somewhere in the Antarctic Circle*

Throughout most of today, we endure the rough waters of the Drake Passage. At about 5 p.m., Pablo, our expedition leader, announces that we are ahead of schedule and will have an opportunity for a landing before dinner. Yeah! We are all super excited and rush up to our room to put on our warm layers. Then, we make our way to the stern of the ship to load up in the Zodiacs after sanitizing our shoes, so we don't accidentally introduce anything onto land. Our first destination is Livingston Island. It's rocky and there's a light wind as we step out of the boats. The first thing I see is a penguin. It's small and cute, and one of the experts says it is a gentoo penguin. The closer we get to the colony, the more the smell increases, like poop and rotten shrimps. It's awful. After you get over the stink, though, it's amazing to watch the penguins waddle around, hundreds of them, like something I've seen in movies but now it's right in front of me. The penguins have no fear, and we need to move so they don't run us over.

CHAPTER 13

It's 2 a.m. The *Ushuaia*, our home for the next ten nights, bucked wildly on the rough South Seas, sending me flying into the wall beside the bed and back again, rolling into Randy. Groaning, I tried to recenter myself in the tangle of sheets.

"Still awake?" Randy whispered, his voice barely audible over the creaking wood and crashing waves.

"Yeah. I'm so thankful for seasick meds," I mumbled as another shudder rocked the cabin. "These waves are insane!"

From across the room, Aria piped up: "I just lifted up off my mattress! Like, I literally flew up in the air!"

"You're not sleeping either?" Randy called softly.

"No one here is asleep," Finn croaked, pushing against the wall to steady himself in the bed he was sharing with Aria as another wave crashed into the *Ushuaia*.

It was our first night on an old research ship heading south across the infamous Drake Passage, one of the world's most harrowing channels of open water. The deep waterway sits at the convergence of the Atlantic and Pacific Oceans between Cape Horn, the southernmost point of South America, and the South Shetland Islands. Our destination—Antarctica.

It had not been part of our plan. Antarctica seemed far too pricey for our year-abroad budget, yet here we were, hurtling south on a last-minute steal Randy had managed to secure. Months earlier, he started putting out feelers for budget-fare Antarctic options, zeroing in on smaller, older ships with fewer amenities but no shortage of adventure. He emailed operators seeking last-minute cancellations and reduced fares. In November, one of his outreaches panned out.

There was a large group cancellation on the *Ushuaia*, an ice-strengthened polar vessel that once served as a spy ship off the coast of Cuba. It was a relatively small ship, with a ninety-person capacity, and it lacked newer capabilities like wave stabilization. It wouldn't be a luxury cruise. It would be a real expedition.

Basically, ideal for us.

Randy had turned to me after we pored over photos and reviewed and re-reviewed our finances. Going to Antarctica would stretch our budget, but by cutting elsewhere and being even more mindful of our spending, we had decided we *could* make it work.

"What do you think?" he asked.

Even with the steep discount, it was still damned expensive for us. We didn't have the right gear. And I'd probably be horribly seasick for the bulk of the ten-day voyage. But it was also the chance of a lifetime. I didn't hesitate.

"Hells yeah. Let's do this! Should we tell the kids now?"

Randy grinned. "Let me get logistics sorted. Then we can tell them as we make our way down to Ushuaia tomorrow night."

"We have a surprise!" Randy announced. We were gathered in our bunk room at a backpackers' hostel in Iguazu, Brazil. As far as the kids knew, we were staying there for another night before flying to Buenos Aires, our intended destination for the next few weeks. "We need to pack up now, because our plans have changed. We have a new next stop."

Finn sat up, nearly bonking his head on the top bunk. "What is it? What's the plan?"

"In an hour, we'll catch a cab to the airport. We'll fly to Buenos Aires tonight—but we won't stay there. We'll crash on the airport floor for a few hours' sleep before catching a 5 a.m. connection to Ushuaia—"

"Where's that?" Aria interrupted, right as Randy asked, "Do you know where that is?"

"No clue," she replied. Finn shook his head.

"It's the southernmost city in Argentina—actually, the southernmost city in the world."

I added, with emphasis, "It's also the *gateway to Antarctica*."

Finn's eyes stretched as wide as they would go, and he leaped up, gasping. He bounced on the balls of his feet as he waited for Randy to finish.

"Then, on Monday afternoon, we'll board a ship and head to Antarctica!"

Finn yelled and pumped his fists into the air. "Yes!!!" Aria gave us both tackle hugs.

"Wait, when did this all—? Whaa—? How did this happen?" Aria asked, incredulously.

We laughed as Finn jumped up and down and Aria danced around the hostel bedroom.

"Aria, we're going to see snow! Penguins! Icebergs!" Finn shouted. "I can't believe it! We're going to Antarctica!"

And with that, we swiftly shifted into pack-up mode. Clothes rolled, bags zipped, a cab hailed. Our long journey southward had begun, the 54th parallel and beyond beckoning.

Ushuaia, *"Fin del Mundo, Principio de Todo"* ("End of the world, beginning of everything"), greeted us with crisp mountain breezes and a thrill in the air. Exhaustion couldn't dampen our excitement. We had a day and a half to fill critical gaps in our wardrobe for our upcoming icy adventure.

Randy, ever the organizer, whipped out his iPad at breakfast, and started a list. We needed hats, gloves, another warm layer, and waterproof pants. We would be given boots on the ship, but I was skeptical.

"Every passenger has to use the rubber Wellington boots they give us," Randy said.

"Rubber boots aren't insulated, though. They're rain boots," I protested. "That's crazy. Our toes will turn into icicles."

"Wear two pairs of socks. That's what the woman said."

"Humph," I scoffed, already plotting a three-sock rebellion.

We spent the next day comparing prices for outdoor gear at different outfitters and quickly cobbled together a mix of used, rented, and new gear. At Ushuaia Extreme, one of the outdoor rental shops, the owner chatted with us in Spanish, sensing our nervous anticipation. "First time to Antarctica?" he asked.

"*Sí*," we said, excitement bubbling over.

"It's special, that place," he said. "There's a kind of spirituality you'll feel there. Ships even take yogis for meditation retreats. Antarctica does that to you. It's a profound experience."

When I confessed that my one worry was my feet being cold, he agreed with my plan to bulk up on socks. Then he threw in a second pair of waterproof pants for me, free.

"You don't want cold legs or feet," he winked. "This is a life-changing trip. Enjoy it." "*Muchas gracias!*" I said, gratitude warming me more than socks ever could.

The following afternoon, we hoisted on our backpacks and walked toward the port. Massive cruise liners with well-known names—*Viking, National Geographic Explorer, World Traveler*—dwarfed our rusted navy-and-white *Ushuaia* ship, which looked like a toy fishing trawler in comparison. But to us, she was perfect, and we beamed as we approached, gazing up at the Argentinian flag fluttering atop the bridge—our floating home for the next ten days. With great anticipation, we stepped onto the gangplank and climbed aboard.

We made our way to room 201 in the bow of the ship. It was comfy and spacious, with a private bathroom and two double beds. We unpacked, then hurried to the common room, duck-walking down the steep vertical stairway, as the crew kicked off our voyage.

The captain, a portly man in his mid-sixties with a crisp white uniform topped at the shoulders with navy and gold stripes, set the tone. "Welcome aboard the *Ushuaia*. We will do everything we can to make this a fun and safe journey, but Antarctica is not for the faint of heart. Listen to what the crew and I tell you. We may encounter rough seas, and safety is paramount."

He recounted an incident on a recent voyage in which a passenger fell during a turbulent crossing through the Drake Passage, causing an emergency return to Argentina. He emphasized the ship's safety procedures before passing the microphone to Pablo, a dark-haired Argentinian with smiling brown eyes who would be our expedition leader. Pablo raised his champagne flute in toast: "To a safe, successful expedition! *Salud!*"

Pablo introduced the guides, scientists, and doctor on board, then gave us details of what to expect in the coming days. We would be in the throes of the Drake Passage by evening, and they expected an average two-day crossing—not overly bumpy but not calm either. Waves of approximately three to four meters were expected. The doctor ("Call me Doc") recommended anyone prone to sea sickness should start medicating at once. He handed out anti-nausea pills, which nearly everyone accepted.

Later, as we stood on deck watching the shore recede into the distance, the sun dipped below the horizon, lighting up the sky in a brilliant wash of orange and yellow. A flag reading Antarpply fluttered high over our heads, thumping in the wind.

"That's our expedition flag," one of the scientists, Martin, told us. "Every voyage has one. *¿Estas lista para ir?* Are you ready?"

"*¡Sí!*" We nodded.

Our expedition was under way.

After a tough first night in the Drake Passage, we felt up for attending a series of *charlas*, or talks, in the common room. While the ship continued to rock as we continued southward, we learned about the Antarctic Treaty, marine biology, and penguins with Martin, a mechanical engineer passionate about environmental conservation.

Post-*charla*, Randy and I brainstormed with Martin how to structure science assignments for Finn and Aria. Antarctica, we knew, would be an amazing outdoor science classroom, with opportunities to learn about everything from marine life and conservation to climate change. We aimed to complement their hands-on experiences with targeted projects focused on experimental science.

We landed on two that we felt were age appropriate, engaging, and doable in the time we had. Aria would observe and document in her journal the differences between penguin species, while Finn's task was to research, observe, and make hypotheses about changes in the region over the next ten years. He was to draw on his own observations, the ship resources, and conversations with the scientists.

In addition to their science assignments, we had already begun reading *Endurance*, the true story of Sir Ernest Shackleton's expedition across the Antarctic continent on foot, an intense two-year struggle for survival. I had writing assignments for them, too.

"Finn, I'd like you to imagine you're Ernest Shackleton and write a series of journal entries in his style, reflecting the era. Aria, your writing prompt is to create a series of journal entries as if you were Sir Francis

Drake. We'll give you both time to complete this after we return to Argentina, so there's no need to cram it all in while we're in Antarctica—focus on the science, reading, and just soaking up all this amazingness on our excursions."

They nodded, agreeing.

Aria headed to our cabin, swaying down the corridor like a tipsy partygoer as she braced against the ship's motion, to start her penguin research right away. In contrast, Finn plopped back on the common room couch for a nap in between *charlas*.

"I'll work on it later," he declared. "I need sleep before our first outing."

THE EVERYWHERE LAB: FIELD SCIENCE PROJECTS FOR YOUNG EXPLORERS

Turning travel near or far from home into field science projects is an incredible way to use the world as a classroom. This approach transforms every trip into an interactive learning experience, immersing children in hands-on science connected to their surroundings. It not only fuels their curiosity but also instills a deeper understanding of the environment. Here's how to integrate field science into your family travels:

- *Start with a Field Journal*: Equip your child with a notebook for observations and sketches, encouraging them to detail sights, sounds, smells, and textures.
- *Select Relevant Reading Material*: Choose age-appropriate books or articles related to your destination to spark discussions and deepen understanding. (Google can help!)
- *Engage in Simple Experiments*: Look online for easy and safe experiments that relate to your travels, offering hands-on learning opportunities.
- *Encourage Nature Observation*: Guide your child in observing and respecting wildlife and plant life, noting behaviors and growth patterns.
- *Utilize Local Resources*: Make use of museums, science centers, or guided tours for expert insights and knowledge about the area.

- *Teach Basic Photography Skills*: Show your child how to take quality photos as a way to document and add visual elements to their learning experience.
- *Create a Project Presentation*: At the end of your trip, have your child prepare a presentation of their findings, whether a scrapbook, a slideshow, or a short talk.
- *Reflect on the Experience*: Talk about what they learned and their impressions, reinforcing the educational value of their adventure.

By turning outings into field science projects, children learn to observe, question, and analyze, gaining invaluable skills and a broader perspective on the world.

The loudspeaker crackled on. "*Hola, queridos passajeros.* Hello, dear passengers. This is Pablo, speaking to you from the bridge. We made good time and anticipate being able to do two landings today. Please make your way to the common room, and I'll explain more shortly."

Everyone buzzed with excitement. Our first landings!

Back in our cabin, we layered for the cold, starting with my three pairs of wool socks, thermal bottoms, waterproof pants, a thermal top, fleece, down jacket, and a windproof layer. Our black Wellington boots, reaching mid-calf, were next. Then, sunscreen, wool hats, sunglasses, and finally, our life jackets.

"Who's ready to meet some penguins?" I asked, waddling out of the room.

"Me!" Aria chimed in, and Finn echoed her enthusiasm.

At the lower deck, we lined up to wash and disinfect our boots. This ritual, essential to protect Antarctica's environment from foreign contaminants like non-native seeds or bird flu, involved meticulous cleaning in soapy vats.

Boarding the inflatable Zodiac boats, each holding ten passengers, we zoomed toward Yankee Harbor amid overcast, misty skies, and a cool breeze. Zigzagging through the dark waters, we dodged small icebergs before approaching the rocky beach.

As we hopped ankle-deep into the frigid Antarctic water near shore, Randy turned to me, "Aren't you glad for the Wellington boots now?"

"Let's see if I'm still thankful after an hour out here," I replied, admitting silently that the boots were indeed doing a good job keeping my feet dry and warm.

"Ohhh, look, Mama," Aria exclaimed as she splashed ashore. "So many penguins! I think these are gentoos, but that one might be an Adélie. I need to find Martin or Alan to check!" She ran off to seek a scientist's confirmation.

Our boots made a satisfying crunching sound on the rocky, uneven terrain. We walked across a vast ice field, in awe of hundreds of chinstrap and gentoo penguins parading across the snow. Our guides reminded us to maintain a fifteen-foot distance, even if the curious penguins approached us, to preserve their natural behavior.

A massive leopard seal, unfazed by our arrival, lounged on the ice, casting a lazy eye over the group on its beach. Nearby, a line of gentoo penguins padded across the rocks, wings spread.

"What's that disgusting smell?" asked Finn.

Pablo pointed to the white marks all over the ground. "Penguin poop. Stinky, isn't it?"

Finn nodded, whispering to me, "I wish I had a Berber gas mask right now."

That evening, we embarked on the Zodiacs again, this time to disembark at Half Moon Island. The clouds had parted, leaving a stunning display of shell-pink, peach, and lemony light that bathed the snowy peaks in a pale pastel glow. We trekked across a snowfield, passing a Weddell seal that playfully covered its eyes before peeking at us, then resuming its nap. Chinstrap penguins tobogganed down a snow-covered slope, while terns and gulls circled and cried overhead.

"What a day, huh?" Randy said as we settled into bed that night. It was blissfully calm, and we welcomed the quiet, rhythmic hum of the ship's engines as we fell asleep, feeling utterly at peace in the seas at the ends of the earth.

"*Buenos dias, queridos pasajeros, este es Alvaro.* Good morning, dear passengers, this is Alvaro," the bridge officer announced. "Breakfast in fifteen minutes, followed by a briefing on today's activities."

"How'd everyone sleep?" Randy stretched.

"Great," Aria beamed.

"Mm, good," Finn's muffled voice came from under a pillow.

"Amazing," I added. "Ready for whatever today holds!"

Over a breakfast of scrambled eggs, *media lunas* (our favorite, sweet, doughy mini croissants), yogurt, fruit, and granola, we chatted with fellow passengers. In the calmer seas, everyone on the ship became friendly and talkative. We quickly bonded with our diverse group: a German-Belgian couple on their honeymoon; a Dutch couple vacationing; Marcelo from Bariloche; two American brothers fresh from the Arctic; Joyce, a Californian on a year-long sabbatical; Steffi, a German woman six months into her travels; a group of twelve college students studying abroad; and a Polish family with a quiet fourteen-year-old son, who once sat silently next to Finn, neither of the boys speaking a word, to the bemusement of us all. All were budget travelers who had leaped on the last-minute reduced fare.

Unsurprisingly, Aria quickly befriended everyone. In no time, she was exchanging playful banter with the waiters, who teased her lightheartedly like they'd known each other for years. She taught the college students to play Hearts and Trash on the common room floor. Leo, the bartender, greeted her with fist bumps.

In her downtime, Aria dedicated herself to her penguin project, hunched over her notebook, sketching and painting gentoos, Adélies, and chinstraps. She enthusiastically shared her newfound knowledge with anyone who'd listen.

Finn was also chipping away at his observation journal, albeit with decidedly more nagging from us. We prompted him to talk to the scientists and reminded him to use the ship's resources for research. He waved us away, assuring us he had it.

That morning, our attention shifted to Alvaro and Pablo's briefing. We'd be landing at Deception Island. An active volcano in the South Shetland Islands, it's known for its distinctive horse-shoe shape and large, flooded caldera. We had navigated there through the Neptune Bellows, a hazardous passageway infamous for a needle rock on the eastern side, notorious for sinking ships.

"This is one of the only places in the world where ships can sail directly into the center of a restless volcano," Pablo informed us. "We'll

NO BRAVERY WITHOUT MADNESS: ANTARCTICA

be hiking up the caldera. Enjoy the black glaciers; they're a rare sight only seen here and in Iceland. The dark hue comes from layers of ash and ice accumulating over the years."

Continuing, he added, "And later, for the thrill-seekers, you can do a polar plunge from shore. We'll have towels ready for those who want to swim. Remember the old saying, 'No bravery without madness!'"

We headed back to our room to suit up. "So, who's going to do the polar plunge?" Aria looked around at us. "I am!"

"Me!" Finn declared excitedly.

Randy gave a thumbs-up. "Definitely. 'No bravery without madness,' right?"

They looked questioningly at me. I snorted. "Not a chance. I'll be the videographer."

Bundled up, we ventured into the chilly, overcast day, hopped into a Zodiac, and sped to shore. We walked to the caldera's peak along a trail of hard-packed snow. Begrudgingly, I conceded that the Wellington boots were perfect for the journey.

After taking in the stunning views from the top, we trekked back to the rocky beach. There, the first group of bold swimmers stripped down to bathing suits and charged into the frosty waters, their shouts echoing off the ice. I, bundled in my many layers, whooped and clapped while inwardly applauding my own sensibility.

"You guys are serious about this?" I asked Finn, Aria, and Randy, who were already peeling off their layers.

"For sure," said Finn.

"No doubt about it," Randy chimed in.

"If they're going, so am I," Aria stated firmly.

I pulled out my phone. "All right, let's document this act of stupidity—I mean, bravery."

Finn was the first to dash toward the ice-cold sea, with Aria close at his heels. They plunged in and emerged almost instantly, spluttering, with looks of shock on their faces. They scurried back into the warmth of waiting towels, shivering but looking pleased with themselves.

Randy, hamming it up, strolled confidently forward, adjusting swim goggles with a seriousness as if preparing for a leisurely swim at a local pool.

"You're using goggles?" I chuckled, incredulous.

"Oh, yes," he smirked, then took long strides into the water, diving in smoothly and swimming a few strokes before returning to shore, his composure barely disrupted by the cold.

The Polish family, fresh from their own quick plunge, came over with smiles. "Happy Thanksgiving," the father said warmly. "Quite a different way to celebrate, isn't it?"

I laughed; having utterly forgotten the holiday we would have been celebrating had we been home. "Yes, trading turkey for polar plunges and penguins; that's quite something."

And just then, as if on cue, a curious gentoo penguin ambled by, tilting its head as if to take in the strange sight of us mingling on shore. With an air of nonchalance, it waddled into the water. Spreading its wings slightly, it dipped and resurfaced gracefully, weaving through the waves, before vanishing into the dark, cold depths of the Antarctic waters.

Our next few days were filled with amazing sights: whales breaching, pods of dolphins racing the ship, penguins sliding around on ice flows, and icebergs revealing their vivid blue secrets beneath the surface. Alan, one of the ship's marine biologists, explained the science behind the ice's blue color. He explained that the deeper and older the ice, the more it presses out air bubbles. This increases the ice's density, enabling it to absorb every color in the spectrum except blue. So, what we were seeing was the intense blue light that's reflected.

Up on deck, we spotted massive glaciers and lone seals. Albatrosses and terns glided on the air currents, and whenever someone yelled "Whale!," we all rushed to see. Evenings were filled with *charlas*. Between adventures and educational talks, we munched on snacks and watched early-round World Cup soccer games, especially when Argentina was playing.

Landing at Brown Station on the Antarctic peninsula under a curtain of thick, fast-falling snow was particularly special for Randy and me—it marked our seventh continent visited together. Spotting orcas at breakfast and then stepping into knee-deep snow on the peninsula felt like walking into a dream. Martin led the way, shoveling a path through the snow.

Penguins were everywhere—walking, sliding, and breaking the silence with their occasional caws. Suddenly, a snowball zipped past, sparking a full-blown snowball fight among our group. The kids joined in with gusto, pelting new friends and crew alike and rapidly getting covered head to toe in snow themselves.

As we prepared to return to the ship, Finn took a playful dive onto a snowbank, sliding belly-first down the slope. Nearby, a chinstrap penguin mirrored his action, seemingly racing him downhill.

"Ha-ha, check out Finn and the penguin!" I called out, chuckling.

"Go, Finn!" cheered someone from our group.

Covered in snow, Finn stood up with a grin. "Did you see that? I think I won!"

It was an afternoon I knew none of us would ever forget.

We didn't realize that it was going to be one of our last excursions. The weather was turning bad, fast. A confluence of storms was barreling toward the Drake Passage, making our trip back look dicey.

That evening, the captain broke the news in the common room. "We've been tracking these storms," he said. "They're big, and they're not letting up. We planned to leave tomorrow night, but that would put us right into the worst of it—we're talking winds over fifty knots and waves higher than nine meters. It'd be a rough ride through the Drake."

"So, we're leaving tonight," he continued. "It'll still be bad, but we should avoid the worst. Expect rough seas and possibly to stay in your cabins for a couple of days. We'll make sure you have some food, but you'll need to stay put if we tell you. We've got time for one more *charla* and excursion before we buckle down for the journey."

Everyone seemed rattled by the update, but the new plan gave us some comfort.

Martin led our last *charla*, expounding on how unique Antarctica is—its huge size, intense cold, fierce winds, and untouched, isolated nature. He drove home how important it was for us all to protect this special place.

"You're Antarctic ambassadors now," he said. "This isn't just about sharing cool stories. It's about pushing for conservation and science. Imagine if we cared for other places like we do for Antarctica. That could change the world."

The *Islas sin Nombre*—or Islands with No Name—were small rock formations capped with fresh snow, resembling dollops of buttercream frosting or oversized marshmallow puffs. On our final Zodiac ride, Aria dubbed them the "Marshmallow Isles," a fittingly sweet label.

That afternoon, the light was extraordinary, like a watercolor wash of palest yellow and peony pink. Our friends in the other Zodiacs skimmed ahead, their boats darting between the little islands, which glowed softly in the ethereal light. We watched as icebergs radiated their teal hue and floated past a Weddell seal, content on its icy perch. Overhead, a solitary cormorant sailed through the air.

After absorbing the wild, raw beauty around us, we headed back to the ship, knowing that we needed to batten down our belongings for the voyage ahead.

The crossing that followed was challenging. The crew and passengers alike braced themselves as the storms chased us. Seasickness and anxiety were rife, evident in the quiet, sparsely attended meals and the careful way people navigated the crazy lurching of the ship. Thankfully, the conditions never forced us into lockdown, but most people chose to stay in bed as much as possible anyway through the crossing.

Upon reaching the safer waters of Cape Horn, relief washed over us. Finn presented Pablo with a watercolor painting he had made of the ship early on, a token of his appreciation. Aria once again was the life of the party on our final afternoon on the ship, dealing cards and regaling fellow passengers with her newfound penguin expertise.

Our last night aboard the *Ushuaia* was marked by a special ceremony. The captain handed out Antarctic Expedition certificates to each passenger. When he called Aria's name, Pablo had a surprise. "For our little ray of sunshine," he said, handing her solemnly a folded, white bundle along with her certificate. It was the now-frayed expedition flag, with the navy insignia of Antarpply Expeditions, which we had seen flying on our first night.

"Like you, it's been with us on two crossings of the Drake Passage," Pablo said.

"It's a special maritime tradition to be given the expedition flag," Martin added. "Congratulations."

As applause filled the room, Aria hugged each crew member, her joy contagious. They wrapped her in the flag for a photo.

I took a picture of them all, peering over the top of my camera to savor the moment even as I snapped the image. Picture perfect.

ALMOND FAMILY REPORT CARD ON ANTARCTICA

- *High Marks*: Antarctica's raw wilderness, from vast icebergs to penguins and whales, is one of Earth's most extraordinary landscapes.
- *Needs Work*: For significant cost savings, skip buying a ticket in advance. Travel to Ushuaia, Argentina, and get a last-minute deal from vendors selling tickets at discounts of 50 percent or more. Target older ships with fewer amenities but no shortage of adventure.
- *Learning Tips*: Embrace the role of a naturalist by observing wildlife behavior and engaging in on-ship educational offerings. This immersive approach enhances your understanding of Antarctica's unique ecosystem.

CHAMPIONS OF THE WORLD
Argentina

Excerpt from Aria's Journal
December 3, 2022 | Buenos Aires, Argentina

Today, we watch the Argentina vs. Australia World Cup game. It is the Round of Sixteen, and everyone in Buenos Aires is excited to watch Messi and the Argentina team play. I am wearing my light blue-and-white striped Argentina jersey and blue face paint, which tickles a little, but you get used to it. We go to a bar in Palermo Soho to watch the match. It is filled with locals dressed just like us. Every time Argentina gets close to scoring, the crowd screams. Then Messi scores to put Argentina up 1–0, and the crowd goes wild (I swear I'm half deaf now). In the end, Argentina wins the game 2–1. There's a total uproar. Screaming, cheering, laughing, hugging, whistling. It's a very happy atmosphere, and it's so cool to be a part of it.

CHAPTER 14

On our first Sunday in Argentina, we took a bus to San Telmo, one of the oldest *barrios*, or neighborhoods in Buenos Aires. Pavement soon gave way to cobblestone streets packed with street vendors. In the narrow ribbon of space between the stalls, thousands of people strolled, checking out the wares at the Sunday flea market, an institution in the city. The *Feria de San Telmo* began in the 1970s as an antiques market and evolved into a weekly kaleidoscope of vendors, artisans, and performers stretching for thirteen blocks.

"I'm hungry," Finn announced when we arrived.

Randy sighed. "You just had breakfast at the Airbnb."

"I know. But everything smells so good. Can we get *empanadas*?"

Suddenly, my stomach gave a traitorous little growl. "I could go for an empanada, too," I confessed. The smell of fried dough wafted toward us, as if carried on a mischievous breeze.

"You guys," Randy said, exasperated. "We ate a couple hours ago."

"Yeah, but—empanadas," we wheedled, angling our way to the vendor. Despite his protests, Randy ordered one for himself too. For under a dollar apiece, we bought four piping hot empanadas—golden, flaky pockets stuffed with stewed beef, hard-boiled egg, olives, and potatoes or thick with ham and cheese, Aria's favorite.

"These are unreal," I breathed. "I'm going to need bigger pants soon."

Empanadas in hand, we wandered through the outdoor marketplace, jostling with the crowd and checking out art, jewelry, intricately carved bowls, trinkets, and all manner of crafts. A few stalls displayed ornaments and Nativity scenes, reminders that Christmas was approaching.

"Keep an eye out for your Secret Santa gifts," Randy suggested. "This would be a good place to find a little something."

"I have my money ready," Aria said, patting her pocket. "I know exactly what I'm getting my person, too. I just need to find it!"

"Remember, it has to be a gift under 7,000 pesos, or $20," said Randy.

"We know," Finn replied, then walked over to check out a stall of t-shirts with funny sayings on the front.

As a family, we had agreed on having a quiet Christmas: a multiday trek in Patagonia with a Secret Santa gift exchange to keep things festive. Finn took the lead, placing our names into a hat for us to draw. The challenge was set: we had two weeks to find the perfect, packable gift for a unique Christmas morning in the wild.

In Argentina, the holiday spirit was eclipsed by World Cup 2022 fever—known locally as the *Copa Mundial*. Everywhere, locals flaunted sky-blue and white jerseys, many emblazoned with the name Lionel Messi, the Argentine captain. Storefronts and restaurants were decked out with flags and timely quotes, the nation's enthusiasm for *fútbol* (soccer) palpable. Knowing the depth of their passion for the game, Randy had arranged for us to be in Argentina for the World Cup, syncing our journey with the fervor of football and the welcoming austral summer.

As the hot, humid afternoon wore on, the crowds of San Telmo thinned. We meandered onto a side street, where the sound of a live band drew us closer. A pianist played an upright piano on the sidewalk. A bass guitarist, accordion player, and violinist accompanied him.

In front of them, a couple danced the tango in the paved crosswalk. They moved fiercely, passionately, slowly, then faster to the melody. The woman's silver sequined dress shimmered in the late afternoon light. Her stiletto heels made a clicking sound against the asphalt. Her partner wore dark sunglasses, a black vest that showed off large tattoos across his bare shoulder and arm, and tight black pants. His dark hair was pulled into an austere bun. We watched, awed, as the dancers conveyed with their bodies all the emotions of the tango, the Argentine national dance of love and sadness, longing and desperation, last chances and tormented dreams.

As a light drizzle began to fall, onlookers popped open umbrellas and continued watching as the group, the *Cuarteto Extraordinario*, wrapped up their show in the streets. We clapped as the dancers, dripping with sweat, took final bows. Then, before the downpour began in earnest, we darted under an overhang to wait out the passing shower.

Spending a few weeks in Buenos Aires before heading out to see more of Argentina afforded us a nice, slow travel vibe. Buenos Aires, a dynamic and cosmopolitan city, captivated us with its friendly people, delicious food, well-maintained parks, a rich urban art and music scene, good museums, and colorful neighborhoods to explore. Its heritage, a blend of European influences and distinct Latin character, earned it the nickname "Paris of South America."

Our daily routine had a relaxed, predictable rhythm. In the mornings, Finn and Aria took Spanish lessons at Vamos Academy, a language school in the heart of the capital. Finn, already conversational, was fine-tuning, while Aria focused on expanding her vocabulary. During their classes, Randy and I wandered the city and took care of errands.

In the afternoons, we delved into the city's contrasting neighborhoods. Vibrant La Boca revealed its Italian immigrant roots through Caminito Street's colorful houses. Elegant Recoleta contrasted sharply, its streets leading to the famed cemetery housing notable Argentinians, including Evita Peron. In San Nicolas' heart, the pink Casa Rosada on Plaza de Mayo symbolized Argentina's political saga. Each area showcased a slice of Buenos Aires' identity, mixing European and Latin American influences.

We made time in the evenings for worldschooling, and on days with World Cup matches, we joined locals in parks or restaurants, engrossed in the wild atmosphere of the games. We were bullish on Argentina's chances and increasingly excited about being in the soccer-obsessed capital of a soccer-obsessed country as the *Copa Mundial* progressed.

WORLDSCHOOLING WOBBLES: NAVIGATING THE HIGHS AND LOWS

Worldschooling your children is an adventurous path with invaluable rewards, but it can be challenging. It's a learning experience for you and your kids, especially if you're not a professional educator. Here are some tips to help you navigate:

- *Understand Your Teaching Comfort Zone:* Assess how much you want to personally teach and create curricula versus outsourcing to online courses or local tutors. Balance is key in keeping it manageable and enjoyable for both you and your children.
- *Regular Check-Ins:* Discuss as a family how you are all coping with the worldschooling lifestyle, what's working, and what's not. Identify opportunities to improve.

CHAMPIONS OF THE WORLD: ARGENTINA

- *Be Flexible*: Worldschooling is not about a strict curriculum, and you may not get the approach right from the start. Be open to adapting along the way.
- *Customize to Your Family's Dynamics*: Every family is unique, and so are the learning styles of children. Figure out what works best for your family and adapt accordingly.
- *Set Realistic Goals*: Set clear, achievable educational goals based on your travel plans. Remember, it's about the overall experience, not textbook learning.
- *Join Worldschooling Communities*: Connect with other worldschooling families online or in person. This can provide support, advice, and a sense of community.
- *Take Time for Yourself*: Don't underestimate yourself in this! Carve out personal time to recharge. A happy, relaxed parent makes for a better teacher and travel companion.

At the end of the day, worldschooling is as much about educational development as it is about personal growth and family bonding. Enjoy the journey!

Hearing sobs one evening from Finn and Aria's bedroom, I went in to check.

Finn lay in a heap on his bed, tears on his blotchy face, journal entangled in sheets, pen askew on his pillow.

"Aw, buddy," I comforted him, sitting and rubbing his back. "What's up?"

"I just can't keep up," he sniffled. "It's all too much."

"Your worldschooling assignments?" I guessed.

He nodded. That afternoon, we'd discovered he was a week behind in his trip journaling, hadn't made much headway on his science report from Antarctica, was barely through *Endurance*, and hadn't begun his writing assignment to imitate Shackleton's journal. We'd insisted he catch up that evening, heightening tensions.

"But, Finn, you've had plenty of time," I said, struggling to mask my frustration. "You need to focus on your work, not YouTube or texts."

"I know, but we're busy with Spanish school in the morning, our days are packed, and by the evening, I'm just too tired," he lamented, face buried in his pillow. "Maybe I should just drop a grade."

In the Airbnb living room, I briefed Randy, who came to join the conversation.

"We need to work through this, Finn," I encouraged, hugging him. "Managing time and balancing responsibilities are part of growing up. You'll face more demands in high school. It's important to stay organized."

He nodded, more composed.

Randy advised, "Learn to prioritize; I understand there's a lot going on, but when you do have time, you often spend it on other things. Let us help you better plan your weekly tasks, so you don't get too off track, OK?" He nodded.

"What's been hardest?" I asked.

"Math with YouTube is tough, because the videos are a little boring. And I think it would be easier if we could print out the worksheets; they're hard to do on my iPad," he admitted.

Randy offered to help, saying we could tweak the approach to math.

"And the Antarctica assignment got overwhelming," Finn added.

"We can adjust, but you need to communicate earlier if you're struggling."

I suggested Finn create daily checklists, and we promised to carve out more structured time for worldschooling. We also said we could easily print out math assignments.

Hearing our plan, Finn brightened. "Does that mean I don't need to drop a grade?"

"No, you're doing really well overall. Just stay on top of your work," we reassured him.

Aria peeked in the doorway. "Can I come in now?"

We smiled and patted the bed. "Sure, come join us."

We snuggled together for a while, listening to the sounds of the city buzzing outside the open window. Then, before heading into the living room to start drafting up a weekly spreadsheet of worldschooling assignments, we tucked the kids into bed.

We had anticipated that worldschooling would have its ups and downs. But as I looked at our kids, burrowing comfortably under blankets in Argentina after a day of immersive Spanish lessons and wandering the city, I reflected on how much they had grown and matured since the start of the trip. How many lessons they had learned along the way. It was a learning process for all of us—and clearly not a linear path—but one I wouldn't trade for anything.

The World Cup semi-final match approached in a wave of excitement that swept through the country. Argentina, after a shaky start against Saudi Arabia, was now battling Croatia for the chance to advance to the finals. On the morning of the semi-final, we headed to a public park, which was broadcasting the games on a mammoth screen. The atmosphere was electric, with everyone off work and focused on the game.

We reached the park early, jostling for a shady spot among the crowd. Everyone was decked out in Argentine colors, some in elaborate costumes, and chants filled the air. As the match unfolded, the fans' energy intensified. Argentina led 1–0, then 2–0, and finally clinched the win with a decisive 3–0 final score. Each goal unleashed waves of joy and celebration, each more deafening than the last. When Argentina secured their victory, the park exploded in cheers.

We joined the triumphant procession of jubilant fans back to our Airbnb, the streets alive with celebration. Cars honked in solidarity, and victory chants sparked impromptu dance mobs on every corner. We knew the party would go on all night, and sure enough, we went to sleep hearing the sound of *"Vamos, Vamos Argentina"* and *"Ole, Messi"* carried on the breeze.

"Maybe we should have postponed our flight south by a few days," Randy lamented, not for the first time, as we headed to the airport in Buenos Aires. We were bound for El Calafate, a town in the southern Patagonian region of Argentina. We had booked it a week earlier, before we knew that Argentina would earn a spot in the World Cup final.

"Don't be silly," I replied. "It'll be awesome to be in El Calafate for the final. I have no doubt the whole town will shut down. Everyone will be watching the match there, too."

When we arrived and checked into a backpacker hostel, surrounded by mountains and crystal-clear lakes, he conceded that we'd made the right call to continue south as planned.

El Calafate, in the Santa Cruz Province of Patagonia, is named for a native bush with yellow flowers and dark blue berries. The town, filled with adventure operators and outdoor outfitters, is a gateway to Los Glaciares National Park, including Perito Moreno Glacier, a massive ice formation fed by the Southern Patagonian Ice Field.

We were excited to get back into nature after weeks of being in a big city, and planned to spend our time trekking, camping, and kayaking. And, of course, watching the World Cup final.

Our first stop: a day trip to Perito Moreno Glacier. After taking in a panoramic view of the glacier and moraine from a walkway, we then took a catamaran to its imposing southern face. At the edge of the glacier, we clamped on helmets and strapped crampons to our hiking shoes at the edge of the ice.

"Wow, these are heavy," said Finn, stomping around a dirty patch of ice in the spiked iron plates now affixed to his trail runners. "It feels like I have bricks under my shoes."

"Bricks with long spikes," Randy reminded him. "Don't step on yourself; you'll stab your toe off if you're not careful."

Our guide taught us glacier walking techniques and pointed out its features like deep cracks and turquoise ponds, while we discussed glaciology and climate disruption, a theme we'd been exploring throughout our travels. Dahr Jamail's book *The End of Ice* had been an insightful worldschooling read for Finn and Aria, underscoring the global impact of melting glaciers. Interestingly, Perito Moreno is one of the few glaciers that's currently in equilibrium, neither growing nor shrinking significantly.

Before we left the ice field, our guides invited us to share a toast of whiskey over—what else? Glacier ice. Even though I'm not usually a whiskey drinker, I joined in, reveling in the sensation of fire and ice.

The mood in our hostel on the morning of the World Cup final between Argentina and France was one of pent-up energy and excitement. Along with everyone else, we donned our blue and white jerseys and painted stripes of sky blue on our faces. We headed into town hours before the match started, intending to find a place to watch with the locals. When we arrived, the bars were already overflowing, spilling out with spectators into the street. We finally found one with a sliver of space and tucked ourselves into a corner.

In a tense, nail-biting final, Argentina finally triumphed over defending champions France, securing a 4–2 victory in a penalty shootout after an electrifying 3–3 score. Messi scored two of the goals then another in the shootout, taking Argentina to its third World Cup win—and his first ever. The roar of the crowd when Gonzalo Montiel fired home the winning penalty was deafening.

After the victory, we chatted with the staff at the hostel about the win.

"You guys sure know how to make a match exciting," Randy teased them. "First the Netherlands game, where you gave up a 2–0 lead to win in penalty kicks—then to do the same thing against France in the final! It made for amazing soccer, but wow, the team almost gave everyone across the country collective heart attacks."

"*Sí, bueno,*" one of the women said, laughing. "It's like the tango, right? We're a country that needs to torment ourselves, to have that tension and longing, right? If it came too easy, it wouldn't be Argentina. That sense of almost-despair—it's in our DNA."

We laughed and went back to watching the celebration continuing to unfold, which we knew would continue for a long, long time.

A day later, we took a bus north to the mountain village of El Chaltén, the starting point for our Christmas camping excursion. Our plan: a four-day, three-night circuit to Laguna de los Tres and Laguna Torre.

After renting the necessary gear, we set off on December 23. The morning of our departure was a sunny, bluebird day; the air was crisp and cool. After several hours of steady hiking, we arrived at Poincenot Campground and pitched our four-person tent in a dappled beech grove. As we lay back on our sleeping bags, the front tent flap open, we soaked in the spectacular views of rugged Mount Fitzroy thrusting above the countryside. At 11,072 feet (3,375 m), the jagged spire of rock and ice is the tallest peak in Argentine Patagonia.

CHAPTER 14

On Christmas Eve, after a day of exploring nearby trails, scrabbling over rocks, and fording rivers to picnic in the shadow of stunning Cerro Torre, we relaxed at our campsite. In the fading afternoon light, we played Hearts, sitting on beech stumps and using a piece of scavenged wood as our card table. For dinner, Randy cooked rice and lentils seasoned with a soup packet over the small gas stove. Then we crowded into our tent and nestled into our sleeping bags as night fell.

"I downloaded a playlist of Christmas songs before we left," Finn said. "Do you want to listen to any?"

"Oh, yes, let's please listen to 'Silent Night,'" I replied. When my brother and I were young, we would stand with our parents around the tree on Christmas Eve, holding hands, and reflect on what we were grateful for. It's a tradition I passed on to my children.

"Cool! I have 'Michael Bubble Sings Christmas Favorites,'" he said.

I snort-giggled "That's Michael Bublé, not Bubble."

It was dark, but I was pretty sure he blushed while we all chuckled.

"OK, then, Michael Boo-BLAY is singing," Finn amended. "Here's your song, Mom."

We lay back in our sleeping bags, holding hands, and listening to the Christmas classic playing softly from Finn's iPad, before falling asleep to the hooting of a pygmy owl from high in the trees above us.

At the first rays of light on Christmas morning, we got up to hike to Laguna de los Tres, a lake at 3,860 feet (1,176 m) above sea level. The climb was a hard, rocky uphill scramble, but worth it. Glistening in the early morning sunshine, the placid lake looked like a mirror reflecting "Los Tres," or the three towering peaks visible from the shore: Fitz Roy (3,405 m), Poincenot (3,002 m), and Saint-Exupéry (2,558 m). We walked the rim, taking in the hanging glaciers dripping narrow waterfalls into the water at the far side, and then sat on boulders for long minutes to take in its beauty.

We stayed for about an hour enjoying the views before returning to our campsite. Over the little gas stove we'd rented, Randy made us Christmas morning coffee and hot chocolate, then piping hot bowls of oatmeal, into which we stirred spoonfuls of *dulce de leche*, a thick, caramel-like sauce popular across Latin America.

After breakfast, sitting on logs beside our tent, we exchanged our Secret Santa gifts. Finn had selected for Aria a handmade silver bracelet and earrings engraved with *calafate* flowers. I gave Finn new wireless ear buds, which he really wanted to be able to listen to music. Aria had selected a cool graphic T-shirt of Patagonia for Randy. And Randy gave me a silver necklace of a mountain range, which he had bought weeks earlier in San Telmo from a street vendor.

Under the shadow of Mount Fitz Roy and its neighboring peaks, we sat enjoying the last of our hot drinks, lost in the beauty of the morning. The range's rugged outline seemed to mirror our own journey through Argentina—a story of resilience, discovery, highs and lows, wins and losses, and the vibrant spirit of a country that captivated our hearts and challenged our perspectives.

ALMOND FAMILY REPORT CARD ON ARGENTINA

- *Top Marks*: Choosing where to explore in Argentina might be your toughest decision! From the vibrancy of Buenos Aires and vast pampas to rugged Patagonia and serene Bariloche, each area offers stellar experiences; you can't go wrong.
- *Needs Work*: Navigating Argentina's economic challenges can be tricky, making accessing cash and essentials like metro cards difficult (or at least it was in 2022). Bring U.S. dollars and stay informed about economic conditions.
- *Learning Tips*: Immerse yourself in culture by watching free tango shows and taking Spanish lessons to enhance your understanding of local customs.

III

THIRD-QUARTER WORLDSCHOOLING GOALS
(January–March)

January 2023
Dear Finn and Aria,

In some ways, it's hard to believe we've been on our family trip for six months already! But when we reflect on how much we have experienced together since leaving home last summer and how much you have learned through worldschooling so far, the magnitude of what we packed into our first half year on the road is clear.

Over the last few months across Greece, Jordan, and Egypt, we stepped into the past, not only reading about but exploring firsthand ancient sites from Mycenae to Petra, the Great Pyramids, and the Valley of the Kings. We went from the birthplace of democracy in Greece to seeing a seminal presidential election unfold in Brazil. In Antarctica and Argentina, you learned about different species of animals and the importance of ice and glaciers to our planet, as well as the threat of climate change. You got to learn enough Greek, Arabic, and Portuguese to get by, and put your Spanish to work in Argentina. And, of course, from Buenos Aires to Patagonia, we got to experience Argentine culture to the max while being immersed in the soccer-obsessed country as it went on to win the 2022 World Cup.

THIRD-QUARTER WORLDSCHOOLING GOALS

Looking ahead, the next arc of our trip will take us to Asia Pacific, and we will continue our worldschooling curriculum there for your next quarter. We have adjusted our worldschooling approach based on your feedback, including developing clearer weekly goals across all subjects to help you stay on track, printing more materials, and carving out more dedicated time for journaling each day. Beyond that, the overall curriculum in the next quarter will be like the last. Our expectations for you are as follows:

1. *Continue to read the country guidebooks.* We will continue the practice we began in Argentina, with Dad writing a set of questions about each country we visit for you to answer. We don't want you to just hunt for and jot down the answers, though, we want you to read more about the countries and learn about the places we're visiting.
2. *Continue reading fiction and nonfiction texts related to where we are in the world.* In Argentina, you helped select the books that we read, and seemed to like having a say in the selection. So, where it makes sense, we'll research books together. You also like a mix of audio and Kindle books, so we'll aim to alternate. Here is our starter list for the next few months:
    - India: *The Bridge Home* by Padma Venkataram, *The Night Diary* by Veera Hiranandani
    - Thailand: *All Thirteen: The Incredible Cave Rescue of the Thai Boys Soccer Team* by Christina Soontornvat
    - Cambodia: *First They Killed My Father: A Daughter of Cambodia Remembers* by Loung Ung
    - Vietnam: *Escape from Saigon: How a Vietnam War Orphan Became an American Boy*
    - Nepal: *Buried in the Sky* by Peter Zuckerman and Amanda Padoan
3. *Watch documentaries or TV series to enrich our on-the-ground experience.* We have all enjoyed finding films that give greater context to historical events or broader themes, so we'll keep trying to find relevant movies or shows. Here is our target list:
    - Cambodia: *Angkor Awakens* (a portrait of Cambodia decades after its genocide, examining how *baksbat*—Khmer for "broken

courage"—continues to affect the country, with a look to its future).
- Vietnam: *Good Morning, Vietnam* (a 1987 war comedy based on a true story. Set in Saigon in 1965 during the Vietnam War, it's about a radio DJ who is popular with the troops but infuriating to his superiors).

4. *Continue the daily practice of writing in your journal.* Since you now have a clear sense of our expectations, we want you to get more disciplined about writing every day. When you get behind, you forget the details that make for rich journal entries. Focus on your impressions as we travel—what surprised you, disappointed you, what you loved, what made you laugh, and of course, what you learned.
5. *Continue learning the basics of the languages in the places we visit.* We're also committed to finding an opportunity for Finn to take Mandarin lessons in China or somewhere else in Asia, and in the meantime, dedicate fifteen to twenty minutes every day to Duolingo Mandarin. Aria, focus on improving your Spanish, by continuing with Duolingo app lessons and/or listening to *Harry Potter* in Spanish.
6. *Write shorter essays based on questions we assign and one short story.* As we visit certain sites, we will assign short essay questions requiring some research to answer.

We'll also turn to fiction this quarter and have you write one short story.

- India: Before we visit Varanasi, considered India's holiest city, you will research why this is the case and why it's considered lucky to die there and write a one-page essay on this.

Researching and writing these shorter essays—then discussing them as a family—will help you develop a deeper understanding and enrich your experience of being in these places in person.

In addition, you'll write one short story this quarter:

- Nepal: Write a short story about kids from the United States who are in Nepal on a multiday trek. Draw sensory details from what you experience as we do our own twelve-day trek through the Himalayas. The narrative needs to follow the arc of a good story, with an inciting incident (an event that triggers the main conflict) followed by rising action (a series of related events that create more tension), climax (the point at which this tension reaches its peak), falling action, and resolution or denouement.

7. *Continue your math curriculum.* You have been doing a good job working through the chapters in your online courses. We will continue printing worksheets and working together to make sure you understand all the concepts and complete the assignments as outlined in the detailed calendar we created for you.

There's a famous proverb: "The journey of a thousand miles begins with a single step." We're excited to take our next step with you into Asia. India, here we come!
Love,
Your worldschooling teachers (Mom and Dad)

15

AND THAT, MY FRIENDS, IS KARMA
India

Excerpt from Finn's Journal
February 7, 2023 | Delhi, India

I don't like riding camels. I mean, it's fun, but super uncomfortable. . . . This afternoon, we ride camels into the Thar Desert in western India, near the border with Pakistan. After twenty minutes' riding, we get down to play in the dunes and watch the sunset. Aria gets flipped onto her face by dad accidentally and gets all sandy. I laugh, and she gets huffy with me.

On the way back to camp, my camel won't stop farting. Aria and mom are behind me on their camel and keep smelling the farts. I laugh again, and mom tells me karma is going to come back to bite me in the butt.

When we arrive at our tent, we shower then walk to the main pavilion for dinner and a traditional Rajasthan show. It starts with nice, lively music, followed by dancing and singing. One of the dancers stacks seven pots on her head and dances with that on top! Mom says she can't even balance a book on her head. We have daal and rice for dinner. Then, everyone in the audience is invited to join in dancing. I do the best I can.

Today I learned I'm not a good dancer. I also learned how sandy a person can get in just a few seconds. The answer—so sandy that it looks like they were caught in a sandstorm.

AND THAT, MY FRIENDS, IS KARMA: INDIA

Landing in Delhi, we were greeted outside the arrivals terminal by Salman, a short, dark-haired man holding a sign with our names.

"Welcome to India," he said warmly. "I'll be your guide here in Delhi." Beside him was our driver, a soft-spoken man named Surendar.

They placed garlands of orange marigolds around our necks and assisted with our luggage. Salman noticed we were one backpack short.

"Only three?" he inquired.

Randy explained that Aria's bag was lost in transit and that we had filed a lost baggage claim with the airline. In addition to her clothes, it had her journal and special stuffed animals in it, so she was distraught but hopeful it would be returned soon.

After the introductions, we piled into a van to head to our Airbnb. As we inched forward in the congested traffic, a woman with a baby slung over her chest banged on the car windows, gesturing for food. She rapped on each pane then cupped her hands on the glass, peering inside.

Salman advised from the front seat, "I know it's hard, but you must ignore the beggars. If you say 'no,' that just gives them hope. Ignore them completely, and they'll move on." I nodded at Finn and Aria, silently urging them to listen. But inside, I felt conflicted.

Back in Colorado, we kept small bags with essentials to give to homeless people. The scale of poverty in Delhi was a stark contrast, though, with dozens of beggars seen in just minutes. Salman explained the overwhelming numbers in cities like Delhi and Mumbai, and reiterated the dangers in acknowledging even one, which would lead to being swarmed by others, and noted they were sometimes associated with organized crime.

"Trust me, just ignore them. You'll get used to it," Salman reassured us, but I questioned whether we should ever become accustomed to such sights. Our worldschooling book for India, a young adult novel called *The Bridge Home*, had touched on this issue, depicting the invisibility of the homeless in India.

As Surendar navigated us through the frenzied traffic—a crush of rickshaws, tuk tuks, trucks, cars, bicycles, livestock, and pedestrians—the woman and child faded into the thick haze. I sighed. Even having mentally prepared myself for the crushing poverty and intense wealth disparity of the world's most populous country, India was clearly going to be a lesson in worldschooling for me, too.

When we got to our Airbnb, we immediately crawled into bed and let sleep heavy with jet lag carry us away.

India is a land of extremes, a teeming, complex whirlwind. It's a third the size of the United States but with four times the population, upward of 1.4 billion people. On the afternoon we arrived, Salman told us that India's population had just surpassed China's, a statistic he said was dubiously celebratory as so many of its people lived in abject poverty. We had deliberately planned our travels there for the second half of our trip, after Finn and Aria would be more seasoned travelers and hopefully better able to navigate and appreciate its chaotic rhythms.

Unlike our independent travel style in other countries, we decided to lean on local expertise in India. We connected with Pradeep Kumar, a local entrepreneur who balanced running a small travel agency with a nonprofit dedicated to helping youth from Delhi's slums. Pradeep offered us a unique window into various facets of India.

He helped organize our journey across northern India, which would take us from Delhi to Agra to see the Taj Mahal, then across Rajasthan—to Jaipur, Udaipur, Jodhpur, and the far western desert town of Jaisalmer—before we'd fly east again to culminate our travels in the Holy City of Varanasi. He'd arranged guides for us in each city as well as our transport with Surendar. In Delhi, he personally escorted us for a day through the Sanjay Colony slum, which he said wasn't on most tourist itineraries but would give us a broader view of life in India.

"Before we go in, I'd like to know—what do you think of when you think of a slum?" Pradeep asked. On either side of us, cows rummaged through heaps of trash.

"A place where many people live, and there aren't enough bathrooms. So, they sometimes need to pee or poop on the ground," Aria said. I knew she was recalling our time in Alexandra township in Joburg.

"No electricity or running water," said Finn. "A lot of poverty."

"In general, not enough infrastructure to support the people living there," Randy added. "I think of transient, temporary structures of cardboard or tin where people end up living longer term."

Pradeep nodded. "Different slums have different characters in India. There are more than 750 in Delhi alone, with 2 million people living in them. This one is near the textile factories, so it is slightly better off than others.

"The government provides electricity, public toilets, and water tanks," he continued. "Not everyone has toilets in their homes, though some do; others use communal facilities. Children go to government school at least through eighth grade. Residents pay for medicine, but doctors are free. Parents work in the garment industry, recycling unwanted clothes or waste fabric from the factories in Okhla."

That explained the scraps of brightly colored cloth we'd seen in piles along the street. Men in flip flops squatted among the heaps of fabric, sorting through the swatches, like gold panners sifting for a prized nugget.

"What do they do with the larger fabrics if they find some?" Finn asked.

"Resell it. The margin for this work is about 200 rupees—$3—for an eight-hour day."

"That's not a lot of money," Aria said.

"For people living here, it is a lot," replied Pradeep in his soft voice.

Turning a corner, we saw five children crowded around a little girl who was clutching a snack-size bag of chips. They were barefoot or in flip flops, dirt streaking their faces and arms. They waved to us brightly as we passed.

"In India, we are a big sharing culture. We don't have much, but what we have, we share," said Pradeep. "We believe in karma—what you put into the universe will come back to you.

"See," he continued, gesturing to the kids. "This girl has gotten herself a small bag of chips. She took one or two, then shared the rest. That's just what we do."

He steered us to an alcove and gestured for us to take a seat atop canvas sacks lining the walls.

"Would you like chai? This woman makes fabulous masala chai—Indian tea."

"Yes, thank you," I replied. A woman in a brightly colored sari stirred cardamom, ginger, nutmeg, and cloves into milk simmering on a pot over the stove. The fragrant, spicy aroma filled the small space with a warmth not present in the cool winter afternoon. I shrugged into my jacket and thought about the kids—and the woman—in their bare feet and tattered clothes. She ladled the creamy tea into terra cotta cups the size of shot glasses and handed them to us. We murmured, "*Shukriya*"—thank you in Hindi. The tea was sugary and smelled like Christmas in a cup.

"Pradeep," I asked after a moment. "What do people think when they see Westerners like us in the slum?"

"In India, we have another belief," he said. "We receive guests with the spirit of *atithi devo bhava*—the Hindu-Buddhist philosophy that a guest is akin to a God. It's why you'll find many locals asking to take selfies with you and why we greeted you with marigolds, a holy flower. People are happy to have you; you are welcome here."

When we finished our tea, Pradeep guided us through the alleyways of the slum, stopping at a doorway to pull off his shoes, which he placed on a low wooden rack. A sign read, "Learning by Locals: Empowering Youth."

"Come, meet my students," said Pradeep. "They love to meet new people and practice their English. Then Sukhmani will do henna for you and Aria. She's a former student who grew up in the slum. Then she got a scholarship to the United States like I did, became a teacher, and now runs our center."

We peeked our heads into three rooms: a computer lab filled with donated laptops and desktop computers; a classroom with world maps and a patchwork of well-worn rugs on the floor; and the library, with a collection of books and games.

We placed our shoes alongside Pradeep's, then plopped down on the rug at the front of a classroom with about twenty teens, who ringed us in a semi-circle. We shared a bit about ourselves and where we were from. Finn and Aria showed them on the map what state we were from and told them it was snowing in Colorado.

The kids' eyes got wide. They had never seen snow and were excited to hear Finn and Aria talk about skiing. We asked what their hobbies were, and they told us about themselves. They ranged in age from fourteen to twenty-two and loved soccer, dance, and video games. When they grew up, they aspired to be police officers, accountants, programmers, teachers, doctors, and tour guides.

After visiting with the students, Pradeep led us up to the roof balcony. We could see the maze of streets in the slum stretching below us, the cacophony of sounds muting as we ascended. Through the gray haze of the choking Delhi smog, we saw vibrant pops of color—the green, white, and saffron-colors of the India flag flapping in the breeze and bright saris drying on clotheslines across the rooftops.

"Look at the kites," Finn called out, pointing to colorful diamonds dancing in the breeze. Pradeep smiled and nodded. "Kids here love to play games with their kites, battling each other for the skies. They fly two kites close together, and the one that is cleverest and strongest wins and snaps the other's string. The trick is to capture the other kite before it falls to the ground."

Scanning the nearby buildings, we traced the kites to dozens of children scattered across the rooftops, working the strings. They had little room to maneuver, but they kept their kites aloft with ease, their smiles obvious even from a distance as they gazed upward, tracking their toys above the din.

"Up and at 'em," Randy called as his alarm rang at 6 a.m. "Time to see the Taj Mahal."

"Mmmph," Finn moaned. "It's so early. Five more minutes."

"Nope, you can nap later. Let's go see one of the world's greatest wonders."

It was dark outside as we made our way to the car, where Surendar was waiting for us.

"It's pretty with all the little white lights," Aria noted, walking along the long pathway to the famed monument.

Crossing through the main gates, we saw the iconic white marble building framed before us. Walking into the gardens, we took in its reflections in the "rivers" of water that gathered in a central pool, all designed to depict heaven on earth. A mausoleum commissioned by the Mughal emperor Shah Jahan to house the tomb of his beloved wife, the Taj Mahal is said to have been "designed by giants and finished by jewelers," the most beautiful building ever constructed.

As the first rays of dawn tinted the marble pink and gold, we sat on nearby benches and stared up for long minutes, easily seeing how it earned its accolades. The semi-precious stones inlaid into the facade glinted in the soft sunlight, like glimmering sequins.

"This is one of those sights that lives up to every hype," I murmured. "You see it in pictures, read about it in books, hear about it from travelers, but the reality of it really does take your breath away."

BEYOND THE COMFORT ZONE: TACKLING TOUGH TOPICS ON THE ROAD

When worldschooling through travel, you and your children are bound to encounter challenging situations and ethical dilemmas. From witnessing poverty to navigating cultural differences, these experiences can be as educational as they are complex. Here's how you can approach these moments with sensitivity and openness, turning them into learning opportunities:

- *Open Honest Conversations*: Use these encounters to have honest discussions with your kids. Acknowledge that you don't have all the answers, and it's okay to feel unsettled or confused.
- *Research Together*: When facing tough topics, research them together. Look for books, documentaries, or reputable online resources to better understand the context and history.
- *Encourage Empathy and Respect*: Foster empathy in your children by encouraging them to see situations from multiple perspectives. Remind them of the importance of respecting different cultures and lifestyles.
- *Seek Local Insights*: Engage with local communities respectfully. If appropriate, seek opportunities to learn from them directly about their experiences and viewpoints.
- *Reflect and Debrief*: After encountering difficult situations, take time to debrief. Discuss what you've learned and how it might impact your views or actions.
- *Teach Critical Thinking*: Encourage your kids to think critically about what they see and experience. Ask questions that prompt them to analyze and form their own opinions.

- *Be Aware of Your Impact:* Consider the implications of your choices, like the decision to visit a slum or township. Weigh educational value against potential risks or ethical concerns.
- *Balance Exposure with Age Appropriateness:* Tailor these experiences to the age and maturity of your children, ensuring they are not overwhelmed.
- *Utilize Support Networks:* Connect with other worldschooling families or educational forums for advice and support in navigating these complex topics.

Remember, worldschooling isn't just about exploring new places but also about confronting and understanding the realities of our world. These experiences, while challenging, can significantly contribute to your children's growth into well-rounded, compassionate global citizens.

"This is not ice cream, Mom," Aria muttered, sniffing warily at the *Kulfi Faluda* the street vendor handed her.

Sony, our guide in the Pink City of Jaipur, told us that this sweet treat was centuries old, passed down from the Mughal rulers who came from Persia. The vendor scooped heaping spoonfuls of neon yellow *faluda* noodles into small cardboard cups, then ladled on the *kulfi*, a traditional Indian "ice cream" made from slowly simmered whole milk flavored with pistachio, rose water, and saffron.

Aria eyed it suspiciously. "It smells like soap. You try it first, Mom."

I gamely drove my spoon into the radioactive-looking concoction and took a bite. I felt like Simba when he tried a grub in *The Lion King*.

"Slimy but satisfying," I announced. "Seriously, it's tasty. You try it, Aria."

She still looked dubious but dipped her spoon in a millimeter. Sony laughed.

"It's a different texture, I know, but truly, it's tasty."

Aria nibbled the world's tiniest bite.

"Well? What do you think?"

"It's . . . better than a grub."

We laughed and ate as we walked. Poor Finn had stayed back at our homestay, felled by a stomach bug. Our hosts were warm and caring, assuring us they'd keep an eye on him. They offered to make him mild rice or yogurt and toast. He had no appetite though and just wanted to sleep.

While he recuperated, Randy, Aria, and I continued a culinary journey through Rajasthan. While we all loved Indian food back home, we had quickly realized that our favorites—like mild and creamy masala—are heavily tailored to Western tastes. Everything in India was spicier than we were used to, which Randy and Finn loved but took more getting used to for Aria and me. We learned to pair meals with yogurt-based dishes like a yogurt *raita* or *lassi* (a thick, sweet drink similar to a smoothie).

We enjoyed sampling a variety of street food with our guides in all the cities we visited, arriving early at roadside stalls to see how they prepared the dishes, like *samosas* and *kachoris*. In the alley outside an open-air stand, we watched as they mixed diced vegetables and spice fillings in huge, circular bowls; kneaded and then rolled the dough; and stuffed it. In the front, atop giant fires, they fried the pastries, which we tried, piping hot. At another stand, we tried the fresh, sticky sweet *boondi laddu*, a popular Indian sweet made by combining tiny dots of fried, sugar-soaked batter with seeds and fragrant spices.

Aria's favorite, though, was seeing how traditional naan bread was made.

"A tandoor is a large, urn-shaped oven made of clay," Sony told us as we peered inside. She explained that, since antiquity, tandoors have been used to make unleavened flatbreads, like roti and naan, as well as to roast meat. The cooks worked the dough in their hands, then slapped the round, flat disks onto the side of the tandoor oven, where they stuck to the curved surface.

Within minutes, the dough puffed with flaky bubbles and browned. The cooks used long prongs to pull the baked rounds out, then brushed them with butter and let us try, still bubbling from the fire.

"This is easily the best naan I've ever eaten," breathed Randy.

"Sony, this food is delicious," I echoed. "I just wish Finn could have been with us. He would have loved seeing all this."

When we got back to our homestay, we found Finn feeling a little better. In fact, the first thing he asked—and a good sign—was, "Did you bring me back any leftovers?"

❖ ❖ ❖

On our first afternoon in Jodhpur, nicknamed the Blue City for its vibrant indigo buildings, we stumbled upon a lively street celebration. Women in dazzling saris and men in sport coats and vivid turbans danced in a raucous parade, beckoning us to join and snap selfies with them.

At the heart of the festivities was a boy in a crimson jacket, adorned with marigold garlands and a *tika* on his forehead, a mark of success or rite of passage. Our guide, Rishi, had to shout over the cacophony of drums, maracas, and the city's buzz, explaining this was a traditional coming-of-age ritual, part of Hinduism's sixteen sacraments.

While Finn suddenly feigned interest in a distant cow, Randy dove right into the dancing throng. A man in a striped turban, his face beaming with joy, grabbed Randy's hand and pulled him into the heart of the circle. They danced side by side, Randy following the man's lead in an enthusiastic, if slightly awkward, imitation of the local dance steps.

Aria was drawn in next by a woman in a pink sari. She quickly found the rhythm, surrounded by a sea of color and sound, becoming part of the intricate dance.

As they whirled, the revelers suddenly started stuffing *rupees*—Indian money—into Randy and Aria's mouths, a gesture that surprised them but was clearly meant as an honor.

"Um, what was the *rupee* thing about?" Aria asked Rishi later, swishing water in her mouth to get rid of the stale taste of the bills.

"They were thanking you for joining in with them," he replied.

"Ah," Aria said. "They could have just said, '*shukriya*.' I'd have been fine with that."

"That was amazing," I told Rishi. "Why am I not surprised that this kind of thing would happen here? India seems a place where chance encounters lead to meaningful moments."

Rishi smiled. "There's a Hindi saying called '*apnaayat*.' It means friendliness, closeness, a feeling of belonging. It's the soul of Jodhpur—of India—selfless love and kindness. When you open your heart to people, you'll see, people open their hearts back."

Continuing our journey westward, we arrived a few days later in the Golden City of Jaisalmer, a former medieval trading center in the far west of India, near the border with Pakistan. Known for its imposing hilltop citadel, Maharaja's palace, vibrant bazaars, and intricately decorated temples, Jaisalmer sits in the great Thar desert.

This is the world's seventh largest and most populated desert in the world; with 30 million people, it's known as the teeming desert. And it was our destination for the night.

"Somehow, I'm not surprised that India's desert is the most populated," said Finn. "There doesn't seem to be anyplace here that doesn't have people in it."

We piled into the back of an open-air truck and held our breath as swirls of dust rose from the barren back roads. The landscape was parched, undulating with sand dunes and low-lying scrub brushes. Goats and camels crossed the street at intervals. Young children in school uniforms blew kisses as we drove by.

After settling into the desert camp, we headed toward a herd of camels. Aria scrambled onto one, whose name we were told was Lalu. At the guide's signal, I climbed up onto Lalu's back also, grabbing hold behind Aria.

"Guess we're sharing a ride this time," I told her.

"Yep," she said "Off we go!"

As Lalu lurched upward, we watched Finn and Randy get set for the ride.

Finn mounted a camel named Raju, while Randy made friends with a dromedary called Papaya.

"Tsk, tsk," our camel driver clicked at Lalu, who took off, into the setting sun.

We were disappointed to see trash littering the landscape. First it was a lone paper bag, then a pile of discarded juice boxes and plastic water bottles, followed by a banana peel, old shoe, and paper wrappers half buried in the sand.

When we arrived at the dunes, we walked away from the large groups that had arrived by jeep. We settled into the curve of a dune to take in the setting sun, then turned at the sound of dozens of voices chatting and shouting into their phones. We turned to see several Indian men, all on mobiles, loudly speaking into their screens and walking into the sand.

"This feels fitting of our experience in India," Randy noted. "Even here, in the farthest reaches of the country, literally the middle of nowhere, it's loud. Busier than I'd imagined. Less pristine than it should be. But also beautiful, joyful, communal."

Abandoning the idea of a quiet, solitary experience in the desert, we embraced the atmosphere and had fun playing in the sand, doing cartwheels, and finding patterns in the wind-blown ridges.

Later that night, in our tent, Finn teased Aria for being a sandy mess—even post-shower—after Randy accidentally dumped her onto a dune while they were playing.

"Finn, you clearly don't understand the concept of karma," I called after him. "You should be nicer to your sister."

Shortly afterward, as he was getting ready for bed, Finn stubbed his toe on the dresser and hopped around the room.

"And that, my friends, is karma," I said, smothering a chuckle. Aria let out a satisfied snort from her bunk while Finn stomped to the bathroom in a huff.

Our final stop in India was Varanasi, the spiritual heart of the country and a pilgrimage destination for devout Hindus. Known for millennia as Kashi, this temple-laden city in Uttar Pradesh, attracts pilgrims to bathe in the Ganges River and perform funeral rites along its *ghats*, or riverfront steps. It's the place where Hindus aspire to end their days for *moksha*, liberation from the cycle of birth, death, and rebirth.

Before arriving, we had Finn and Aria write essays about Varanasi for their worldschooling, to grasp its significance and brace for its intensity.

From the deserts of Jaisalmer, we flew via Delhi to reach Varanasi. During a brief layover in the capital, we met up with Pradeep, who had recovered Aria's lost backpack, much to her elation, reuniting with her globetrotting stuffed animals, Kaleb and Jordan. To her traveling menagerie, she had added a new friend, a small plush elephant named Hindi.

Our guide in Varanasi was Shailesh, a shaman and a brilliant storyteller with a PhD in archaeology. With his thick glasses, handlebar mustache, and saffron smear on his forehead, he was the embodiment of a wise, holy figure.

"In Hinduism, we revere a pantheon of over 330 million deities, all manifestations of a singular divine essence," he explained in his deep, resonant voice. "Among these, three deities hold paramount importance. Can you name them?"

Aria responded promptly, a result of our earlier reading from a book we picked up at a roadside stall titled *Hindu Gods and Goddesses*. "Brahma, Vishnu, and Shiva."

"Exactly," Shailesh acknowledged with a smile. "Each embodies a cosmic function: Brahma the Creator, Vishnu the Preserver, and Shiva the Destroyer."

Finn chimed in: "They're like the Generator, Observer, and Destroyer, right? G-O-D."

Shailesh nodded, leading us in the early morning through the warren of Varanasi's alleyways. "This city venerates Shiva. People often question the worship of a destroyer. But Shiva's destruction is transformative, cleansing sins and bad karma, making Varanasi a city of positive destruction."

As we reached a bustling *ghat* by the Ganges, Shailesh shared a belief: merely entering Varanasi absolves half one's sins, while a dip in the Ganges purges all, transcending lifetimes.

We climbed into a boat and pushed off into the dawn, taking in the scene unfolding on the west bank before us. The sound of bells rang out, almost drowning out Shailesh's rumbling voice. Men sat cross-legged, eyes closed, praying on the stone steps at the river's edge. In the water, pilgrims bathed, splashing their arms and heads or submerging themselves completely. Floating candles bobbed in the current, and camel caravans loped along on the opposite shore.

Our eyes stung from the thick smoke curling into the early morning haze from pyres lining the banks. Shailesh pointed out Manikarnika Ghat, the largest cremation *ghat*, where he said more than a hundred bodies were cremated every day. Dead bodies swaddled in cloth were carried through the old town to the Ganges, to be dunked in the river prior to cremation.

"We will see the traditional cremations tonight, after dark," Pradeep said.

"I don't want to see people's bodies being burned," Finn said, looking pale.

"Me neither," Aria echoed, her eyes wide.

"You will see. Here, it is a different experience than you might think. Don't forget, for Hindus, this is what we want most—to die in Varanasi, so our souls can attain salvation."

"Look," Shailesh, said, pointing toward the east. "It has been too hazy in recent days to see the sunrise, but you are going to be lucky."

The sun, a massive red orb, slowly rose over the eastern bank of the Ganges, casting ripples of scarlet in the river. Our driver shut off the boat's motor so we could glide along, listening to the soundtrack of ringing bells, chirping birds, and the voices of tens of thousands of people carried on the wind.

After spending the day exploring Varanasi's temples, we arrived at Dasaswamedh Ghat at dusk for the Ganga Aarti ceremony. Shailesh, squatting along the bank, showed us how to place offerings into the river for the Goddess Ganga.

"With the first candle you light and place in the water, give a prayer to those who have passed on. With the second, give thoughts to loved ones back home. With the third, you may ask for a small personal wish."

As Shailesh chanted, we knelt to light candles nestled in foil cups and adorned with marigolds, releasing them into the dark waters of the Ganges. We watched in silence as our candles drifted away, joining a constellation of flickering lights.

"Now, the Ganga Aarti awaits," Shailesh announced, leading us through the crowd.

We settled on a wooden deck, securing a vantage point amid thousands who had come to witness the sacred nightly ceremony. The air vibrated with anticipation as *pandits*, young priests clad in vibrant saffron, commenced the Aarti. Their synchronized movements, offering of flowers, and the hypnotic sound of conch shells being blown created an otherworldly ambiance.

As they waved incense and circled brass lamps in devout motions, Shailesh whispered, "Each element symbolizes an offering to the divine. It's a dance of devotion, a spectacle of faith."

The ceremony culminated in silence, punctuated only by the lapping of the river. We then navigated our way to the cremation *ghat*, our path lit by the flickering lamps of street vendors. We walked to an outcropping overlooking the traditional pyres, our senses assaulted by the sounds of hundreds of voices and smells of burning wood mingled with incense and curdled milk from the temple offerings that pooled along the banks.

"Oh my gosh," Finn said, pointing quietly to the fire closest to us. "You can actually see a body in that one. And in that other one, too."

We followed his gaze and could, indeed, clearly see the charred remains of a head and torso in the flames. On another, a rib cage.

People mingled along the shore. It wasn't a particularly sad atmosphere. Nor was it a celebration. There was more of a sense of communion.

We watched as one of the Untouchables—those belonging to the lowest caste in India—monitored the fire and stoked the flames.

"One of the things that strikes me most," Randy said, "is how different of a sentiment people seem to have toward death here. At home, it's something so unspeakably sad. Something people endure and get through alone or surrounded only by close family and friends. Here, there seems to be a sense of broader community to it, that you're part of something larger as you give your loved ones their ultimate peace and salvation."

"It's still eerie to see the bodies," Finn said, "but not as scary as I thought it would be."

We watched a while longer before heading back to our hotel where, as we had on so many of our nights in India, we collapsed into bed, exhausted and spent.

On our final morning in Varanasi, we navigated the labyrinthine old town toward the airport, backpacks in tow. The alleyways, barely wide enough for the occasional rickshaw or wandering cow, were an obstacle course of everyday life. We dodged trash and "cow land mines," a euphemism one of our guides had used for the ever-present cow droppings.

As we reached the bustling main street, the symphony of Varanasi in mid-morning hit us. We were seasoned now in the art of moving through the crowds without our packs becoming unintentional battering rams. We paused to observe a group of women adorned in intricate henna and heavy jewelry, a stark contrast to a nearby holy man whose dreadlocks were caked in ash as he bestowed blessings.

Street vendors hawked their goods—fresh fruit, chai, *kachoris*—each a sensory note in the city's vibrant mosaic.

This mix of experiences brought me back to a visit on our first day in India, to Delhi's Lotus Temple with Salman. Inside its serene walls, we had listened to soulful prayers and beautiful song, a world apart from the clamor of the city outside. Salman had posed a question to us: "Do you know why the lotus is sacred in Hindu culture?" We didn't. He'd explained that it was revered as something pure and beautiful, which grows from murky waters—a metaphor I now more deeply understood reflected in the essence of India.

Varanasi, and India as a whole, was a land of contradictions: chaotic and spiritual, dirty and joyful, overwhelming and beautiful. A country where unexpected encounters became lasting memories, where our hearts felt both shattered and healed by the people's warmth.

Initially, India hadn't been high on my travel list, its intensity a daunting prospect. Yet, it was a destination I felt compelled to explore—how could we worldschool Finn and Aria, aiming to expose them to diverse cultures, and omit the world's most populous country?

India confronted us all with harsh realities, many questions, and few answers. But it was also a lesson in seeing beyond the struggles to the deeper beauty of a complex nation.

As we left, I realized that this journey through India had been as much an education for Randy and me as it was for our kids. We were all worldschoolers here, learning from a land that defied simple explanations and which bloomed from adversity.

ALMOND FAMILY REPORT CARD ON INDIA

- *Top Marks*: Don't miss India's holy city of Varanasi. Participate in the Ganga Aarti and watch the sunrise over the Ganges, moments that give a glimpse into the spiritual heartbeat of the country.
- *Needs Work*: Prepare for intense sensory and emotional experiences, especially the stark contrasts between wealth and poverty. Handle begging sensitively and respectfully, understanding its complex social implications.
- *Learning Tips*: Engage a local guide who can help you navigate the chaos, show you which street foods to try, offer cultural insights, and reveal lesser-known spots, enriching your understanding of India's diverse cultural landscape.

16

NO MANGO STICKY RICE FOR YOU

Thailand

Excerpt from Aria's Journal
February 21, 2023 | Bangkok, Thailand

At breakfast, Mom and Dad tell us that Finn and I can plan our day today in Bangkok, yea! We spend time researching the city and writing down our detailed plans. Then we present those to Mom and Dad, who like our itinerary. We leave at noon to get to the first activity. By then, it is already hot, so the twenty-minute walk to Wat Pho is hard. We wander around until we finally get to see the reclining Buddha statue. It is huge, golden, and its feet are patterned with pearl. After the temple, we go to a local restaurant for a quick lunch, then head to a "What is Thai?" museum. I find it very interesting and informative. Lastly, we take a boat to the Icon Siam mall. We spend hours wandering around. There is a lot to look at! The mall is huge and fancy! Soon it is time for dinner. There is a huge street market on the bottom level, which is why Finn and I wanted to come here in the first place. It has everything from bao buns to fried chicken to candy! I would call our "Kids Plan It" day a success. What I learned is that you can't pack too much into a day of exploring or you will be exhausted. Dad does a good job planning most of our days.

"OK guys, social studies time! There are important cultural dos and don'ts that we all need to know about traveling in Thailand," I said, swiveling in my seat to look at Finn and Aria. On our way to Ko Yao Yai, a Thai island in the Andaman Sea, I used the drive to give a cultural primer.

"Thailand is the 'Land of Smiles,'" I explained, "so no sibling fights or frowns, or you'll be arrested."

Finn gave me a withering look, and Aria rolled her eyes. "No, we won't," she scoffed.

"Just kidding, but it *is* the Land of Smiles. From your reading thus far, have you come across any Thai customs we should keep in mind as we travel here?" I asked.

Aria, enjoying pop quizzes, replied, "In Thailand, respect is key. Be calm, polite, and don't lose your temper. People greet each other with a *wai*, a bow with palms together. There are rules for it, like who bows first and how deeply."

"You got that from *All Thirteen*?" I asked, impressed. They were reading it for our worldschooling literature, a book about the rescue of a Thai soccer team, which included sidebars on Thai culture and customs.

"It's one of my favorites," Finn added. "We also learned that causing someone to lose face is bad in Thai culture. Even if they're wrong, it's disrespectful to call them out."

"Good start," I said. "Remember to dress modestly, especially in temples. Never disrespect the Thai government or Royal Family. Don't point with your feet or touch heads, as they're sacred in Buddhism. Greet with a *wai* or say *'sawadee ka'* for women, *'sawadee krap'* for men. Lastly, always say things calmly and with a smile. Sound good?"

The kids nodded. "Sounds good."

"Awesome. Now who's ready to chill on the beach for a few days?"

A chorus of "me's" sounded from the back of the van. Randy woke with a start and gave a sluggish "me" as well; he had gotten an early start on relaxing with a nap.

"Me four," I said and settled back to take in the fresh sea breezes as we drove past wooden houses on stilts, banana trees, and a handful of local restaurants and bars lining the road. There was very little traffic, only an occasional scooter or bicycle.

Though it's less than thirty minutes by boat from Phuket or Krabi on the Thai mainland, Ko Yao Yai, which means "long and large island," is still little known among travelers and largely undeveloped. Located in the middle of Phang Nga Bay, it has sandy beaches, mangroves, small fishing villages, and a sleepy vibe—something we were all craving after the intensity of India.

By this point in our travels, we knew our rhythm. We could go for a while at a faster pace as we did across northern India, but then we needed a period of slower travel to regroup. Finn and Aria needed concerted time to work on worldschooling assignments. Randy and I needed to get caught up on TripAdvisor and Google reviews, logistics planning and budget reconciliation, social media updates and writing. More than anything, though, we needed time and space to recenter so that we'd be able to continue to fully appreciate everything we were seeing and experiencing as we went forward.

We figured a week in the islands of southern Thailand would be a perfect place for that.

"Do you hear that?" Randy asked as we walked up to our hotel, steps from the beach.

"What? I don't hear anything," I replied.

He smiled. "Exactly."

At our hotel's outdoor restaurant overlooking the ocean, Finn and I savored our lunch. He juggled geometry problems with a protractor, while savoring bites of spicy *massaman* curry. I munched on chicken with cashew nuts, glancing up from the guidebook.

"This is the way to work," said Finn.

"Totally agree. I hope Aria and Daddy are enjoying their one-on-one time too," I said, thinking of them exploring the island by motorbike.

After a bathroom break, I rushed back to Finn, bursting with news. "Huge epiphany, Finn! I just realized that the hose attached to the wall, which we've been seeing in bathrooms across India and here, may not be only for washing the toilets or cleaning the bathrooms!"

"What else would it be used for?"

I paused for dramatic effect. "For washing . . . ourselves!"

I pulled up Google to test my hypothesis. "Yes! Apparently, that hose is sometimes called a 'bum gun.' I can't believe I never knew that. It's apparently more hygienic than toilet paper."

Finn's reaction was lukewarm. "Eh. Toilet paper's fine."

"It's a cultural thing! Plus, it's cleaner," I argued, excited to share with Randy and Aria.

Finn went back to his geometry and muttered under his breath. "I doubt they're going to be as excited as you are."

When they returned from their daddy-daughter time, I regaled them with my discovery. "I admit, it's weird trying it at first, and I don't think I did it right. I ended up drenching my pants. I bet that's part of the reason women here wear skirts."

"Mom, you are oddly obsessed with the bathroom hose," Aria noted.

"I accept that. But everyone needs to try the bum gun at least once, okay? Practical cultural lessons in worldschooling! Who's with me?"

Finn folded his arms over his chest. "I will think about it if you stop calling it a 'bum gun.' And no posting about this to Instagram."

I grinned. "Deal."

EMPOWERING KIDS TO PLAN A TRAVEL DAY: A GUIDE FOR PARENTS

By involving your kids in the planning process, they'll feel like they have skin in the game—and learn more than if they're just passive participants. A "Kids Plan It" day is a great way to make educational travel exciting. Here are some tips we've found that work well to help your kids—especially if they're older (tweens and teens)—take the lead:

- *Start with Research*: Encourage them to research the destination. Steer them to resources like travel guides, websites, and local tourism information. Let them explore various attractions, historical sites, museums, and outdoor activities. This research phase can spark their interest and give them a sense of ownership over the trip.
- *Budgeting Skills*: Give them a budget for the day and let them figure out how to allocate it. Teach them about the local currency and how to handle money, including understanding conversion rates

and estimating costs. This not only teaches financial responsibility but also practical math skills.
- *Logistics Planning*: Challenge them to plan the logistics for the day. This means figuring out transportation options, travel times, and the most efficient route to cover their chosen attractions. It's a great opportunity for them to learn about time management and navigation.
- *Decision Making*: Encourage them to make decisions collaboratively. If there are younger siblings involved, let the teens consider their preferences too. This fosters a sense of responsibility and teamwork.
- *Presentation and Feedback*: Have them present their plan to the family. Listen to their ideas and provide constructive feedback. This enhances their communication skills and boosts confidence.
- *Be Supportive, but Hands-Off*: Provide guidance and support, but resist the urge to take over. Mistakes are part of the learning process. A missed train or a miscalculated budget can turn into valuable life lessons.
- *Enjoy the Day*: Finally, go with the flow and have fun on the day they planned. Celebrate their effort and initiative, regardless of any minor hiccups.

By empowering your kids in this way, you're not just planning a trip; you're equipping them with skills for life while creating lasting family memories.

"Daddy, is that our boat?" Aria asked a couple of days later, her eyes fixed on the shore where several long-tail boats bobbed in the shallows. Each boat, with its long pole extending from the back, was adorned with colorful ribbons and flower garlands. These offerings to the water spirits were a traditional Thai gesture, for safe passage and good fortune.

"That's the one," Randy confirmed as a man from one of the boats waved us over.

We waded through the warm water and climbed aboard. The driver fired up the engine, lowering the propeller at the end of the boat's long tail, and we sped off toward towering limestone karsts that jutted out of the sea.

Our driver soon pulled up to a gorgeous island with a long pier. Part of a marine park, Ko Hong is uninhabited. Two soft sand beaches curled around twin bays, each with clear turquoise water. Finn and Aria immediately strapped on their goggles and dove into the sea.

"Whoa, check it out," said Randy, nudging me.

I turned and leaped back as a huge lizard sauntered across the sand. "What is that?"

"I think it's a water monitor."

"He's gigantic."

The monitor clicked its tongue at us then slithered into the water and paddled around a huge karst.

"I'm glad I didn't turn around in the water and find that thing next to me," I noted, adding "Should we tell the kids about it?"

"Maybe we wait until they're done swimming for the day."

At Monkey Island, our next stop, a troop of macaques greeted us, spurred on by our boat driver, who threw them bananas. One particularly daring monkey swam to and boarded our boat, startling Aria with its Gollum-like appearance. After some tense moments and clever maneuvering by our driver, the scary monkey leaped back in the water and swam back to shore.

Aria, a bit shaken, declared, "Let's never feed monkeys again. He was creepy."

Just before sunset, our driver navigated to one last tiny island, this one just a small slip of beach surrounded by tall cliffs and a clump of mangroves.

"Our own private island," Finn cried, jumping into the shallows.

He and Aria ran to the rugged limestone walls jutting over the water. Finn climbed to an outcropping then did a back flip into the Andaman Sea. Aria followed him with a spread-eagle jump, making a big splash as she landed.

I sat on the beach, burying my feet in the sand. I quietly watched my teen and tween laugh and play together as the sun dipped lower on the horizon. Finn was almost as tall as Randy now. Aria's hair, which she had clipped short when we left home, now fell past her shoulders and had golden highlights from time in the sun. Both seemed more confident and settled, content to just be.

CHAPTER 16

Finn found a long bamboo stick in the jetsam on the shore and twirled it around like a martial artist before planting it into the sand at the water's edge.

"There," he said solemnly. "I name thee, Almond Island."

"It's got a good ring to it," I agreed.

"I love this place," he said.

As our driver revved the motor and we zoomed across the sea toward Ko Yao Yai, the setting sun sent orange ripples across the sea. I hugged Finn, feeling profoundly grateful for our time together.

A few days later, we took a ferry to another Thai island, Ko Samui. Thailand's second largest island, Ko Samui is more developed and touristy than sleepy Ko Yao Yai. But we were ready for a little more action and culture after a few low-key days.

On my forty-sixth birthday, to explore the island, we rented a red, rickety Suzuki jeep with a tiny backseat. Too big to cram inside, the kids ended up squatting in the open-air flat bed at the back.

"Never a dull moment," I said as we set off under overcast skies for the Big Buddha Temple. At its center sat a massive golden Buddha, which, at 40 feet high (12 m) was visible across much of the island. We then attempted to visit some waterfalls, but the battered old jeep struggled on the muddy hillside before stalling completely. It had also started to rain, leaving the kids soaked in the back.

"It's character building," Randy shouted at them as they banged on the window.

Luckily, the jeep restarted, and we returned it as quickly as possible.

"You look like scary, wet pirate monkeys," I teased the bedraggled kids as we piled into a communal truck with a dozen or so wet locals and tourists, to head back to our hotel.

That evening, while the kids stayed in, Randy and I went out for my birthday dinner. We tried a nearby restaurant, which was clearly popular since it took over an hour to be seated. Another hour later, we still didn't have drinks or food, and I was starting to get hungry and grumpy.

"Try to enjoy the slow pace," Randy suggested. "Island time, you know?"

Thirty minutes later, our food arrived. By then, I was over the meal. Randy eyed the desserts, reminding me it was my birthday, but I was ready to go home.

"No mango sticky rice for you!" I said. "Time for bed."

Randy smirked, "You're cute when you're hangry."

The next morning, Randy recounted the previous night's escapades to Finn and Aria, who found the whole saga a hoot.

"Mom lost her cool! Does that mean she failed Thai customs 101?" Finn crowed.

"Seems like it," Randy chuckled.

Aria nudged me, teasing, "You need remedial social studies, Mama!"

"Okay, I may not be great at staying calm," I conceded, then changed the subject. "Who wants to hear a joke about Bangkok?"

Both kids perked up. "I do!"

I paused for effect. "A Wise One once said: A man who walks naked through revolving doors is going to . . . BANG-kok!"

Finn burst into laughter. "I have to tell that one to my friends."

We arrived in Surat Thani late afternoon, hours before our overnight train to Bangkok. Leaving our packs at the station, we explored a nearby night market for dinner.

The market buzzed with vendors selling kebabs, pastries, and tropical fruits. Aria marveled at a woman spiraling a pineapple with a machete. The market's sounds engulfed us: motorcycles, sizzling grills, frying food, and vendors calling out.

Aria beelined for a Waffle House cart, opting for a Nutella and banana waffle. We chose local foods like grilled pork skewers, sweet potato balls, and spring rolls. Randy bought a small container of mango sticky rice, happy to have a second chance at the dessert.

Finn jokingly pointed to a cart selling fried bugs. "Anyone interested in insects?" he asked. We declined, citing full stomachs and our train's imminent departure.

Back at the station, our train arrived. Randy had booked top bunks, not realizing bottom ones were more spacious. My backpack wouldn't fit in the luggage holder, so I squeezed it into my bunk.

As the night progressed, the cabin grew cold. I layered up with all my warm clothes, glad now to be squeezed in with my backpack. Later, Aria whispered across the aisle, "Are you freezing, too?"

I popped out in my wool hat. "Nope, I'm wearing everything I own!"

"Oh, man, I'm so jealous," Finn said, poking his head out from his bunk.

Randy laughed at my over-preparedness but admitted he was cold, too.

Stepping off the train the next morning into Bangkok's hot, humid morning, Aria sighed contentedly, "Ah, now that's more like it."

"OK, we have two full days in Bangkok," Randy said at our early breakfast in the hostel café. He proposed a "Kids Plan It" day to Finn and Aria, where they'd be our tour guides. They eagerly agreed and got to work researching options.

Randy relaxed, looking forward to a day off from planning. A couple of hours later, Finn and Aria returned with their itinerary.

"We're starting at the lovely Wat Pho, known for its reclining Buddha. This fabulous experience will cost 800 baht," Aria told us, hamming it up in her best tour guide voice, with Finn adding, "Lunch will be at the traditional restaurant Sawasdee, around 650 baht."

"Then, we'll visit Museum Siam's 'Exploring Thainess' exhibit," Aria continued. "That's a fantastic, interactive educational experience. Afterward, we'll relax at Chaloem Phra Kiat Park before dinner at the mega-mall's indoor Street Food Market."

Finn added, "Finally, King Power Mahanakhon's sky bridge. It's the highest building in Bangkok, and it has a cool glass floor high above the capital. But no pressure to walk on it."

Randy reviewed their plan and budget. "It's ambitious, but let's give it a go. Lead on!"

NO MANGO STICKY RICE FOR YOU: THAILAND

After a successful day orchestrated by the kids, Randy took the reins again for our last morning in Bangkok. We decided to get traditional Thai massages at an affordable place he had found nearby.

"Thai massage is like 'lazy person's yoga,'" I told the kids. "It combines assisted stretches with pressure techniques using hands, elbows, knees, and feet."

Finn quipped, "That's my kind of yoga!"

Without a reservation, we learned only three of us could get massages simultaneously, each costing $8. Aria opted for a $4 foot massage, apprehensive about the full body experience anyway.

We soaked our feet in warm, petal-filled water before heading to the massage area with mattresses on the floor. In our separate curtained rooms, we donned robes and lay down.

The massage was intense, involving poking, prodding, and stretching.

Afterward, Finn admitted, "That was painful."

I asked Finn if he felt refreshed, though. "Not really, I think I pulled something."

"My masseuse told me 'No breathing!' during a deep stretch," said Randy.

Aria wasn't a huge fan of her choice, either, describing her foot massage as odd, especially the toe-popping part.

Laughing, I concluded, "Maybe Thai massage isn't for everyone."

"Do you know what I just saw in the bathroom?" I burst out of the ladies' room at the Bangkok airport.

"No, but I have a feeling you're going to tell us," Finn said dryly.

"There was a sign that showed how to use—and how NOT to use the Western-style toilets. It shows a person squatting on top of the toilet and has that crossed out, saying 'Please don't step on the toilet seat.' I feel vindicated!"

"Um, why?"

"Because!" I exclaimed, feeling that it should be obvious. "It's clearly not just us that needs an instruction manual for how to use different style toilets. More cross-cultural potty training is needed! Ooh, I could make that the title for my Thailand chapter, what do you think?"

"Veto that," Randy said. At the same time Aria said, "Definitely not!"

"Did any of you even try the bum gun in the end?" I asked accusingly.

"Yes, but I'm not a fan," Finn said. "It was about as painful as that massage we had."

"Fair enough. I'm glad you tried it, though."

"Yeah, well, just remember . . . what happens in Thailand, stays in Thailand, OK?"

I smiled and nodded, winking at him. "Absolutely."

ALMOND FAMILY REPORT CARD ON THAILAND

- *Top Marks*: Explore less-touristed islands like Ko Yao Yai. Enjoy longtail boat rides through turquoise water dotted with limestone karsts, offering a peaceful escape from bustling tourist centers.
- *Needs Work*: Thailand's popularity can lead to overcrowded tourist spots. You may need to make a concerted effort to discover authentic experiences away from key attractions.
- *Learning Tips*: Dive into Thai culture by mastering the traditional *wai* greeting and respecting local customs, such as avoiding pointing with your feet. Reading up on dos and don'ts in advance can enhance your understanding of Thailand's rich heritage.

17

HAPPY LIFE, HAPPY LOVE
Cambodia

Excerpt from Finn's Journal
February 25, 2023 | Siem Reap, Cambodia

This morning, we ride in a tuk tuk to Ta Prohm. This is one of the Buddhist temples in Angkor. At Ta Prohm, we see mystic ruins being eaten by strangler fig trees and overgrowth. We see a massive tree—the biggest tree I have ever seen. I enjoy this temple a lot because it is in a forest and nicely shaded. Next, we drive to Banteay Srey, a Hindu temple dedicated to Shiva and Parvati, the mother goddess. Banteay Srey is super interesting and so different from Ta Prohm. It is made of pink sandstone, supposedly entirely by women! While it is beautiful and I like the carvings, overall, I enjoy wandering less because of how unshaded it is and how hot it is in the sun. Six hours of exploring temples in the blazing sun is a bit much, and I start feeling dizzy, so I am glad when we head back to our homestay.

"Ah, hello! Hello, Andi! Hello, Andi husband and children! Welcome BunYong Home! My name Bun. James Bun. You get it? Double-oh-seven?" The slim man threw back his head and laughed, his dark eyes crinkling with mirth. "You can call me Mr. Bun!"

His laugh was infectious. "I love it!" I said, grinning. "Nice to meet you, Mr. Bun!"

I had been put in touch with Bun via a friend and arranged for us to stay for three nights with him and his family at their home in rural Cambodia. The house was set off a dirt road pitted with potholes and bordered by palm and mango trees, open fields, and a murky pond dotted with magenta lotus flowers.

Bun, his mother, brother, brother-in-law, and niece all lived on the main floor of the homestay, while the upper level had rooms for guests.

"We glad to have you here!" Bun continued enthusiastically. "We have many visitors from France. United States, not so much after COVID. We have family from France arriving today also. They old friends, visited us before and now come back. You meet tonight at dinner!"

Bun led us upstairs, where we removed our shoes and entered a spacious common room. Scrawled in permanent marker on the walls were inspirational quotes, drawings, and advice on traveling in Cambodia (or "Scambodia," as one set of handwritten tips warned). Many of the quotes were Buddhist teachings. "We are shaped by our thoughts; we become what we think," read one in block lettering. Another said, "When the mind is pure, joy follows like a shadow that never leaves. –Buddha."

A photo of a much younger Bun hung in a gilded frame by the door. His hair and eyebrows were shaved, he held a set of folded saffron robes, and he wore an enigmatic smile.

"Are you being ordained as a monk here?" I asked.

"Yes! Me becoming Buddhist monk. I was twenty years old," he replied. "Now, forty-seven years old!"

"Oh, we're close in age," Randy noted. "I'm forty-nine, and Andi just turned forty-six."

Bun clapped his hands, a smile lighting up his eyes. "We are like brother and sister then! Born on different sides of the world, but maybe brother and sister in another life! Found our way back to each other now! Energy is like that, always find a way!"

CHAPTER 17

Bun led us to our rooms.

"This your home for the next few days!" said Bun, then turned to leave. "We have dinner later all together; you meet my family and also friends from France, OK?"

"Amazing," I said. "*Arkun.*"

"Oh! You speak Khmer?"

"No, no," I laughed. "Only a few words."

"Ah! Ha-ha, good, good! OK, see you later. Bye bye, *lear hi*!"

"Bye bye, *lear hi*!" Finn and Aria chorused.

Finn looked around after Bun closed the door. "Hey, check it out! You know what the password is for the Wi-Fi? Bunyong-007! He really is Bun, James Bun! This is going to be a cool experience here."

I looked around at the quirky bedroom with bright pink mosquito netting falling like a princess canopy over the bed and the sunflower-yellow walls graffitied with names of past guests and messages they left like, "All you need is love!" and "Forgive and let go." This place was unlike anything I'd ever seen before.

"It'll definitely be a one-of-a-kind experience."

After unpacking, we wandered downstairs to greet our *tuk tuk* driver for the next few days. *Tuk tuks* are two-wheeled open carriages pulled by motorbikes. They're the main way of getting around in Cambodia and other parts of Southeast Asia. It's common to see them filled with anywhere from one or two people to entire families.

Bun was lounging barefoot in a hammock beside the open-air kitchen in the front yard. A young girl in a Daisy Duck T-shirt, her short black hair in spiky pigtails, smiled shyly at us from behind a banana tree. We waved at her, and she darted behind the trunk.

"This Mr. Two," Bun told us, pointing to a man in a helmet beside the *tuk tuk*. He had on a T-shirt with the American flag on the front. "Because he have two kid before! In COVID, he have another baby! Now he Mr. COVID-Baby! Ha-ha!"

The man pulled off his helmet and bowed. "I Mr. Three now," he said, adding to the joke.

"Hello, Mr. Three," we said and piled onto benches in the carriage. We were heading to a traditional Cambodian floating village on our first afternoon in Siem Reap, a destination best known for its massive temple complex of Angkor. Before visiting the temples, though, we wanted to get a sense of life in a local community, far from the well-trodden tourist track.

For worldschooling literature, Finn and Aria had been reading a sad but powerful memoir, *First They Killed My Father: A Daughter of Cambodia Remembers*, about the Cambodian genocide under the brutal Khmer Rouge regime. The Khmer Rouge held power for about four years, from April 1975 until January 1979, leaving up to 3 million Cambodians dead through starvation, torture, execution, forced labor, and other forms of violence. Both civil war and the threat of the Khmer Rouge carried on until the 1990s, when Cambodia began opening to the outside world.

Four decades later, Cambodia, a developing nation in Southeast Asia of about 16 million people, is still recovering. Its economy has grown rapidly, but most of its citizens continue to live in poverty in rural areas, experiencing malnutrition and lack of access to basic health care.

As we drove along the desolate country roads, we noticed women cooking something in bamboo tubes over fires. "What are the vendors selling?" Finn called to Mr. Three. We had been riding for about an hour in the *tuk tuk*, and our T-shirts stuck to our chests in the hot, humid morning.

"This *Kralan*," Mr. Three told us, pulling over at one of the stands. "Khmer sticky rice with beans and coconut milk. You want?"

We nodded but quickly realized we had no idea how to get inside, so we got a crash course in Cambodian snacks from Mr. Three. He showed us how to peel back the stripped bamboo bark to get at the sweet rice inside, which molded together like a thin popsicle.

"I like it," Finn said, then turned to Mr. Three. "How much longer until we get there?"

"Thirty minutes. We go?"

"Yes, let's go. *Arkun*."

As we drove further, we began to pass more wooden houses set atop high stilts along the river, and we talked about the floating communities we were heading to see.

"There are around 170 floating villages across Cambodia. More than eighty thousand people live on the water permanently," I read aloud, skimming from an article as we bounced along. "Most are based on Lake Tonlé Sap, the largest freshwater lake in Southeast Asia.

"In the rainy season, the lake swells to six or seven times its normal size. In the dry season, the flow reverses, and it drains back into the Mekong. Locals live on stilted homes like these or on the water in floating villages that rise and fall with the level of the lake."

"Where do kids go to school if they live way out on the lake?" Aria asked.

"Or what do they do if they get sick?" Finn added.

"There are whole communities on the water," I answered. "Floating schools, medical centers, gas stations, temples—even floating basketball courts and karaoke bars."

Finn's eyes grew wide. "Wow, playing basketball on a raft? Think we'll see that?"

"We'll find out soon."

At the village, we walked to the banks of the muddy river. We greeted a woman in a wide-brimmed hat who would be our boat driver. She didn't speak English, so we bowed in greeting then stepped onto the open-air, wooden boat.

She revved the motor, which sat exposed at the back and looked like an old car motor. We drove along a tributary lined with stilt houses for about twenty minutes before we spilled into the vast lake.

There, we spotted dozens of homes bobbing on the surface, surrounded by nothing but open water. Some were decorated with bright bougainvillea or trees in pots adorned with red Lunar New Year ornaments. People lounged in hammocks on their raft-houses, and men fished from boats in the distance.

"The income from fishing is steady," I continued reading, "but conditions living on the water are tough. Twelve percent of children die before the age of five from malnutrition or lack of access to adequate medical care. Climate change and drought, pollution, and overfishing mean the ecosystem of the lake is changing, making it harder for villages like these to sustain themselves in the future."

"The kids seem happy though," Aria said, watching two children splashing in the water in front of a colorful house. "How funny that instead of a front porch, they have a front lake!"

Most kids and adults were hard at work, paddling in their boats, washing clothes or hanging them to dry, and mending nets in the water. They barely gave us a second glance as our driver revved the engine again and steered us back into the narrow canal. Soon, they receded into the distance behind us.

> **NAVIGATING WORLDSCHOOLING FOR NON-TEACHERS AND EXPERTS**
>
> Embarking on a worldschooling journey doesn't require you to be an expert in every subject. Here's how you can facilitate learning and embrace discovery together:
>
> - *Use Local Resources*: Explore libraries, museums, and historical sites for hands-on learning experiences and resources to help you put learning in context for your kids.
> - *Learn from Locals*: Engage local guides or residents for authentic insights and stories.
> - *Read and Discuss Together*: Share articles, books, or blogs related to your destinations, and read them aloud or discuss them as a family to enhance understanding.
> - *Embrace Digital Learning*: Use online courses, educational websites, and videos to explore unfamiliar topics.
> - *Incorporate Documentaries*: Watch and discuss documentaries, which can visually and engagingly bring subjects to life.
> - *Admit Knowledge Gaps*: Be honest about not knowing everything and research new topics as a family; it's a great way to model lifelong learning.

"You like rum?" Bun asked us at dinner that night. "Juliette is making rum drinks for all of us! OK?"

We nodded, greeting the French guests who had arrived earlier that afternoon.

"Wow, these are strong," I coughed as I took a tiny sip.

Bun grinned widely and leaned over to clink glasses calling, "Happy life, happy love!"

We raised our drinks and repeated after him, "Happy life, happy love!"

"OK, eat, eat!" Bun gestured to the family-sized plates of food before us at the long table. "This green beans! This one pumpkin! Fried fish! This last one—crocodile!"

At that, he glanced at Aria, whose head had popped up rapidly, eyes wide.

"Nah, just kidding! Kidding!" He threw back his head and howled, then pointed at the older woman at the far end of the table. "My mother made these! She Michelle! Michelle Obama, first lady, ha-ha!"

His mother gave a weary smile. A short woman, she sat hunched over and said little. We weren't sure if she spoke much English. She sat beside Bun's brother-in-law and brother, who we learned had been born mute. They didn't say much, but Bun was gregarious enough for all.

"Another toast for new and old friends!" Bun cried, then sat back for a moment, as though reflecting. He continued in a quieter tone. "All we have is here and now. What happened in the past—any pain, any happiness, it does not matter. Tomorrow? We not know if it comes. So, we have to live today. Travel, embrace family, friends! Buddhism tells us everything impermanent. My brother sick? Impermanent! COVID happen? Impermanent! It is to us to enjoy every moment we have today!" He raised his rum a second time, exclaiming "Happy life, happy love!"

We echoed him again in the sticky Cambodian night, our clinks accompanied by the whir of the fan overhead and the sound of crickets chirping in the nearby mango trees.

Hidden in the jungles between the Tonlé Sap Lake and the Kulen Mountains, lies the sprawling Angkor Archaeological complex. Spanning more than 154 square miles (400 km) and comprising hundreds of temple ruins, it is the largest religious complex in the world. From the ninth to the fifteenth century, Angkor was the center of the Khmer Kingdom. At its peak, the city was home to more than a million people, the largest preindustrial city in the world.

After the empire fell, the temples were largely abandoned and reclaimed by the jungle. Many have been restored to their former state. Ta Prohm, in contrast, has been left in much the same condition as it was when it was rediscovered by French explorers in the nineteenth century. Thick roots of fig and silk-cotton trees tangle and twist around its crumbling walls, as though being crushed by a massive boa constrictor.

Finn was particularly awed by Ta Prohm. "These trees are amazing. It looks like they are literally eating the temple."

"Can you imagine being one of the archaeologists working to piece the building back together?" Aria said, practically bursting with excitement. "There are *so* many carved stones all over the place. It must have been gorgeous when it was first built."

Picking our way across the ruins, it felt like we were bearing witness to a battle between civilization and wilderness, and it was still unclear who the victor would be.

"It's not just archaeologists working on preservation of this temple," I told Aria, reading a sign by one of the doorways. "There's a team of archaeologists, hydrologists, arboriculturalists, structural engineers, architects, and historians working together to keep the temple stable and prevent it from being further taken over by nature."

"It's crazy how much work it takes to make it look like it's about to collapse into the jungle!" remarked Finn.

"Ha-ha, so true."

After Ta Prohm, Mr. Three drove us to the elaborately carved sandstone temple of Banteay Srei, originally dedicated to the Hindu god Shiva. Its modern name means "citadel of the women" as it is believed to have been built entirely by women. Banteay Srei was the first temple to be restored so, unlike Ta Prohm, it had been given a full makeover.

"Is it bad to say I liked Ta Prohm better?" Finn asked in the *tuk tuk* ride back to Siem Reap. "Banteay Srei was neat, too, but I really liked the way Ta Prohm made you feel like you were the first person there in centuries."

"No, it's not bad," Randy answered. "I think Ta Prohm is a lot of visitors' favorites. But just wait, tomorrow, we'll tour Angkor Wat, the largest religious monument in the world. See *wat* you think then."

We pointedly ignored his pun.

CHAPTER 17

After leaving the serenity of the temple, our next destination offered a stark contrast—the Cambodia Landmine Museum, a short journey from Banteay Srei. Pulling up, we were immediately struck by a foreboding red sign hanging from a jackfruit tree, bearing a skull and crossbones above the words "Danger!! Mines!!"

A man in a green shirt, limping slightly, approached us. His name tag read Kak Hort, but he introduced himself as Hak. "I'll be your guide today," he said. "I'll share the history of landmines in Cambodia, including my own story. I was just ten when I lost my leg to a mine. My brother and sister weren't as lucky—they died in the same blast."

As we followed Hak inside, his gait was steady, his prosthetic leg almost imperceptible beneath his trousers.

"Cambodia's landmine issue is one of the worst globally," Hak began. "Children, often boys, make up a third of the victims."

He told us about the 6 million active landmines scattered across Cambodia, legacies of decades of war, making daily life perilous for many.

Hak pointed to a grenade, its long metallic form resembling a gourd. "Just yesterday, a woman and her family died because of a similar object. She found it in the forest. She didn't know what it was and brought it into her kitchen to use with her mortar and pestle."

Aria gasped. "She used a grenade to crush spices?"

"Yes," Hak confirmed. "She and whole family were blown up."

Finn and Aria looked horrified, as I'm sure I did as well.

Hak told us about the United States' bombing of Cambodia as they sought to destroy the Ho Chi Minh Trail, the North Vietnamese supply route in the 1960s and early 1970s. Many of those bombs are still active and hidden, deadly surprises lost across the countryside.

"Dad," Finn asked quietly as we looked at a huge arsenal of deactivated bombs, grenades, and mines. "Do the Cambodians hate the Americans?"

"I don't think so now," Randy replied. "Cambodia's history over the last century has been complex, but the people seem pretty good at moving on."

"Has the United States helped with clearing the mines?" I inquired.

"Yes," Randy said. "The United States made some pretty bad choices during the Cold War when we justified all kinds of questionable foreign policy decisions to contain communism. But we've been pretty good at trying to help fix some of the damage we caused."

Hak guided us to an area of jungle, mines, and grenades hidden among the foliage to demonstrate the immense challenge in finding and removing the weaponry.

"Should we be worrying about landmines as we explore the temples?" Finn asked.

"No," Hak reassured him. "Used to be a big problem because many sacred temples were surrounded with mines to protect them from being robbed. All safe now, they clear."

In the *tuk tuk* on our way back to the homestay, we sat in silence.

"Why doesn't the government warn people about the landmines?" Aria asked. "Can't they educate kids and adults not to pick up explosives or wander into the jungles on their own?"

"Well, they're trying to, but many people live in remote and rural areas without access to proper education," Randy said. "There are also many types of mines and bombs, and they're spread across a massive area, so it's a real challenge."

"It was interesting to learn some of the ways they're trying to find and deactivate them," Finn said, "like using specially trained rats and dogs that can sniff out the mines and bombs without getting hurt. Maybe that will help."

"Maybe," I answered, looking out at the expanse of fields around us. "There's a long way to go."

At 4 a.m. the following morning, we awoke and crept quietly into the darkness, stepping lightly to avoid waking the French guests and our hosts downstairs. It was surprisingly cold in the pre-dawn. We had all donned jackets and wind breakers for the *tuk tuk* ride to Angkor Wat, where we were headed to see the sunrise.

Bun had left us to-go breakfasts of bananas, hard-boiled eggs, and mango slices, which we gratefully carried with us in the *tuk tuk*. Mr. Three drove us to the entrance, and we walked with hundreds of other tourists to the edge of a lake in front of the most famous and largest of all the temples, Angkor Wat.

Our eyes and throats felt itchy from the air pollution, which had been bothering us more in recent days. A smoggy haze hung heavily over the silhouette of the famed temple. We plopped down in the grass and ate our breakfast, listening to the murmur of the crowds around us.

The hazy sky slowly lightened, first to a purplish blue, then pale pink and orange. The magnificent figure of Angkor Wat, meaning City Temple, reflected in the pond at our feet. In the crisp morning, we explored the corridors and chambers of the twelfth-century temple. Considered the most magnificent example of classical Khmer design, Angkor Wat is said to represent Mount Meru, the home of the gods in Hinduism.

"We climbed Mount Meru in Tanzania!" Aria exclaimed. "Do you think it's named that because of the Hindu belief?"

"Not sure," I said. "I love how you're making that connection. Let's look it up later."

After exploring Angkor Wat, we toured other temples nearby—Angkor Thom with its carved stone faces, the Leper King Terrace, and the Terrace of the Elephants. By noon, we were hot, exhausted, and hungry. Mr. Three drove us to a local Khmer restaurant before returning to Bunyong homestay to relax and reflect on all that we had seen over the last few days.

"OK, kiddos, change of pace," I announced later that night. "Let's go to the circus."

Finn looked up from his journaling. "Will there be creepy clowns?"

"Not sure, but I doubt it. The Phare Circus is billed as a performance that draws from recent Cambodian history, folklore, and modern society. The photos in the brochure Bun gave us look very different from any circus you've seen before."

"OK, let's do it! To the *tuk tuk*!" cried Finn.

Arriving at the circular tent, we took our seats in the small arena. A set of pre-show videos gave us more insight into the background of the circus, its mission as a social enterprise, and stories of the performers' lives.

Bun had told us that the circus's profits go toward supporting free education, professional arts training, and social support programs for the more than 1,200 students at the Phare school. The school was founded in 1994 by nine young Cambodian men returning home from a refugee camp after the fall of the Khmer Rouge. At the camp, they had realized that art could be an outlet for healing—to help them process what they had experienced. When they returned home, they began offering free drawing classes to local children from difficult backgrounds and eventually opened a school, providing formal education and a professional arts curriculum.

When the lights dimmed, we were awed by an hour of storytelling, acrobatics, athleticism, and showmanship—and also, humor.

"That's my favorite performer," Aria whispered to me, pointing to one of the men who had a particularly expressive face and kept making exaggerated, pained expressions. At one point, he leaped into the lap of a spectator in the front row and planted a kiss on his bald head. The man in the audience looked startled but laughed good-naturedly at having a sweaty Cambodian performer suddenly sitting on him and hammed it up for the crowd.

It was a spectacular show. And, best of all in Finn's opinion? No clowns.

On our last evening at the homestay, Finn was working at the main dining table on his latest geometry assignment. Aria was writing in her journal. I was catching up on emails, and Randy was finding us places to stay for our upcoming stop in Vietnam.

Around 6 p.m., Bun came out of the main house carrying a plate piled with something that looked like candied almonds in the fading light.

"You try fried crickets! They very tasty! We make fresh, with lots of spices! You try!"

"You're joking, right?" Aria said warily, leaning back as though afraid the crickets might leap off the platter. "Like you joked about the crocodile?"

"No, no! Crickets for real! Tonight you try!"

"Sounds great," Finn said, grinning maliciously at Aria. "I'm game to try anything!"

"You want beer with your crickets?" Bun asked us. Randy and I nodded.

Finn inspected the plate carefully. "Did you catch these from the trees around here?"

Bun laughed and shook his head. "No! We buy in market and my mother make!" He grabbed a handful and tossed them into his mouth. "So good! You try!"

Randy grabbed one, popped it in his mouth, and chewed it.

"The spice is awesome. Honestly, if you didn't know it was cricket, you'd never guess."

"But I *do* know it," I muttered in an undertone. Aria giggled.

"OK, Finn. You're up next," I said.

Finn reached over, grabbed a tiny cricket, and popped it in his mouth. He chewed slowly, keeping an even expression as he swallowed then chased it with water.

Bun leaned close to him. "Well? You like?"

"Eh," Finn hedged. "It was kind of chewy, like it had cream in the middle or something."

"So, Aria? Are you going to try?" I asked.

"I would, but I have gum in my mouth."

"You could throw that out."

"I could, but I don't want to."

Sigh. My turn.

I took a breath and told myself it was a candied almond. That was it, just a little cricket-shaped candied almond. With long, hairy legs.

Bun leaned over and tossed some more into his mouth.

"We ate many cricket when I was little growing up under the Khmer Rouge. Crickets saved us when we didn't have food. Good protein, easy to find! Taste good!"

I gamely grabbed one and tossed it in my mouth. It was disconcerting to feel the spines from the legs on my tongue, but overall, Randy was right. It didn't taste horrible.

I took a big swig of beer as Bun threw back his head and roared with laughter.

"Well?" he demanded.

"It tastes nutty, almost smoky! Not bad!"

As Bun drank his beer, he sat cross legged and told us about his childhood and perspectives on his home country now. He was born the year after the Khmer Rouge came to power. He doesn't remember that time, but his mother and older siblings do. He said he wishes the government would do more now to help the people of Cambodia.

"Anyway," Bun continued, sitting back on his heels on the bench and smiling. "No matter! All impermanent! This what Buddha tells us. In Buddhism, you not blame the world, you not ask the world or any god to forgive or help you. He teach you to focus on inner peace and on what you do."

"The most important thing," he concluded, "is to do good things today. This is much better than living a hundred years and doing a bad thing. The mind will be so relaxed and at peace. Travel, love, spend time with friends and family. These are good things."

He beamed and lifted his beer toward us for a final toast. We leaned forward to clink our glasses together. This time, we knew immediately what to say.

"Happy life, happy love!"

ALMOND FAMILY REPORT CARD ON CAMBODIA

- *Top Marks*: Beyond the renowned Angkor Archaeological Complex, venture to one of Cambodia's floating villages and visit Siem Reap's Landmine Museum. Places like these can round out a richer understanding of the country's complex culture and challenges.
- *Needs Work*: Navigating rural Cambodia can be challenging due to its underdeveloped infrastructure. Prepare for rough roads and basic amenities as part of the experience.
- *Learning Tips*: Dive into Cambodia's culinary diversity by trying traditional snacks like fried crickets or ants. Embracing these unique flavors enriches your travels by connecting you with local customs.

GOOD MORNING, VIETNAM

Vietnam

Excerpt from Aria's Journal
March 11, 2023 | Da Bac, Vietnam

Today, we are heading from Hanoi to a village in the mountains. The people we're going to be staying with only speak local dialects, so we need a translator. His Vietnamese name is Dat, but he told us to call him Jack. He is very nice. It is a three-hour trip to a remote area on a windy road, and I feel nauseous by the time we arrive. Lunch is served family style. We meet two girls who are also staying here to see more of Vietnam—parts that tourists don't always see.

    In the afternoon, we walk to a cave with a local guide, who gives mini waffles as an offering to the "crying mother" goddess at the cave entrance. I am a little sad because the waffles look tasty. In the end, he brings them out of the cave, and we get to eat them! We then learn how to make paper in a traditional way. It takes a lot of patience! They use tree bark, boil it, hand pick all the bugs, lay it flat, let it dry, and peel. Patience!! When it starts to rain, we head inside and get to take herbal baths in big barrels. Herbal baths are supposed to help with illness. They pour boiling water into the barrels, then you add cold water until you have the temperature you want. When I get into my barrel, I accidentally knock the plug out of the drain without realizing it, and all the water drains out. So, when I get in, it's only up to my ankles. That's sad because I'm cold and hoped to get warm in the bath. I quickly get out and wait until everyone else is done. Oh, well. Today I learn that it's much easier to soak in a modern bathtub than the old-fashioned way they do it.

CHAPTER 18

We hoisted our packs onto our backs and headed in the direction indicated by the sign reading, "Nhat Quy homestay" in neat green lettering. Hibiscus and wild poinsettia trees lined the dirt path. A handful of stilted wooden homes with thatched roofs were visible through the woods, each flying a red Vietnamese flag with a yellow star in the center. A rooster ambled in front of us, crowed loudly, then disappeared behind a shed. Three pigs grunted; one stuck his snout under a slat in its sty and eyed us as if to say, "We don't see the likes of you here often."

Approaching the Nhat Quy homestay, our host, Mr. Nhat stepped forward to greet us.

"*Xin chao*," he said. We echoed the hello back, "*Xin chao*."

Jack, our twenty-year-old Vietnamese translator, pushed open the door into the large bunk room, and we followed him inside. About fifteen twin beds lined the perimeter of the room, each swathed with mosquito netting and curtains that could be pulled around for privacy.

"Aw, look at this handsome fellow," cooed Finn, squatting to pet a puppy that had wandered in behind us. The dog wagged its tail excitedly as both kids knelt and stroked its fur.

We plopped our backpacks on four beds, then meandered into the open-air common room, the puppy bounding at our heels. Mrs. Quy, our other homestay host, was preparing tea. She wore traditional Dao clothing, a black tunic and skirt with block-print patterns at the hem and a black headscarf embroidered with red-and-white pinwheels and edged with red fringe. She motioned toward the glasses and addressed Jack, who translated, though her intent was clear.

"This is local Shan green tea—a specialty of Sung Village. Would you like some?" Jack asked us. The Sung villagers spoke no English, only Dao and Vietnamese. Jack didn't speak Dao, so they communicated in Vietnamese, and he translated into English.

"Sure, thanks," we replied.

I settled into a hammock overlooking the valley and sipped the bitter tea. On the roof of the pig sty, a tabby cat stretched and rolled over in the sun. "I think these next few days are going to be a nice mix of down time and cultural immersion. I'm glad we changed our plans to come here before leaving Southeast Asia."

"Definitely," Randy said, settling back in a neighboring hammock as a fluffy chick scurried across the floor and into the vegetable garden.

A week earlier, Randy and I had been reflecting on our journey thus far across Vietnam. We were enjoying salted Vietnamese coffee in the sleepy town of Tam Coc, surrounded by lush rice paddies. While our experience across the narrow nation in Indochina had been beautiful, it had also felt inauthentic, as we'd followed a very typical tourist itinerary.

Our adventures began in Ho Chi Minh City with Nana, our wonderful local guide. A lively woman in her twenties, with shoulder-length dark hair and a Pac Man hat, she greeted us enthusiastically at our Airbnb. Finn complimented her hat, and she made a mini finger heart with her thumb and index finger, a gesture of love in Vietnam.

Nana started our tour at a local street market, where she explained the custom of buying fresh food daily. We marveled at the wide array of seafood, including live snakes and frogs, which kept leaping out of their baskets onto the street, as well as the rich scents of herbs and exotic fruits like jackfruit, dragon fruit, and tiny bananas. I was fascinated by the local vendors, sporting traditional *nón lá* leaf hats, and their vibrant stalls.

Finn's curiosity about Nana's favorite street snack led us to a vendor making crispy bananas, a delicacy she adored. The fried bananas, reminiscent of corn dogs, were a hit, especially when paired with traditional Vietnamese salted coffee—a flavor akin to salted caramel.

Nana then took us to a series of historical sites, including the statue of Thich Quang Duc, the Buddhist monk who set himself on fire in 1963 in protest of the persecution of Buddhists by the South Vietnamese government. Standing there, we gained a richer understanding of the period through Nana's narration and her family's experiences. A visit to an underground bunker in downtown Ho Chi Minh City and the Cu Chi Tunnels outside the city deepened our insight. These sites, significant during the 1968 Tet Offensive, showcased the tactics of the Viet Cong, emphasizing the importance of their tunnel networks.

This part of our journey offered the kids—and us—a more well-rounded, nuanced understanding of history, one from a very different perspective than they'd gain back in the United States.

From Ho Chi Minh City—still called Saigon by residents—we headed north across the length of the S-shaped country, traveling by small plane, bus, and train. In the ancient town of Hoi An, once an important trading post in the sixteenth and seventeenth centuries, Finn and I took a cooking class one afternoon, learning how to make delicious local specialties. After shopping at an open-air market for ingredients, we were shown how to make *goi cuon* (fresh rice paper salad rolls with pork and shrimp, accompanied by a tangy peanut hoisin dipping sauce); *pho bo* (a flavorful beef rice noodle soup infused with cinnamon, ginger, and star anise); and *banh xeo* (crispy Vietnamese crepes filled with pork, shrimp, bean sprouts, and green onions, served with lettuce leaves and fresh herbs). Randy and Aria, who had decided to go to the beach and explore by motor scooter, visited us during our class to try some of our tasty homemade dishes.

"Yum!" Aria exclaimed after taking a big bite of the *banh xeo*.

"Always the tone of surprise," Finn said grumpily, then added, "I want to make a Vietnamese feast for my friends when we get back home."

I nodded appreciatively. "I bet they'd like that. You could make a variety of foods from around the world—all your favorites! That would be special."

He nodded. "I have so many favorites. I'll have to think about what to make!"

"Luckily, you have time to figure it out," I said.

Later that evening, we wandered the cobblestone streets of Hoi An's old quarter. We had timed our visit with the monthly Lantern Festival celebrated every full moon, a sacred time in the Buddhist calendar. On these nights, the quaint town of Hoi An cuts the electricity, so that it's lit solely by candles and lanterns. Hundreds of boats glide along the Thu Bon River, and small paper lanterns float in the water. We bought four candles from a young girl along the riverbank and placed them in the current, watching them join hundreds of others bobbing on the surface.

A couple of days later, we caught a train north, to the imperial city of Hue, along the Perfume River. We explored the citadel and modern section of town. Then, we continued toward Tam Coc, south of Hanoi. Our hotel had cruiser bicycles we could borrow, so we spent hours biking through the rice paddies. We took a ride in a *sampan*—a traditional wooden boat—and marveled at how the locals rowed with their feet. At the large Bai Dinh cultural complex, we climbed to the top of the modern temple, built by more than five hundred artisans and craftsmen from nearby villages, and marveled at the massive gold-plated Buddha statue—the largest in Asia.

Our intent had been to continue to the northeast to spend our last few days in Ha Long Bay, with its emerald waters and iconic limestone karst formations.

But as we drank our coffee and began to map out our last few days in the country, we were struck by the fact that while we had traveled the length of Vietnam and gotten a primer into its history, we hadn't had a chance to interact meaningfully with many locals or get a deeper sense of life outside the typical tourist stops.

So, we scrapped the original idea and decided to head in a different direction.

One nice thing about traveling with few set plans is that there is no penalty for shifting gears last minute. I did some research online and found an opportunity to experience village culture by staying with local families at homestays in two remote ethnic towns, only a few hours—but worlds away—from Hanoi.

We booked a trip for two nights, three days to Da Bac, in Hoa Binh province. We arranged for a translator to accompany us, as villagers spoke no English, only local dialects.

Before leaving Tam Coc, we told our hotel manager where we were headed next. He looked puzzled. "Da Bac?" He said. "I've never heard of that."

We smiled. Perfect.

Located in northern Vietnam, Hoa Binh Province is known as one of the wellsprings of ancient Vietnamese culture. Surrounded by green valleys and rolling hills, it is home to a range of diverse ethnic minority cultures and hill tribes, including the Muong, Dao, Thai, and Tay, who have remained largely untouched by the outside world.

In Da Bac, through a community-driven tourism initiative, sustainable income opportunities were being created for residents of three remote villages. Facing poverty rates above 42 percent, these communities relied heavily on agriculture. The construction of a hydro-electric dam had uprooted many families, however, forcing them into the less fertile hills and exacerbating financial hardships. Families began offering homestays, trekking, and cultural experiences, adopting a community-based tourism model that emphasizes local participation, equitable profit sharing, environmental conservation, and cultural preservation.

Our hosts in Sung Village, Mr. Nhat and Mrs. Quy, had embraced this model to supplement their farming income. Their home, one of the few homestays in the village, sat on the slopes of Bieu Mountain.

Upon arriving, we met Jack, who would be our English-speaking guide throughout our time in Da Bac. A tourism student, Jack was as eager to learn about the local life of the villagers as we were. He introduced us to our Dao guide for the afternoon, a man in traditional attire who led us to Sung Cave.

As we started our hike, Aria noticed him holding a packet of mini waffles. "Are those for us?" she asked curiously.

"No," Jack explained after conferring with the Dao guide, "they are an offering for the Goddess of the cave. There's an old legend here about Hoang Lan and her lost daughters."

The air was heavy with smoke from small fires dotting the landscape. "What's with all the fires?" Randy inquired.

"They're clearing their fields," Jack responded. "It's an ancient practice, though it does make the air quite thick."

Inside the dark, damp cave, our Dao guide placed the waffle offering at a shrine. Finn discovered tiny shrimps in water pools, gently observing them. "Look at these little guys!" he exclaimed.

Exiting the cave, Aria's face lit up as our guide handed out the waffles. I laughed, "A snack and an offering, all in one. Efficient and tasty!"

EMBRACING CULTURAL IMMERSION: MAKING THE MOST OF HOMESTAY EXPERIENCES

Homestays can vary widely, from living in a room at a local family's house in a bustling city to participating in the everyday activities of a rural community. These experiences might include helping with household chores in a small village, staying with a family in a suburban neighborhood to learn about their day-to-day life, or living on a farm where daily activities are intertwined with the rhythms of nature. Each type offers a unique window into the local culture, customs, and lifestyle. Here's how to fully embrace these diverse experiences:

- *Be Flexible*: Prepare for different standards of living. It's an authentic peek into local lifestyles, and standards can vary widely.
- *Enhance Communication*: In places with language barriers, consider a translator to help you understand local customs and stories.
- *Choose Relaxation over Screens*: Bring a book or sketch pad for downtime, a perfect way to unwind and engage with your surroundings. Also, Wi-Fi may be nonexistent.
- *Carry Cash*: Have small bills for buying local products, as remote homestays may not support card transactions.
- *Respect Traditions and Join In*: Show interest in local customs and participate in daily activities to gain a sense of the local way of life.
- *Finding Homestays*: Research online platforms that specialize in homestay arrangements, check travel blogs, or consult travel forums. Local tourist information centers can also be valuable resources once you're in the area.

Homestays can profoundly impact your worldschooling journey, offering authentic experiences that textbooks simply cannot match. By fully engaging with these opportunities, your family can gain invaluable cultural insights and create lasting memories.

Back at the homestay, Mr. Nhat laid out a family-style lunch. He set a large circular platter on the table with neatly arranged stewed pumpkin, crispy chicken, cabbage, tofu, and delicate Vietnamese spring rolls on palm fronds. Beside the platter were tiny cups of *nuoc mam*, a tangy fermented fish sauce.

Sharing the homestay with us were two women: a twenty-year-old from Germany and an eighteen-year-old American. They, too, were seeking a quieter, more genuine experience in Vietnam. We all reached for chopsticks, eager to enjoy the communal feast and swap travel stories.

After lunch, we continued our immersive experience into the villagers' cultural traditions, learning about healing herbs gathered from the surrounding area. We were treated to herbal baths in half-barrel tubs. After adjusting the water to a comfortable temperature, I settled into the tub's embrace, knees drawn up, the herbal aroma filling the air.

"This is divine," I sighed contentedly.

From the next stall, Aria's voice sounded forlorn. "I accidentally unplugged mine and lost all the hot water. Now I'm sitting in a chilly puddle!"

"Aw, honey, I'm sorry! I wish I could share my tub, but it's a snug fit."

"At least the herbs smell good," she conceded.

That evening, our hosts invited us for Shan tea in the kitchen, a cozy wooden building beside the communal bathroom. As rain pattered outside, we gathered around a central wood-burning fire to warm up.

"Do they cook all their food over this fire?" Finn inquired.

Jack shook his head. "No, they mostly dry pig food over the fire"—he pointed to a shallow wicker basket hanging above the flames—"and it's mainly for warmth."

We settled on squat plastic stools, common in Vietnam due to their portability for sidewalk cafés. Gathered in a circle around the fire, Mrs. Quy served tea from a porcelain pot. Despite the language barrier, we enjoyed the quiet camaraderie.

The light melody of a flute intertwined with the rhythm of the rain. I asked Jack about it.

"It's their son who is playing," Jack relayed after a quick exchange with our hosts.

"Oh, nice! How old is he?"

"Twenty-five," Jack translated.

"Do they have any other children?"

Again, a quick conversation, then Jack conveyed, "Yes, they have three boys and a girl. They consider having a boy and a girl as lucky, so they say you are lucky."

I smiled at them and nodded my head. "Jack, I'm curious, could you ask Mr. Nhat and Mrs. Quy how they feel their life has changed since having a homestay? Since their village opened to tourists?"

There was one more, longer conversation, then Jack shared the reply.

"They are happy that they can share their culture and lifestyle with tourists," he said. "They never imagined having visitors to their town, but by doing this, they are able to earn enough income to support three generations of family."

I nodded again. "Please tell them we're so grateful to be here. They have a lovely home."

They bowed their heads to us after Jack translated. A quiet settled in again as we drank our tea and enjoyed the sounds of the flute and the rain. Hoa Binh means "peace," in Vietnamese. It felt an apt name for this untouched pocket of the world.

The next day, we spent time with other villagers going about their days. We learned about and took part in dyeing fabrics, creating patterns with natural indigo colorings; making paper in a traditional way; and drying Shan tea leaves. Before we left, Randy joined in a volleyball game with the locals on an outdoor court on a steep hill. It seemed to be a favorite community sport. Men played barefoot, with cigarettes hanging from their mouths, spiking the ball with ease as other villagers looked on. When the ball escaped downhill, the local kids pelted after it.

In the afternoon, we packed up and hiked for six miles to a neighboring village, another in the community-based tourism network of the region. The trail took us along steep terraced hillsides and a thick grove of bamboo trees before descending toward the riverbank, where a rusty ferry awaited to take us across to the small Muong Ao Ta village of Da Bia.

With its sleepy waterfront vibe, Da Bia had a very different feel from Sung Village. We could see only a handful of homes on the hillside as we pulled up in the ferry.

"How big is Da Bia village?" Randy asked Jack.

"Smaller than Sung," replied Jack. "Forty homes with maybe two hundred people. There used to be many more, but over the years, people moved to the big cities."

"Ah," Randy said. "That makes sense. Do you see a lot of shifts to the cities from these smaller communities? I would imagine as everyone has more access to technology and exposure to the outside world, traditional ways of life might be eroding a little."

"Yes, that is true," Jack agreed. He walked up to a two-story wooden home with a thatched roof, set high off the ground on stilts.

"Does it flood here often?" Finn asked.

Jack nodded. "In the rainy season."

A group of four young children played on a wooden swing outside the house, laughing and waving as we looked over.

A little boy walked over to us, then brightly gave us the middle finger and said with a huge smile, as though in greeting, "Go to hell!"

Finn and Aria's eyes went wide, then they began giggling.

"No," Randy shook his head and said gently, "That's not nice."

The little boy grinned back at us, waved, and ran to his friends to resume his play.

Finn and Aria alternated between surprise and thinking that was the funniest thing they had ever seen. "Hmm," Randy said. "Methinks some visitors have been teaching that kid things that he might not even realize what they mean."

Our Muong host, a young woman I guessed to be in her early thirties, greeted us warmly then gestured for us to sit at a long picnic table for lunch. She had on the traditional dress of the tribe, which was quite different from that of the Dao villagers: a long-sleeve white blouse with a black-and-red embroidered stripe down the center. A green belt edged in red trim cinched her waist atop a black skirt. Her dark hair was pulled back into a low ponytail.

She brought out plate after plate of local foods: a large bowl of rice, a Vietnamese omelet, pickled lotus root, fried tofu, and marinated pork. We were the only guests there, so the four of us and Jack sat down to eat.

In the evening before bed, we took turns using the toilets and brushing our teeth in the open communal bathroom, feeling a light mist from the rain that had rolled in around dusk. I shivered, huddling into my rain jacket and listening to the chirping of the crickets.

"Mama?" Aria called from within the mosquito cocoon of the mattress across from me.

I switched off my headlamp and burrowed under the light blanket. "Yes, honey?"

"Can we do more tie-dye when we get back home? That was fun to do today."

"Sure! The patterns they made were lovely, weren't they?"

"Yeah. It was cool to see how they get the natural blue color."

"It was. Night-night, I love you."

"Love you. Sleep tight. Don't let the crickets bite—because there are a lot of them!"

We turned off our headlamps and fell asleep to the patter of rain overhead.

"Ack! Guess what creature I saw just now in the bathroom?" I asked Randy and the kids as I plopped down next to them the next morning at breakfast.

"What?" Finn asked.

"I saw a few cockroaches and a ton of mosquitoes yesterday," Aria offered. "But at least they were only on the walls, not actually *on* the toilet!"

"I saw a moth," Randy added.

"Nope, this was new. I saw a frog hop out of the stall before I headed in. Outdoor bathrooms are always quite the adventure!"

"Thank goodness I didn't find a frog in there at night," Aria exclaimed. "In the daytime, fine, but at night, when you only have your headlamp, that would be terrifying."

"Ready to see the fish hatchery before heading back to Hanoi?" Jack proposed. We agreed and followed the path to explore more of the town.

"Do they raise all the village's fish here?" Finn queried.

"They still fish in the river, but these hatchery ponds contribute significantly," Jack said.

Spotting the large fish, the kids were eager to feed them. A woman handed them fish pellets, and they delighted in watching the fish frenzy.

Wandering back to our homestay, past the stilted houses, each displaying the Vietnamese flag, I reflected on the village's future. "I wonder how these small tribes will fare in the coming decades."

Randy speculated, "More villagers might move to cities, but tourism like this could help to retain their culture, as we heard."

Before leaving, we asked our Muong host if we could all take a photo together. She seemed pleased and nodded. As we raised our arm to take a selfie, she put her hand up and gave the mini love sign. We grinned and mirrored her, all of us holding up our thumbs and index fingers one more time before saying goodbye and heading back to the bustle of Hanoi.

ALMOND FAMILY REPORT CARD ON VIETNAM

- *Top Marks*: Embrace the diverse experiences Vietnam offers. Discover the enchantment of Hoi An during a full-moon festival, bike through lush rice paddies, and savor the flavors of traditional Vietnamese salted coffee.
- *Needs Work*: Vietnam's well-trodden tourist trail can obscure more genuine experiences. Exploring rural areas like Da Bac requires patience due to undeveloped infrastructure and language barriers, but it rewards with deeper cultural insights.
- *Learning Tips*: Engage with locals through culinary classes, crafts, market walks, and city tours, which can bring a more well-rounded perspective to your explorations.

19

MOUNTAINS AND MOMOS

Nepal

Excerpt from Finn's Journal
March 21, 2023 | Ghorepani, Nepal

It is blissfully clear when we wake up this morning high in the Himalayas. We get amazing views of Annapurna South before the clouds roll in and consume everything. After breakfast, we start on the trail with a steep uphill climb before a downhill through dense forest. It's misty and muddy, and Dad slips and falls on his pole, breaking it. Luckily, he is OK. I give him one of my poles, because I don't really need both. We stop a little while later for lunch. I have dal bhat, a Nepalese lentil curry, which is so good! We keep walking downhill when we're hit with a hailstorm. The hail is the size of marbles—they are so big and painful! We walk a miserable thirty more minutes uphill until we arrive at the tea house where we're staying for the night. When we get there, we are drenched. We quickly strip off our wet outer things and hang them up to dry, then go to the common room to sit around the fire. It's toasty warm. We eat dinner then immediately crash in our sleeping bags in our cold rooms. So tired . . .

MOUNTAINS AND MOMOS: NEPAL

Arriving on the outskirts of Pokhara on a propeller plane from Kathmandu, the first thing we noticed as we stepped onto the tarmac was the chewy air. It hung thick and heavy, like syrup. I felt my eyes prickle, then sighed. I doubted whether the scratch in my throat, which I'd felt throughout Southeast Asia, would recede anytime soon.

"Bummer," Finn said, wrinkling his nose. "I hoped the air quality would get better when we got into the Himalayas. Aren't we supposed to be able to see mountains from here?"

"I thought it'd be better too, buddy," admitted Randy. "And yeah, Pokhara is famous for its views of the Annapurna range. Maybe it'll improve as we gain elevation on our trek."

I gave another sigh as we headed into the gray afternoon. We crammed into a taxi then set off, watching a Buddha Bobble Head on the dashboard wobble all the way into Pokhara.

Nepal's second largest city, Pokhara is in a valley about 125 miles (200 km) west of the capital, Kathmandu. Situated on Phewa Lake, it is a haven for boating, paragliding, zip-lining, and bungee jumping. It's also the starting point for some of the best treks in the world.

"Listen to this description of Pokhara," I read grumpily from our guidebook as we waited for our hotel room to be ready. "Pokhara's *pristine air*, spectacular snowy peaks, blue lakes, and surrounding scenery make it the 'jewel in the Himalaya.' Whoever wrote this must not have been here in March."

"Let's think positively," Randy said. "What would Mr. James Bun have to say about this? Impermanence! Bad air quality today, but tomorrow? Who knows? Let's channel our inner Buddhists and be optimistic."

"Mmm," I replied. Randy is annoying when he is right.

"I saw a Nepali restaurant with good reviews nearby," he added. "Shall we grab lunch before we meet up with our trekking guides?"

"Definitely!" Finn said. "I need to keep up my *momo* count! I had twenty-four yesterday in Kathmandu. I can't fall behind!"

Finn loved *momos*, the national dish of Tibet, commonly found in Nepal, Bhutan, and parts of northern India. These dumplings, stuffed with meat or vegetables and seasoned with coriander and cumin, were his obsession since arriving in Nepal.

At the restaurant, we ordered a mix of local specialties: chicken *shapta*; *thienthuk*, a Himalayan noodle stew; and Finn's favorite, pan-fried chicken *momos*.

"*Momo* Count for the day—sixteen," Finn noted, wondering aloud if he could find them on our upcoming trek.

"We'll see," Randy replied. "Tea houses along the way might have a limited selection."

We had planned a twelve-day Himalayan trek to Annapurna Base Camp. We chose Three Sisters Adventure Trekking, a local company promoting women's empowerment through adventure tourism, as our guides.

Approaching their lavender-colored office, a sign read, "Changing the world, one woman and one girl at a time."

"Do you know why this matters?" I asked Finn and Aria.

"Because women haven't always had the same rights as men here?" Finn answered.

I nodded. "Correct. Nepal has long been a patriarchal society. Women are traditionally seen as subordinate, lacking equal rights, education, healthcare, careers, or property ownership. There's been progress—they elected their first woman president in 2015—but there's still a long road ahead. Initiatives like Three Sisters are important for empowering women by giving them skills and a career path."

"So, our guide and assistants will all be women?" asked Aria.

"Yep," Randy confirmed.

"That's so cool."

I nodded. "Let's go meet them."

"*Namaste*," a dark-haired woman in a yellow sweater greeted us. She had a red *bindi* on her forehead, a dot of color known as the third eye chakra, representing the universe.

"You must be the Almonds," she continued. "I am Mana. Welcome to Pokhara."

"*Namaste*," we echoed.

Mana was one of the senior guides. She gave us an overview of the Annapurna Base Camp trek.

"ABC is one of my favorites," she said. "It has varied terrain, beautiful scenery, and a chance to get a glimpse into local culture. You'll interact with villagers of Magar, Tamang, and Gurung ethnicities and learn about Hindu and Buddhist traditions in the shrines you'll pass. You'll stay in local teahouses and enjoy traditional meals. It's a perfect high-mountain trek to experience the customs and hospitality of the kingdom of Nepal."

Mana unfolded a glossy topographical map, smoothing it across the table. She outlined our route. "You'll drive from Pokhara to Birethanti, then trek to Hille on the first day," she explained.

Pointing to the map, she continued. "The next day you'll climb over four thousand steps to Ghorepani, a challenging but gorgeous route; you'll see many rhododendrons in bloom. After that, you'll start at dawn for Poon Hill, then trek to Tadapani, Chomrong, and onward, reaching Annapurna Base Camp after several days. The return trek includes stops at Jhinu Danda's hot springs and Ghandruk before returning to Pokhara."

Aria and Finn bounced in their seats, jittery with anticipation.

I was concerned about the weather forecast. "Looks like rain every day. Should we delay our start?"

"No," Mana responded. "In the spring, it's usually clear in the morning with rain in the afternoon. You'll start early each day on the trail to try to avoid it. Danu, your guide, can fill you in more."

Mana introduced us to Danu and assistant guides, Anjali and Swastika. We knew from our travels in India that the swastika is an ancient symbol of good fortune in Hinduism and Buddhism. Initially taken aback when we saw it used across Rajasthan, we soon learned to distinguish it from the Nazi appropriation. So, we were not as surprised by her name as we might have been otherwise.

Danu, short, energetic, and outgoing, asked the kids, "Are you ready?"

"Yes!" Aria and Finn replied enthusiastically.

"We're excited," I added. "We'll go rent the rest of the gear we need and see you in a couple of days!"

As we zipped up our jackets against the wind, we stepped out into a downpour and wondered what we had gotten ourselves into.

SUNDAY, MARCH 19
Annapurna Base Camp Trek, Nepal
Day 1 of 12 // Birethanti up to Hille (6,391 ft / 1,948 m)

- Distance: 5.46 miles
- Elevation Gain: 1,699 ft
- Moving Time: 2 hours 20 minutes

On Sunday morning, the mountains still hidden behind a thick gray veil, we met Danu, Anjali, and Swastika to set off.

"*Jā'aum̐, jā'aum̐,*" Danu said, her smile infectious as we hoisted our backpacks onto the roof of the van. "It means 'let's go' in Nepali!"

The journey took us about an hour and a half, winding through the rugged landscape until we reached the Annapurna Conservation Area. We disembarked in the mountain town of Birethanti. Here, we shouldered our packs, adjusted our trekking poles, and followed Danu's lead, ascending the town's stone steps into the lush green hills.

Our trail meandered through charming Nepali villages and remote countryside. Children eagerly swarmed us as we passed, playfully peeking in our pockets for sweets. Local men worked in the fields with their oxen, while women gathered at communal water spigots, laundering clothes in the frigid spring water.

Around midday, Danu stopped at a tea house painted in shades of pink and blue. Ravenous, we ordered plates of *dal bhat*, a traditional Nepali dish of lentils, vegetables, and rice.

"Can I get *momos*?" Finn eagerly asked Danu.

She chuckled. "Maybe not for lunch. They take a long time to make. For dinner, I'll make them for you at the tea house where we're staying, okay?"

He nodded, content with the compromise. As we ate, the weather shifted, and a gentle rain began to fall. After lunch, we donned our new rain ponchos and covered our packs, thankful that the rain was light.

By early afternoon, we reached Hille. The Dipak guesthouse welcomed us with vibrant red geraniums and wild poinsettias near its sky-blue front door. "*Namaste,*" greeted the owner, and we echoed the salutation.

Our rooms were sparse: twin beds with thin wool blankets, to which we added the sleeping bags we had rented for extra warmth. The guesthouse, like all those we'd encounter on the trail, lacked heating and felt especially cold in the damp spring air. Downstairs were two outhouses, one with a western toilet and the other a porcelain-lined hole in the ground. There were two cold showers in stalls outdoors as well.

After layering on hats and jackets, we gathered on the deck, trying to warm ourselves with mugs of hot green tea as we watched the rain envelop the terraced hills. Finn brought out a deck of cards. "Anyone up for a game?"

Danu nodded enthusiastically, "Do you know how to play 'Less than five?'"

"No, what's that?" Finn replied, curious.

"A Nepali card game. I'll show you," she suggested, leading us to the common room where it was more sheltered, if not warm. Anjali and Swastika joined on one side of the bench, while Randy, Aria, and I took the other.

It was a fun game, and we enjoyed the friendly competition. As dinner approached, Danu kept her promise and made *momos* for Finn from scratch, showing him how it was done.

"*Momo* count for the day—ten," he announced proudly after wolfing them down.

MONDAY, MARCH 20
Annapurna Base Camp Trek, Nepal
Day 2 of 12 // Hille up to Ghorepani (9,429 ft / 2,874 m)

- Distance: 9.5 miles
- Elevation Gain: 5,413 ft
- Moving Time: 5 hours 1 minute

CHAPTER 19

Our second day on the trail began inauspiciously. Aria woke up feeling weak and dizzy after a restless night in the cold bunk room. Concerned about altitude sickness, she kept asking if her headache was a symptom, referencing a pamphlet she'd picked up in Pokhara and details from the book I had—possibly ill-advisedly—chosen for our worldschooling reading, *Buried in the Sky: The Extraordinary Story of the Sherpa Climbers on K2's Deadliest Day.*

I reassured her. "We're only at five thousand feet, Aria; that's less than Denver's altitude. It's likely dehydration and anxiety. We'll speak to Danu and take it slow."

Finn also had a tough night and complained of a churning stomach after breakfast. A quick retreat to the outhouse didn't bode well for the start of the day.

Danu, however, was a beacon of positivity. "*Bistarai, bistarai,*" she told the kids, meaning "slowly, slowly" in Nepali. "We'll stop a lot for water and snacks. OK?"

Finn and Aria nodded. We began the tough but beautiful uphill slog from Hille to Ghorepani. The trail, marked by massive stone steps, wound through lush forests. Magenta rhododendrons bloomed overhead, their petals creating a pink carpet underfoot. As we walked, we caught whiffs of the spicy, clove-like scent of azaleas, the sweet perfume of honeysuckle, and the earthiness of moss and magnolia blossoms.

The rain began after lunch, sending us into our ponchos again.

We reached Ghorepani's tea house around 5 p.m., cold and sopping wet. The tea house had recently been renovated, and while it still didn't have heat, it now boasted heated blankets, which we eagerly snuggled into.

After warming up a little, we pulled back on all our layers and dashed out in the rain to the main building for dinner. An iron stove kicked out heat, creating a bubble of warmth in the center of the room. Nepali locals and hikers crowded around to get warm, and Aria and I nestled in, waiting for the boys to join us.

Then, everything went dark. The electricity had gone out. Glancing out through foggy windows, it looked like it was out across the whole village. A moment later, a flicker, then a subset of lights came back on; there was generator electricity at least in the common room, so we could get dinner. But the larger ramifications were clear.

"This means no heated blankets!" Finn moaned when he and Randy joined us.

"Oh no! Maybe it'll come back on soon."

We played Hearts in the dim light and talked about the trek so far. Aria had her mojo back, and Finn's stomach was no longer roiling. We were all excited for the next few days, though we wished the rain and cold would go away.

Before we returned to our rooms, the electricity returned across the village. As we crawled under our heated blankets, we felt profoundly grateful for the little things.

TUESDAY, MARCH 21
Annapurna Base Camp Trek, Nepal
Day 3 of 12 // Ghorepani up to Tadapani (8,628 ft / 2,630 m)

- Distance: 10.69 miles
- Elevation Gain: 3,489 ft
- Moving Time: 5 hours 46 minutes

At 4:45 a.m., the next morning, I whispered softly to Aria, "Do you want to join Daddy and me for the hike up to Poon Hill, or would you rather keep sleeping? It's not raining, but the fog might obscure the mountain views."

Burrowed under her heated blanket, Aria mumbled, "Keep sleeping. Have fun, Mama."

"Okay, see you later for breakfast," I replied, giving her a kiss.

Bundling up against the cold, I stepped out into the pre-dawn darkness. The air was chilly, my breath visible as I met up with Randy, Danu, Anjali, and Swastika to begin the "side trip" ascent to Poon Hill. Like Aria, Finn had chosen to sleep in.

On a clear day, from the top of the hill station overlooking the Annapurna Massif and Dhaulagiri mountain ranges, Poon Hill offered panoramic views of some of the Himalaya giants—Annapurna II, Nilgiri, Lamjung, Dhaulagiri, and Machapuchare (also known as Fishtail because of its distinctive peak). With the morning shrouded in thick fog, though, we weren't sure what the hike would reveal. The path uphill was dark and quiet, lit only by the beams of our headlamps. As we climbed, we noticed the frost on trees transitioning to blankets of snow.

Reaching the summit at 10,532 feet (3,210 m), we were greeted by a horizon heavy with clouds. At a lone stall, we bought hot tea, letting the warmth seep into our bodies as we quietly awaited the dawn.

Gradually, the clouds began to part, casting ribbons of pale-yellow light across the towering peaks. "Wow," I murmured, shuffling to keep warm. "So beautiful."

The hillside, draped in swirling mist, showcased snow-covered pines and bursts of pink rhododendrons under their snowy veil. The shifting winds created fleeting windows in the clouds, offering us tantalizing glimpses of the colossal mountains beyond.

"I'm so glad we got up for this," I said to Randy.

"Me, too," he agreed, his voice filled with awe.

Back at the guesthouse, Finn and Aria were still asleep when we returned. After rousing them and eating a hearty breakfast, we ventured into the fog-enshrouded forest. The drizzly cold created a moody, otherworldly landscape.

The rain-soaked path was a muddy challenge. We picked our way carefully around roots and down steep embankments, leaning on our trekking poles for stability. Randy slipped at one point, landing on his backpack in the mud, like an overturned turtle.

"You OK, Dad?" Finn asked, sloshing over to give him a hand up.

"Yeah, I'm fine," Randy replied. He held up his trekking pole, which had snapped in the middle. It hung limply in the shape of an L. "But this trekking pole has had it, I'm afraid."

"You can have one of mine," Finn offered. "I don't need both of them."

"Thanks, bud," Randy said, gratefully accepting it.

Danu's calm voice, repeating *"Bistarai, bistarai,"* became our guiding mantra.

After a tea house lunch, with Tadapani still hours away, we braved the rain again. Then, a sudden thunderclap and lightning strike heralded a hailstorm.

"Ouch!" Aria cried as hailstones bombarded us. "They're huge!" She exclaimed, showing us the marbles of ice in her palm.

"Don't just stand there; let's keep moving!" I urged, charging forward.

Freezing and soaked, we finally clomped up to our next tea house in the late afternoon. The common room was toasty warm, everyone crowded around a stove in the middle of the room. Clotheslines crisscrossed the ceiling like a spider's web, laden with everyone's wet garments. We headed upstairs to change into something dry and find spots to hang our gear. With the inside area packed, we strung our clothes outside our rooms in the open air, knowing there wasn't much chance they would dry there overnight.

After dinner, the kids and I cuddled together in Aria's and my room, wishing for heat or heated blankets, and watched a *Friends* episode on our iPad. We could see our breath as we burrowed into our sleeping bags in the frigid bunk room, trying to keep warm. Then we said goodnight to Finn, who dashed off to his and Randy's room, and fell into a deep sleep.

GUIDED JOURNEYS: WHEN AND HOW TO CHOOSE THE PERFECT GUIDE

Selecting the right guide can make a significant difference in your family's travel experience, especially in destinations brimming with options. But it's not always obvious when or how to find one that matches your needs. Here are some tips to help you choose wisely.

When to Hire a Guide:

- *Mandatory Guides*: Some destinations require guides for certain activities or areas.
- *Complex Travel Environments*: In places with underdeveloped tourist infrastructure or overwhelming options, a guide can simplify navigation.
- *Language Barriers*: If you're traveling to a place where you don't speak the local language, a guide can help with communication and understanding.
- *Navigating Complexities*: In culturally or historically dense destinations, guides can provide essential context and insights.

- *Authentic Experiences*: Guides can offer access to off-the-beaten-path locations and deeper cultural immersion, helping you connect with local people and customs.

How to Find the Right Guide

Once you've decided to use a guide, selecting the right one is crucial. Here's how to make an informed choice:

- *Personal Interaction*: If possible, talk to potential guides to gauge their communication style and compatibility with your family.
- *Prioritize Your Needs*: Consider what's most important for your trip—budget, private, or group tours; storytelling; logistical support; or specific insights.
- *Local vs. International Guides*: Decide whether you prefer a local guide for more authentic experiences or an international organization for a more standardized approach.
- *Language Proficiency*: Ensure the guide speaks your language well enough for clear communication.
- *Expertise in Adventure*: For adventurous trips, check the guide's technical expertise and safety record.
- *Community Impact*: If giving back or supporting local communities is a priority for you, look for guides or companies committed to these values.
- *Recommendations and Reviews*: Seek recommendations from others and read reviews to assess the guide's reputation and reliability.

WEDNESDAY, MARCH 22
Annapurna Base Camp Trek, Nepal
Day 4 of 12 // Tadapani up to Chomrong (7,391 ft / 2,253 m)

- Distance: 7.34 miles
- Elevation Gain: 1,820 ft
- Moving Time: 3 hours 47 minutes

"*Jā'auṁ, jā'auṁ,*" Danu encouraged us the next morning, her voice full of energy. Without delay, we set off, determined to reach Chomrong before the afternoon rains.

The morning greeted us with clear skies, a refreshing change. Towering around us were some of the Himalayan peaks we'd been waiting so patiently to see—Machapuchare and Annapurna South. We took a few moments to soak them in, then followed Danu into the forest.

Along the trail, we passed a stupa in a clearing, its white dome and gilded spire adorned with a golden moon, punching into the blue sky against jagged, snow-covered peaks. Colorful Tibetan prayer flags, representing the five elements, fluttered from its corners. Danu shared with us the symbolism of the flags, often described as "blessings spoken on the breath of nature."

At the base of the hill, we came upon a long, narrow suspension bridge over a deep gorge. We crossed in single file, then embarked on an uphill climb. Cows, horses, and sheep grazed in the fields, and we passed through lush terraces and quaint hamlets.

In the early afternoon, we reached the "Excellent View Point" tea house in Chomrong, elated to have stayed dry and feeling like we'd bested the Gods of the Mountains. Danu informed us that from here to ABC, guest houses had no wood fires, meaning no more cozy stoves in the common rooms. Our weather app read a chilling 32 degrees F (0 degrees C), with temperatures dropping. Bundled into all our layers, we congregated in the common room for tea. Soon, the predictable rains arrived, drumming on the tin roof through the night.

"I'm so profoundly glad to be here and dry, if not warm," I remarked to Randy.

"Ditto," Randy agreed, turning to Finn and Aria. "You guys are doing awesome. Despite the challenges, you've stayed determined. We seem to be finding our stride. Well done."

Their faces lit up with pride. We had this.

THURSDAY, MARCH 23
Annapurna Base Camp Trek, Nepal
Day 5 of 12 // Chomrong up to Dobhan (9,393 ft / 2,863 m)

- Distance: 8.39 miles
- Elevation Gain: 2,850 ft
- Moving Time: 4 hours 20 minutes

The morning didn't start well again. Finn had a rough night, waking up with a headache and nausea. Skipping breakfast, he vomited as we were packing up. After resting for a while and taking a Pepto Bismol, he felt better and ready to begin hiking.

The striking fishtail peak of Machapuchare and neighboring Annapurna South stood prominently against another clear blue sky. At a stupa along the way, we spun the heavy golden prayer wheels, wishing for good weather and health.

Unfortunately, our prayers seemed to fall on deaf ears. As we finished lunch, light rain began, escalating to a downpour in the final stretch to Dobhan. Our rain ponchos were no match for the deluge, and soon hail forced us to seek shelter under branches.

As I glumly shook off clumps of ice the size of mothballs, I wondered what on earth we were doing there, freezing, wet, and bone-tired in the remote wilds. I looked at Aria, hunched over beside me, water dripping from the hood of her poncho. Her little face was set in a determined line. She gave me a small smile and nod, and I felt a surge of pride. She and Finn had battled through and been troopers, rarely complaining even in the toughest of conditions. I squared my shoulders and took a deep breath. Worldschooling comes in many different forms; I knew on this trek my kids were learning a lot about resilience and determination, understanding (and pushing) their limits, and growing in adversity. I could too.

"Ready to keep going, Mommy?" Aria asked, taking my hand.

"Ready," I replied. "Onward!"

FRIDAY, MARCH 24
Annapurna Base Camp Trek, Nepal
Day 6 of 12 // Dobhan up to Deurali (10,498 ft / 3,200 m)

- Distance: 4.51 miles
- Elevation Gain: 2,453 ft
- Moving Time: 2 hours 30 minutes

At breakfast, we talked to Danu about whether we could continue to Annapurna Base Camp or would need an alternate plan for safety reasons. The heavy monsoon-pattern rains had dropped a lot of snow on the high camps, elevating the risk of avalanches along critical passes. It was uncertain whether climbing farther was still a possibility.

"Happy news," Danu announced. "I've spoken with villagers and other guides. We can take a longer but safer route. We're still on for Base Camp ascent."

"Yay! So, Deurali will be our stop for tonight?"

"Yes. Let's have a hearty breakfast and gather our energy for the day!" She cast a concerned look at Finn, who'd been fluctuating between feeling okay and unwell. He nodded in agreement, and by 8 a.m., we hit the trail, uplifted by Danu's reassurance.

The morning was beautifully sunny, and we hung our damp clothes on our packs to dry, transforming them into mobile clotheslines. Our spirits were high, buoyed by the sun and the prospect of a relatively easy three-hour hike to Deurali.

Midway, we paused at a guest house in the tiny village of Himalaya, soaking up the warm rays. Randy enjoyed an espresso, and I indulged in an unexpected café mocha from a small coffee shop, surprise luxuries that felt immensely gratifying. By the time we resumed our trek, our clothes were dry, adding an extra spring to our steps.

Optimism coursed through me. "We can do this," I thought.

As we neared Deurali, a dense mist enveloped us, and the rains began shortly after we checked into our rooms. Despite the downpour, our timely arrival meant we had stayed dry—a huge victory. We watched with sympathy as later arrivals trudged in, soaked and weary.

In that moment, we felt like we had outsmarted the elements and obstacles in our path. But, like Icarus, we gloated too soon.

CHAPTER 19

SATURDAY, MARCH 25
Annapurna Base Camp Trek, Nepal
Day 7 of 12 // Deurali back down to Himalaya (9,636 ft / 2,900 m)

- Distance: 3.55 miles
- Moving Time: 2 hours 7 minutes

On the morning of our expected ascent to Annapurna Base Camp, we awoke at 6:30 a.m., prepared for the final push to the top. Finn's condition had taken a turn for the worse, though. He had a restless night, waking weak, dizzy, and nauseous. He couldn't stomach breakfast.

Danu, Randy, and I held a quick conference. "Let's give him a bit more rest," Danu said. "We've seen him bounce back before."

Randy gave Finn another dose of Pepto Bismol, hoping it would settle his stomach, but knowing if he was suffering from altitude sickness—which increasingly felt likely—Pepto wouldn't help. Meanwhile, Aria, Swastika, Anjali, and I started up the trail, moving slowly to allow the others time to catch up. An hour in, Danu called Anjali with an update—we needed to turn back. Finn's condition hadn't improved. We needed to descend to a lower altitude for his recovery.

We regrouped and made our way back to the village of Himalaya, about a thousand feet lower. "We'll see if this helps him feel better," I said, trying to stay optimistic. "We can decide tomorrow whether to try for ABC again or go down further."

By noon, there was a glimmer of hope as Finn managed some plain noodles. He remained lethargic, though. "He doesn't even want any *momos*," I whispered to Randy. "You know it's not good when he says no to that."

"Yeah," agreed Randy. "Let's see how he does overnight and make the final call."

That night, as I tucked Aria into bed, she seemed teary. "I'm just frustrated," she admitted. "I feel terrible for Finn, but why do we all have to turn back? When I had to stop on Mount Meru and go down with Daddy, you and Finn were able to continue to the summit. Can we do something similar here?"

I hugged her, understanding her disappointment. "That's very fair; you've earned the right to try for Base Camp. Let me talk to Danu. I imagine you and Dad can continue with her tomorrow, while I go down with Finn."

Her eyes brightened. "Really? That would be great."

"I'm proud of you for sharing how you feel," I told her. "Let's see what's doable."

"Thanks, Mama. And I do hope Finn gets better."

"I know you do. We all do."

I headed out to find Randy and Danu to talk through our options.

SUNDAY, MARCH 26
Annapurna Base Camp Trek, Nepal
Day 8 of 12 // Randy, Aria, Danu, and Anjali—Himalaya up to Annapurna Base Camp (13,550 ft / 4,130 m)

- Distance: 7.03 miles
- Elevation Gain: 5,129 ft
- Moving Time: 4 hours 26 minutes

Andi, Finn, and Swastika—Himalaya down to Bamboo (7,709 ft / 2,350 m)

- Distance: 4.5 miles
- Moving Time: 2 hours 15 minutes

The next morning, our group parted ways. Swastika, Finn, and I began our descent. Finn's persistent symptoms made it clear that getting to lower altitude was crucial. Randy, Aria, Danu, and Anjali set their sights upward, continuing toward Annapurna Base Camp.

"Bye, guys—good luck!" Finn and I said.

Aria replied with a wide smile. "Feel better, Finny!"

Finn managed a weak smile and called, "Take a picture for us from the top!"

As we descended to the village of Bamboo, Finn's condition steadily improved. By the time we had showered, eaten, and settled in for the night, he was almost back to his usual self.

"It's annoying that I feel better already," Finn lamented. "I wish I could've felt like this at the higher camp."

"I know," I empathized. "Altitude sickness is unpredictable. We'll always have our summit in Tanzania. Right now, I'm glad Dad and Aria have this opportunity."

We spent the afternoon reading and awaiting updates. Four hours later, my phone buzzed with a message from Randy—a photo of all four of them, their faces beaming against gray skies and snow, colorful prayer flags fluttering in the wind, and a sign behind them reading, "NAMASTE. Annapurna Base Camp, 4,130 m."

"They made it!" I exclaimed.

"That's awesome!" Finn's face lit up. "Tell Dad to send a video!"

MONDAY, MARCH 27
Annapurna Base Camp Trek, Nepal
Day 9 of 12 // Randy, Aria, Danu, and Anjali—Annapurna Base Camp down to Bamboo (7,709 ft / 2,350 m)

- Distance: 9.84 miles
- Moving Time: 4 hours 30 minutes

Andi, Finn, and Swastika—Bamboo down to Chomrong (7,391 ft / 2,253 m)

- Distance: 6 miles
- Moving Time: 2 hours 54 minutes

At Annapurna Base Camp at dawn, Randy and Aria awoke to clear skies and a spectacular sunrise over the surrounding snow-covered peaks. They hiked around, their sneakers laden down with heavy crampons for traction in the thick snow. After breakfast and one last look around, they began the long descent, covering six thousand feet to reach Bamboo by early afternoon.

Finn, Swastika, and I had continued down to Chomrong, arriving around lunchtime. With time on our hands, we settled into the common room, reading, journaling, and playing cards.

In the afternoon, the weather took a dramatic turn. The skies darkened, and temperatures plummeted as rain transformed into sideways sleet driven by fierce gusts of wind. All of a sudden, we saw a blinding flash of light followed by a deafening bang. Then several things happened simultaneously.

A lightbulb directly above us exploded, showering us with glass. Finn dove under the table, a woman screamed, and across the room, a credit card machine burst into flames.

"Looks like lightning hit the lodge," I whispered, still processing the sudden turn of events. Swastika stood frozen, her eyes wide in shock and fear.

The tea house manager rushed over to snuff out the fire. The rest of us—a dozen or so haggard-looking trekkers and locals—huddled together, wary of more lightning. I checked the ceiling—scorch marks and dangling wires were all that remained of the lightbulb. The floor was littered with glass and smoldering debris. I peeked under the table at Finn. "You okay?" I asked.

He nodded, visibly shaken. "That was crazy."

"Totally. Ready to come out?"

He nodded again, climbing back onto the bench.

With the storm raging outside, we were left in a dim, gray-blue light filtering in through the windows. "Looks like we're in for a long night," I remarked, pointing out the village-wide power outage. "I don't think the electricity's going to come on any time soon."

We were relieved to get a text from Randy, learning that they had arrived safely at Bamboo and weren't caught out in the storm. Finn and I spent the rest of the afternoon playing hangman and Gin Rummy in the fading light. Dinner was a simple affair of cold fried rice eaten by headlamp light before going to bed, but we were thankful for anything at all.

"Well, we might not have made the summit, but you can't say we didn't have our own adventure," I said as I snuggled under my wool blanket and sleeping bag.

"Uh, yeah, that was insane. Pretty sure we'll remember that experience forever."

TUESDAY, MARCH 28
Annapurna Base Camp Trek, Nepal
Day 10 of 12 // Randy, Aria, Danu, and Anjali—Bamboo down to Jhinu Danda (5,840 ft / 1,780 m)

- Distance: 6.69 miles
- Moving Time: 3 hours 42 minutes

Andi, Finn, and Swastika—Chomrong down to Jhinu Danda (5,840 ft / 1,780 m)

- Distance: 1 mile
- Moving Time: 1 hour

The next morning, Finn, Swastika, and I had a short, easy hike to the hot springs village of Jhinu Danda. We spent the day making friends with the resident cat at the teahouse and enjoying the sunshine while awaiting the others' arrival.

Around noon, we heard a familiar voice. "Hey there, strangers," Randy called. Aria, Danu, and Anjali followed, looking weary but exultant.

"Daddy!" Finn shouted with excitement, rushing to greet him.

I wrapped Aria in a big hug. "You did it! I'm so proud of you! How was ABC?"

"Amazing!" she beamed. "Daddy got loads of photos and videos. You'll see."

"I can't wait."

That afternoon, as we soaked in the nearby hot springs, Aria mused, "Wouldn't it be nice if we could just teleport back to Pokhara?"

Finn half-submerged, gave an enthusiastic thumbs up.

WEDNESDAY, MARCH 29
Annapurna Base Camp Trek, Nepal
Day 11 of 12 // Jhinu Danda down to Ghandruk (6,601 ft / 2,012 m)

- Distance: 5.52 miles
- Moving Time: 2 hours 22 minutes

After more than ten days traversing through tiny mountain villages, our mid-morning arrival at Ghandruk, with its one thousand households and five thousand inhabitants, felt like entering a bustling metropolis. With the whole afternoon ahead of us, we settled in to watch the afternoon clouds gather, as we knew they would, over the distant peaks.

THURSDAY, MARCH 30
Annapurna Base Camp Trek, Nepal
Day 12 of 12 // Ghandruk down to pickup point

- Distance: 3.26 miles
- Moving Time: 1 hour 22 minutes

On the last morning of our trek, we resumed our descent toward the pickup point, where a van awaited to take us back to Pokhara. As we trekked, I turned to Aria with a question.

"Do you think you'll want to finish *Buried in the Sky* once we're back in civilization? It's an excellent book, but it's all right if you don't; I'll give you a one-time pass."

She leaped at the offer. "Pass, thanks! I've had enough of altitude sickness for this trip!"

Finn chimed in, "I finished it already. Can I save the pass for later?"

I laughed. "Nice try; it's a one-off opportunity."

Looking to shift the conversation, Randy asked, "So, what's everyone most looking forward to back in town?"

Aria didn't hesitate. "Nutella crepes at that French creperie in Pokhara!"

"*Momos*," Finn declared. "Gotta get my count back up."

"Fully dry clothes and cozy sheets," I added. "What about you, Randy?"

"A hot shower," he replied. "Trekking makes you appreciate the little things, doesn't it?"

"Definitely," I agreed.

Pulling up to our hotel, we gave Danu, Anjali, and Swastika hugs and thanked them.

"Look, you can see the peaks from town now!" Finn exclaimed. He was right. The sky was blue, the air clear. We could see the distinctive tip of Machapuchare's fishtail punching above the buildings to the north.

"The mountain is saying goodbye to you," Danu said, smiling.

We nodded and stepped out into the pristine Pokhara air, turning away from the Himalayas—until the next adventure.

ALMOND FAMILY REPORT CARD ON NEPAL

- *Top Marks*: Trekking in the Himalayas offers exhilarating glimpses of high peaks and local culture in mountain villages and tea houses. Choose a trek that matches your fitness and interests, with options varying in length and difficulty.
- *Needs Work*: Be prepared for the possibility of poor air quality in the cities and variable weather conditions in the mountains. Invest in a good, inexpensive rain poncho like those worn by locals.
- *Learning Tips*: Learn from community guides about Nepal's rich culture and spiritual practices as you pass stupas (Buddhist dome-shaped monuments) and prayer flags along trails or in towns.

IV

FOURTH-QUARTER WORLDSCHOOLING GOALS
(April–July)

April 2023
Dear Finn and Aria,

Can you believe it? We have been backpacking now for almost nine months, and just like that, we're approaching the last phase of our round-the-world odyssey.

You have climbed mountains, conquered fears, met people in some of the most remote places, learned about new cultures and religions, and challenged yourselves in countless ways. Through a combination of our experiences in Africa, Europe, the Middle East, South America, Antarctica, and now, Asia Pacific as well as the books we have read, documentaries we have watched, and scientists, guides, and locals we have met along the way, you have been gaining a deeper understanding of the world.

Greta Thunberg says in the book that we read by her, "No one is too small to make a difference." As we continue our travels through Asia Pacific—and later, when we are back home—we want you to continue reflecting on this idea and all that you have learned this year. Consider what changes we can all make in our day-to-day lives when we return home to contribute to making the world a better place for more people.

It is a privilege to experience our world as we are doing, and we want to make sure that we not only are traveling through countries, we are listening, reflecting, and carrying the lessons we're learning back home with us for the long term.

Here are our worldschooling expectations for you in the final few months of our travels. Most will be familiar by now, but keep it all up with energy and enthusiasm like you would at home, even as you anticipate the summer holidays approaching.

1. *Continue to read the guidebooks in each country we're in.*
2. *Continue reading books set in countries in which we're traveling.* Continue writing book reviews on each, along with how many stars you give them out of five. Here is our list for the next few months; there are a lot in Japan as many of the books are quite short. We'll also have time on the high-speed bullet trains where you can listen to some of these as audio books.

    - Japan: *Diary of a Tokyo Teen: A Japanese-American Girl Travels to the Land of Trendy Fashion, High-Tech Toilets and Maid Cafes* by Christine Mari Inzer; *One Thousand Paper Cranes: The Story of Sadako and the Children's Peace Statue* by Ishii Takayuki; *Ikigai: The Japanese Secret to a Long and Happy Life* by Héctor García; *Pure Invention: How Japan's Pop Culture Conquered the World* by Matt Alt; *Botchan* by Natsume Sōseki
    - Taiwan: *The Astonishing Color of After* by Emily X. R. Pan
    - The Philippines: *Patron Saints of Nothing* by Randy Ribay
    - Indonesia: *The Rainbow Troops* by Andrea Hirata
    - Australia: *In a Sunburned Country* by Bill Bryson

3. *Continue the daily practice of writing in your journal.* Make sure to review the rubric to capture your impressions.
4. *Study each of your target languages in a focused way.* Finn, you'll be embarking on a solo adventure in Taiwan, studying Mandarin. In many ways, this will be the culmination of all the worldschooling and travel you have done, so we'll not overload you with many other assignments in this quarter. Aria, you will continue to focus on Spanish by continuing Duolingo app lessons. And, of course,

we'll continue our practice of learning the basics of local languages as we explore this region.
5. *Write a few shorter essays on targeted questions we'll assign en route.* Writing short, time-bound essays has worked well in recent months, so we will continue to look for opportunities to do more of this as we make our way through Asia Pacific.
6. *Finish math curriculum.* As we reach the end of our fourth quarter, you will each take placement tests to assess what you have learned and figure out the correct placement for you when you return home. You will likely take these while we are in Australia.
7. *Listen, observe, reflect, and start contemplating ways we can contribute to being the change we want to see in the world.* While we'll wrap up our nomadic lifestyle and return to Colorado in a few months, our hope for you—for us all—is that these experiences stay with us, even if we don't live them every moment any longer, and over time shape the way we think and act, ideally seeking opportunities to bring positive change to the world.

Even though it seems like we're almost at the end of our trip, three months is still a very long time to travel, with many exciting adventures to come. Let's enjoy every moment and soak up all that we can in the Everywhere Classroom!
Love,
Your worldschooling teachers (Mom and Dad)

20

CHASING IKIGAI

Japan

Excerpt from Finn's Journal
April 10, 2023 | Nikko, Japan

This morning, we walk to some temples, which are super cool! There are more than a hundred buildings in Buddhist and Shinto shrines in this complex in the mountains. We see one temple with a cool set of samurai armor. In the Toshogu Shrine, we see a wooden panel showing three monkeys from the phrase, "See no evil, hear no evil, speak no evil." Nana, Aria, and I pose like the monkeys for Mom to take a photo of us with the original behind us. We walk up to another temple to see the burial site of the emperor. I especially love seeing the temples with all the cherry blossoms in bloom. It is what I imagined Japan to be like in the spring, but better.

"Where you are from, if I may ask?" the man behind the desk asked gently, inviting us to sit. His thin white hair was combed back, and he wore a crisp white shirt, a navy vest, and a gray plaid jacket. His charcoal eyes twinkled behind electric blue spectacles.

"The United States," Finn answered, sitting down. Randy, Aria, and I joined him.

"America," the man mused, selecting a piece of red paper from a pile. He folded it expertly, maintaining eye contact. "I visit New York and Chicago many years ago. Beautiful."

His fingers worked deftly, bending and tucking the paper. Within minutes, he created a red-and-white figure with tiny hands, feet, and beard, then added dots for eyes.

"A Santa Claus!" Aria exclaimed.

"Yes, a simple Santa, for you," he replied, bowing with a smile. He gestured at the paper objects around the room. "I am fourth-generation origami master. You like to learn?"

Finn and Aria nodded, their eyes wide, watching as he produced cubes, tulips, maple leaves, a penguin, a crane, and a wedding ring from paper squares. He handed the ring to Randy.

"Would you marry me again?" Randy asked me.

"I'd be honored," I said, smiling. Randy slipped the ring on my finger, and the master beamed.

"It's lovely, *arigato*," I said, and he bowed his head.

Origami, the ancient Japanese art of paper folding, transforms simple sheets into mini works of art. We learned about the tradition in *One Thousand Paper Cranes: The Story of Sadako and the Children's Peace Statue*, a nonfiction book we were reading about a young girl named Sadako who was exposed to radiation from the Hiroshima bombing and folded hundreds of cranes while hospitalized. It is believed that if one folds one thousand origami cranes, one's wish will come true—a symbol of hope and healing in challenging times.

We planned to visit the Hiroshima Peace Monument toward the end of our time in Japan. Finn and Aria wanted to make cranes to leave as an offering. Finding the origami museum in Tokyo and learning more about the art form was an ideal start to our journey.

After thanking the master, Finn and Aria bought origami books and sheaths of paper with their allowance money, excited to practice.

"I can't wait for Nana and Opa to get here tonight!" said Finn. "We can teach them origami now."

"I'm sure they'd love that," I replied. "They should be arriving soon."

"It has been way too long since I've had anyone else to talk to other than you guys," Finn said. "I mean, no offense, or anything."

"None taken," I replied, attempting to ruffle his hair, but he dodged. "We're all looking forward to having them join us for our adventures across Japan."

We had arrived in Tokyo a few days earlier, awaiting Finn and Aria's grandparents from Texas. They'd be joining us for a two-week journey across Honshu, Japan's main island.

In the meantime, we were absorbing the culture and exploring some of Tokyo's diverse neighborhoods. I had assigned several worldschooling books, ranging from fun graphic novels to more thought-provoking nonfiction for our three weeks on the island nation. Finn and Aria started with the *Diary of a Tokyo Teen*, an illustrated memoir by a Japanese American girl, which provided a teen's perspective on Japan's fusion of tradition and modernity.

Within no time, we saw for ourselves the study in contrasts that is Tokyo, a city where you can wander through a serene evergreen forest to a sacred Shinto shrine one minute, then fight your way through the crowded streets of Harajuku, the center of Japanese street fashion and subcultures the next. At a local mall, we discovered floors of capsule toy dispensers, offering tiny toys instead of gum. In Akihabara, the Mandarake complex was a treasure trove of anime merchandise, manga, and cosplay outfits. Street vending machines, one for every twenty-three people in Japan, surprised us with their variety: pizza, balloons, ramen, canned bread, horned beetles, suits, and even beer.

Japanese bathrooms were another source of fascination—and not just to me this time. They were high tech and ultra-modern. Upon entering a stall, toilet lids opened automatically as if in greeting. The seats were heated, a feature we didn't know we needed in our lives until we experienced it. With the touch of a button, the sound of a babbling brook played for privacy.

On the afternoon of my dad and stepmom's arrival, we strolled through a large temple's gardens, leading to a statue of Confucius.

"Who's this dude?" Finn asked.

"Confucius," replied Randy.

"And Confucius was . . . ?"

"A Chinese philosopher," Randy studied Finn thoughtfully. "You know, I think this 'dude' would make an excellent topic for a worldschooling essay. I'd like you and Aria to research and write four hundred words about who he was, his philosophy, and influence in East Asia."

"But . . . but . . . Nana and Opa are arriving soon," Finn spluttered.

"You'll have time," Randy assured him.

After some grumbling, Finn and Aria applied themselves and completed their assignment in their tiny hotel room, then practiced origami in the lobby while waiting. They didn't have to wait long. A short while later, they leaped up, ecstatic, to hug their grandparents and welcome them to Japan, as though they were tenured ambassadors.

After settling in, we all headed out for a quick dinner at a restaurant nearby. We struggled to interpret the menu, Google Translate seeming to be hit or miss with Japanese characters. Thankfully, there were plastic renditions of the food in a display case out front, so we pointed to plates that looked promising and hoped for the best.

And just like that, our traveling group of four became a party of six.

"Will we ride the shinkansen to Nikko?" Shay, my stepmom, asked with enthusiasm. "I definitely want to experience the bullet train while we're in Japan."

"Yes, part of the way," Randy confirmed. "First, we'll take a local train to Omiya, then the shinkansen to Utsunomiya, followed by another local train to Nikko. Don't worry, you'll get your fill of bullet trains over the next couple of weeks!"

With Japan bustling in early April for cherry blossom season, Randy had meticulously—and uncharacteristically for us—mapped out an advance itinerary. We aimed to cover a broad swath of the country in two weeks. Luckily, our Japan Rail passes made it simple, quick, and cost-effective to explore the country. After soaking in Tokyo's vibrancy, from themed cafés to the frenetic Shibuya crossing, we were now bound for the mountain town of Nikko.

Right on schedule, the shinkansen, a gleaming teal bullet train with a pink stripe, pulled into the Omiya station. The conductor, in a crisp navy cap and white gloves, leaned out, offering a friendly finger heart gesture.

"This is the way to travel," my dad, Fred, remarked, stepping aboard into the immaculate interior. "Everything is so incredibly clean."

"Absolutely," Shay, a former nurse with a keen eye for cleanliness, agreed. "It's impeccable."

With punctilious precision, the train whisked us toward the mountains.

"Ohhh, look at all the cherry blossoms," I cried in delight as we emerged from the station into the sunny, crisp Nikko afternoon. "Looks like we hit peak season perfectly here!"

"Exactly what we were hoping to see," Fred said, nodding in contentment. Spring was in full bloom, filling the air with a sweet, floral scent. I lagged the rest of the group with my dad, capturing photos of daffodils, fragrant hyacinths, elegant Japanese camellias, azaleas, and particularly the fluffy pink cherry blossoms that were quickly becoming my obsession.

Upon reaching our hotel, we shed our shoes at the entryway, slipping into the indoor slippers lined up neatly by the door. Fred, Shay, Finn, and Aria claimed the single bedroom with two double beds, while Randy and I settled into the living room, our sleeping arrangements being futon mattresses we'd unfold at night. During the day, the room was furnished with a low table and stools, where Finn was already busy with his colorful array of paper cranes.

"Opa!" Finn called out as we walked in. "Want to learn origami? I'll teach you!"

Fred, looking amused and impressed at Finn's handiwork, chuckled. "Sure, let's give it a try! But mind you, I might need help getting up from these low stools later."

Finn grinned. "Deal." They delved into the intricate world of paper folding until it was time to head out for dinner.

The next morning, we took a bus to the majestic Nikko World Heritage Site. The site, nestled in a grove of fir and cedar trees, was a sprawling complex of over a hundred Shinto and Buddhist shrines and temples. An imposing stone torii gate stood at the entrance, leading us to the Toshogu shrine, adorned with elaborate wood carvings and gold leaf.

Among the intricate decorations, we paused in front of a carving on one of the storehouses. It featured a panel with three monkeys—one with hands over his eyes, the second over his mouth, and the third over his ears.

"You guys are familiar with the three wise monkeys, right?" I asked Finn and Aria. "See no evil, hear no evil, speak no evil?"

Finn's eyes widened. "Is this where that saying comes from?"

"Yep. The three monkeys aren't about ignoring evil, though, as commonly interpreted, but about embodying childhood innocence. I read that they signify the idea that childhood is a time to be shielded from evil, representing the nature of innocence."

Before they could run off to check out the next shrine, I had a request.

"Let's get a picture of you two with Nana standing in front of the panel, posing like the three monkeys, OK?"

They obliged, striking poses, while I snapped away.

ARTFUL ADVENTURES: INTEGRATING ARTS AND CRAFTS INTO WORLDSCHOOLING

Arts and crafts offer a unique and affordable way to immerse your family in the cultures of the world, whether you're at home or on the road. Children gain a greater appreciation for the cultural richness of the places they visit, developing their creativity and broadening their global perspective in a fun, interactive way. Here are tips for incorporating creative experiences:

- *Research Local Art Forms*: Before traveling, research the traditional arts and crafts of your destination. For example, beadwork in Namibia, lantern making in Vietnam, origami in Japan, or calligraphy in Taiwan.

- *Seek Out Workshops and Classes*: Look for local classes offering hands-on experiences in these art forms. They're often affordable and provide a deep cultural insight.
- *Visit Local Artisans and Craft Markets*: Exploring local markets and artisan shops and watching artisans at work is both inspiring and informative.
- *Create a Travel Art Journal*: Encourage your children to keep an art journal, where they can sketch, paint, or collage their experiences and memories.
- *Visit Museums and Galleries*: Many museums have interactive sections for children, where they can learn about art history and try creating art themselves.
- *Look for Festivals or Cultural Events*: These events often feature art and craft activities for children, providing a fun and immersive learning environment.
- *Document and Display Artwork*: Displaying at home the art created during your travels can be a reminder of your experiences and way to celebrate the cultures you've explored.

"I need to stop eating now, I'm 80 percent full," Aria declared, placing her chopsticks across her plate. "That's called *hara hachi bu*. I read about it in our *ikigai* worldschooling book. It's part of having a long, happy life."

We were having lunch at an *izakaya*, a Japanese pub, in coastal Kanazawa. Our table overflowed with pan-fried *gyozas* and bowls of hot ramen topped with sliced pork, *nori* (dried seaweed), bamboo shoots, and scallions.

"How do you gauge when you're 80 percent full?" Shay wanted to know.

Aria thought about that. "Well, if I eat another *gyoza*, I'll explode, so I must be close."

"What about dessert?" Fred joked. "Won't chocolate pudding push you over?"

"There's always room for pudding, Opa," Aria replied seriously.

"Maybe finding the best sweets is your *ikigai*, Aria," I suggested.

"It does make me happy," she agreed, and we all chuckled.

The concept of *ikigai*, a concept meaning purpose or reason for being, was introduced in another book I had assigned for our time in Japan. It explored a Japanese village with a high percentage of centenarians, delving into their lifestyle, diet, and *ikigai*—the secrets behind their meaningful, long lives.

After lunch, we explored Kanazawa, a castle town steeped in history, in which samurai, geisha, merchants, and lords all once lived and left their mark. From a worldschooling perspective, Kanazawa was a fabulous place to immerse ourselves in Japanese culture.

During the Edo Period from the early 1600s to the 1800s, Kanazawa was the seat of one of the most powerful feudal clans and a site of great cultural achievement. It largely escaped the air raids of World War II, so much of the old districts survived. We wandered the cobblestone streets of the geisha quarter; visited a samurai house; explored the beautiful Kenrouken gardens where we loved seeing locals in traditional, colorful kimonos meandering among the pink *sakura* blossoms; and visited Kanazawa castle.

Our last morning there brought us to the D. T. Suzuki Museum, honoring the Buddhist philosopher who introduced Zen ideals to the West. Upon entering, we informed the kids that they would need to write short essays on Suzuki, as they did with Confucius. We knew they'd pay more attention with an assignment due at the end.

Inside the museum, we read Suzuki's writings on nature and Zen, then paused by the Water Mirror Garden. The open-air Contemplative Space allowed opportunity for meditation.

Aria and I sat on the benches, crossed our legs, and closed our eyes, taking in the silence.

"I might start meditating daily," Aria shared softly.

"I've been thinking the same," Randy joined in. "It would be centering."

Aria nodded, then added. "Plus, I might want to explode at Finn less."

We laughed. We all had our motivations.

"So, is everyone still up for staying overnight in a temple in Koyasan?" Randy asked Fred and Shay. "It's quite a journey—multiple trains, cable car, and a bus. You up for it?"

Fred nodded. "Absolutely! Staying in a Buddhist temple is a unique opportunity."

"We're definitely in," Shay added.

"Great, I'll get the train tickets."

After Kanazawa, we spent several days admiring the shrines and bamboo groves of Kyoto before heading to the remote town of Mount Koya, also known as Koyasan. Nestled deep in the forests south of Osaka, it's a sacred Shingon Buddhism center with hundreds of temples and monasteries, many of which offered *shubuku* or temple stays.

Arriving in Koyasan after a long day of travel, the final bus dropped us near Hozen-in temple, our home for the night. A monk, clad in simple robes and a gray cap, welcomed us with a polite *"Konichiwa."*

We slipped off our shoes and shuffled awkwardly, in the oversized black slippers we were given, across the bamboo floors. Our family room, ringed by *fusuma* or sliding paper doors, was spacious and minimalistic, with *tatami* mats and bean-stuffed pillows on the floor. It was chilly, and we sat, bundled in all our layers, until we figured out how to work the electric heater.

Served green tea, we joined the monk to sit cross-legged on the floor. Fred and Shay shifted to try to find comfortable positions on the mat. The monk smiled kindly, then outlined in halting English what to expect that night and the next morning. We'd be free to explore the town and nearby cemetery before dinner at 7 p.m. He'd come get us for morning prayers at 5:50 a.m. Bowing, he left us to settle in.

After finishing our tea, we ventured to explore the small town and serene cemetery of Okunoin, located nearby in an ancient cedar forest. Before dinner, we changed into *yukatas*, or cotton robes, and followed the monk to a private room in the temple, where a spread of *shojin ryori* awaited us.

This traditional Buddhist cuisine was an array of plant-based dishes: bean sprout pancakes, marinated tofu, shiitake mushrooms, baked daikon, sticky rice, and pickled vegetables.

"It's so beautifully presented," Shay commented.

"I didn't know tofu could be this tasty," remarked Aria.

Finn made a face. "I'd still choose steak."

We laughed.

The following morning, we woke before the sky had fully lightened, feeling the effects of an uncomfortable night's sleep on the monastery's firm futons. No one seemed particularly well rested, and the lack of our usual morning coffee only added to our sluggishness. In the communal wash area, I was slightly cheered by the view of the cherry trees in full bloom. I splashed cold water on my face, trying to wake up.

At precisely 5:50 a.m., the monk appeared at our door to escort us to the temple for morning prayers. Finn, doddering in the too-large slippers, muttered under his breath, "I seriously don't know how they don't fall in these."

"You know, I think the slippers are intentionally difficult to walk in," I whispered back. "It probably encourages quieter movement and a more mindful presence."

"Oh, that's a smart theory," Shay replied. "You might be right."

We walked through the tranquil corridors of the temple, passing a meticulously maintained Japanese garden. The air in the temple was heavy with the scent of burning incense, a smoky fragrance that immediately made the space feel sacred and ancient. We settled ourselves on the *tatami* mats, adjusting to the unfamiliar practice of sitting cross-legged for an extended period.

The monk took his place on a raised dais, his back to us, and began a rhythmic, melodic chant. I closed my eyes, allowing the sound to envelop me, trying to focus on the moment and the mantra. But my mind, unaccustomed to this kind of stillness, wandered. I caught my dad glancing around the room, our eyes meeting. He offered a sheepish smile, and I returned it, acknowledging our shared struggle with this exercise in meditation.

As the chant continued, my rebellious thoughts drifted further——to our family's journey, our purpose, our *ikigai*——and what lay ahead. This family trip had been a dream and a goal we'd worked and saved toward for so long; I wondered whether we would feel a void once we returned home and what would fill it. Would there be a sense of aimlessness, or would we find that this adventure was part of a larger journey? How would the kids build on this experience and where would their paths in life lead?

CHAPTER 20

When the monk's chanting ended, I realized that my attempts at clearing my mind had failed miserably. Dad and I probably wouldn't be acing "Intro to Monastery Life" anytime soon. Feeling grateful that most of life's experiences aren't graded, though, I bowed and gave the monk a quiet *arigato* as we rose to leave.

"After breakfast," Randy told Finn and Aria after the morning prayer, "I want you both to take a solo walk through Okunoin. It's Japan's largest cemetery, and it's an extraordinary place. Your mom and I explored it last night and plan to go back this morning. Nana and Opa are interested too. It's a peaceful spot for you to have some quiet reflection and continue our meditative start to the day. Then we'll say goodbye to the monks and continue to Hiroshima."

The kids nodded, their hesitation evident.

"Won't it be scary to walk through a graveyard alone?" Aria asked apprehensively.

Randy explained, "It's not what you might expect. The graves, called *gorin-to*, are layered stone pagodas, each layer symbolizing an element—earth, water, fire, wind, and space. People honor waiting spirits here with offerings. There are *Jizo* statues too, protectors against evil spirits, adorned in red hats and bibs."

"That actually sounds pretty cool," Aria responded, her curiosity piqued.

Randy added, "And, it's beautiful, like redwood forests in Northern California. It's fascinating to see how different cultures honor the dead."

Wandering through Okunoin again in the morning light was enchanting. The sun's rays filtered through the towering cedars, illuminating moss-draped graves of historical and modern figures. Each of us took our own pace along the cobblestone paths, enveloped in a profound tranquility.

The cemetery was almost deserted. We passed a monk in black robes, who nodded silently. A man in a traditional *kasa* hat sat motionless on a bench, immersed in deep contemplation. At the end of the trail was the Torodo Hall, the Hall of Lanterns, aglow with the soft, unceasing flicker of twenty-thousand golden lanterns, said to have burned for over a millennium. Slowly, I turned back, threading my way through the cedar grove to regroup with the family and continue our journey south.

Our final stop in Japan, before my dad and Shay's departure, was Hiroshima. On a rain-drenched morning, we walked from our hotel to the Peace Memorial Park, the site of the city's once-thriving commercial and residential district, now a symbol of peace and resilience. The park, created from the open field left by the atomic bomb's explosion, is home to memorials, monuments, museums, and lecture halls, attracting over a million visitors yearly.

Inside the museum, we gathered around a large clock, marking the days since the first A-bomb detonation. Next to it, a stone statue bore the words "War is the work of man. War is the destruction of human life. War is death. To remember the past is to commit oneself to the future. To remember Hiroshima is to abhor nuclear war. To remember Hiroshima is to commit oneself to peace."

Entering the exhibition hall, a stark date greeted us: August 6, 1945——the day the atomic bomb forever changed the city of Hiroshima. We moved through the exhibits at our own pace, absorbing the somber displays of memorabilia and photographs.

Randy and I pointed out significant pieces to Finn and Aria, relating to their final worldschooling essay: a persuasive piece on whether they felt the United States was justified in dropping the atomic bomb. They were to draw from their readings, the museum's insights, and further research, engaging deeply with this complex, divisive historical debate.

"This panel is crucial," I said, directing them to information about President Truman's decision-making process. "Understanding the alternative options and their implications is key to forming your viewpoint."

Randy added, "Remember, history is often subjective. Being here offers a different perspective, and hopefully starts to give you a more nuanced view of the complexities than you might get just studying World War II back home."

They joined us, taking notes intently.

Toward the end of the hall, we came across glass cases displaying children's belongings—a haunting reminder of the bombing's impact on innocent lives. "Look," I whispered, pointing to Sadako Sasaki's paper cranes. Aria, visibly moved, held my hand as we gazed at the delicate origami.

"Do you have your origami paper?" I asked her.

"Yes."

"Let's visit the Children's Peace Monument then."

We walked to the statue, where a figure of Sadako, arms raised, held a paper crane aloft, flanked by representations of other child victims. Behind the statue, glass cases overflowed with millions of paper cranes from visitors worldwide, symbolizing a collective yearning for a world free of nuclear war.

Sitting beside the statue, Finn and Aria expertly crafted six cranes—one for each of us—and added them to the collection, under Desmond Tutu's quote: "Ordinary acts of love and hope point to the extraordinary promise that every human life is of inestimable value."

They then each rang the bronze bell beneath Sadako's statue, resonating with our hopes and dreams for a peaceful future.

As we zipped back to Tokyo on the *shinkansen*, marking the end of our journey with my dad and Shay before their flight home, I reflected some more on our travels. Our time in Japan had been more than just a series of destinations; it had been an immersion into a culture rich with lessons and surprises. One Japanese concept I'd read about, *ichi-go, ichi-e*, resonated deeply with me. This phrase, meaning "this moment exists only now and won't come again," served as a poignant reminder of the transient nature of our experiences.

The essence of *ichi-go, ichi-e* lies in the appreciation of every encounter's uniqueness, be it with family, friends, or even strangers. It's an invitation to embrace the present, to cherish each fleeting moment without being overshadowed by past regrets or future anxieties.

As I gazed across the cabin at my family, a deep sense of gratitude enveloped me for the time and experiences we shared together. I still had my own journey of self-discovery to continue, exploring my *ikigai*, my deeper purpose. However, for the moment, being fully present in these final hours together in Japan felt profoundly fulfilling.

Outside, the landscape whizzed by, a blur of vibrant pink *sakura* blossoms, a last enchanting glimpse of Japan's spring beauty. Hurtling toward Tokyo, I let the smooth motion of the train lull me to sleep, finally succeeding in clearing my mind.

> **ALMOND FAMILY REPORT CARD ON JAPAN**
>
> - *Top Marks*: Japan captivates with its impeccable cleanliness, efficient bullet trains, fabulous quirkiness, and rich cultural sites, from geisha districts to samurai history. Don't miss the raw beauty of Hokkaido and the iconic cherry blossoms across the country in spring.
> - *Needs Work*: With so many must-see destinations, thorough pre-trip planning is essential. Prioritize and streamline your itinerary to avoid being overwhelmed.
> - *Learning Tips*: Visit moving historical sites like Hiroshima and, for a unique cultural experience, consider an overnight stay in an active monastery.

DRENCHED AT THE DMZ

South Korea

Excerpt from Aria's Journal
May 5, 2023 | Seoul, South Korea

We wake this morning at 5:30 a.m. to visit the Demilitarized Zone (the DMZ) between North and South Korea. You need to take a guided tour, so we meet our group at a McDonald's then board a bus for the long drive. Our guide tells us about Korean history while we go. The weather today is even worse than yesterday. It's raining hard, and we do not have umbrellas. When we arrive at the first stop, we run to an overhang but are immediately soaked. We try to listen to our guide, but it's hard to hear her over the rain. A nice shopkeeper takes pity on us and gives us rain ponchos, which helps. The thing that really stands out to me from the day are the tunnels. North Korea built a bunch of secret tunnels into South Korea. Only four have been found, but there are many more out there. Our guide tells us more than sixty are thought to exist but not yet discovered! Imagine if Canada had tunnels that popped up into the United States where they could attack us from!?! We get to walk through the third tunnel, which runs under the DMZ. We start by walking down a long corridor until it feels like we are at the core of the earth. Then we go down a narrow dirt path. It is tall enough that I don't have to duck, though Daddy does. It's crazy to think an army can creep up on you at any point! Later that night, we get Korean Barbeque, which is awesome because you cook your own food on a grill at your table. And we take selfies of ourselves at a Korean photo booth. We put on funny wigs and hats and huge glasses and make silly faces. It's a fun way to end a long, interesting day.

DRENCHED AT THE DMZ: SOUTH KOREA

Two women in pastel-colored *hanbok* dresses—traditional Korean clothing—and parasols strolled down a cobblestone street, occasionally snapping selfies against decorative doors and temples. Nearby, children in bright dresses and Converse sneakers enjoyed ice cream cones under a tree's shade. A couple in matching blue attire wandered past historic houses and trimmed hedges.

"It feels like we've stepped back in time, aside from the sneakers and Starbucks," Aria noted.

We were wandering through a *hanok* village in Gyeongju, South Korea, with its quaint storefronts and iconic Korean homes. And, anachronistically, a Starbucks, though one unlike any other we had ever seen. From afar, it would be easy to mistake the Gyeongju Starbucks for a temple, with its gently sloping roof, colorful eaves, and a pair of *haetae* —mythical horned creatures—flanking the entryway. The interior boasted a traditional Korean aesthetic as well, with a raised wooden dais reserved for cross-legged floor seating. The mix of ancient and modern embodied the juxtaposition we were beginning to associate with the country.

We had been in South Korea, officially known as the Republic of Korea, for a week. The East Asian country borders North Korea along the heavily fortified Demilitarized Zone in the north, the Yellow Sea to the west, and the Sea of Japan to the east. We had chosen the sleepy southeastern city of Daegu, an agricultural center, precisely because it's rarely on any tourist itinerary. After a period of intense exploration across Japan, we wanted a stint of slower immersion in a place where we could just experience life like locals. We spent our mornings in cafés so Finn and Aria could complete math assignments and finish their persuasive essays on Hiroshima, then ventured out to do a mix of mundane but necessary errands and exploration in the afternoons.

In local markets, we stocked up on granola, yogurt, and Korean melon. Needing haircuts, we continued our global tour of barbershops and salons. Laundry was washed and air-dried at our Airbnb. Evenings were spent watching a documentary series about the Korean War, educating ourselves on the region's recent history. The conflict, which resulted in 3 million deaths, ended after three years in 1953 with an armistice, not a peace treaty, leaving Korea divided.

"So, South and North Korea are still technically at war?" Finn asked one evening.

"Yes," Randy replied. "It's a frozen conflict. More than seventy years since the war's end, the Demilitarized Zone still divides the two halves. The relationship between the two Koreas fluctuates between peace and tension."

Aria looked concerned. "Is it safe? Should we visit the DMZ so close to North Korea?"

"It's safe, or we wouldn't be here," replied Randy. "It's a unique area, worth exploring."

"Think we'll see Kim Jong Un?" Finn asked jokingly.

"Not unless something goes seriously awry."

In the evenings, we tried fried chicken, *shabu shabu* (meaning literally, swish, swish, a type of hot pot cooking style), and Korean barbecue at local restaurants near our Airbnb in Daegu. We were the only Westerners in any of them.

Our first experience with Korean barbecue—a popular style of grilling meat, seafood, or vegetables on a personal grill built into the table—was a worldschooling lesson for us all. We had only a vague idea of what we were doing. Google Translate was failing us. None of the waiters spoke English. So, we studied what locals around us did and mirrored their actions, but we realized too late that we had missed an entire array of side options that came with the meal, like ramen noodles and a salad bar. So, we returned another night and, that time, properly used the scissors at the table that had baffled us the first time to cut meat right over the grill, found the beer opener hidden in a secret drawer, and navigated all the side plates like we had been eating Korean BBQ for years.

After a relaxing week in Daegu, having completed necessary errands and school assignments, we were ready to explore nearby areas before heading to Seoul.

Gyeongju, an hour's bus ride from Daegu, is a UNESCO World Heritage Site and former capital of the Silla Kingdom. This "Museum without Walls" boasts many ancient relics and temples, blending traditional heritage with contemporary attractions. It was an ideal educational destination.

Our day began at the Daereungwon Tomb Complex, featuring over twenty burial mounds from the era of Silla, a Korean kingdom founded in 57 BC. These mounds concealed intricate chambers with historical remains and artifacts. At the Cheomachong Tomb, a reconstructed burial site, we learned about tomb construction and discovered millennia-old relics.

"Still think you want to be an archaeologist?" I asked Aria as we watched a film about the construction and excavation of the site.

"Definitely," she replied. "Can you imagine how it must have been, to be wandering around here thinking, those are nice grassy hills, then maybe you find a piece of pottery or tool in the stones nearby and realize there is something hidden underneath it all? Crazy!"

"It would be unbelievable."

She nodded, her eyes tracing the inside of the tomb.

Later, we visited the Gyeongju National Museum, with its relics and artifacts of the Silla period. We wandered around Donggung Palace and Wolji Pond, then strolled through the Gyochon Traditional Village, where we saw people strolling past handicraft stores, restaurants and cafés, and tea shops in their *hanbok* finery.

Then, because it was the coolest one we had seen anywhere in the world, we sat on the wooden floor of the temple-turned-coffee shop to splurge on Starbucks drinks before catching the late bus back to Daegu.

GAINING A GLOBAL HISTORICAL PERSPECTIVE IN WORLDSCHOOLING

Worldschooling opens the door to understanding history from multiple viewpoints, essential for developing a well-rounded global perspective. Here's how parents can guide their children in seeing history beyond their own "bubble":

- *Explore Historic Sites:* Visit battlefields, memorials, and landmarks to see local narratives come to life.
- *Meet Local Historians:* In each country, local historians can provide unique insights and differing viewpoints on historical events.

- *Museum Visits*: Museums often showcase history from the perspective of their culture, offering alternative interpretations of familiar events.
- *Diverse Reading Materials*: Seek out books by local authors to understand history from the perspective of those who live there.
- *Documentaries and Films*: Watch country-specific documentaries and films for a visual and emotional exploration of their historical narratives.
- *Reflective Discussions*: After learning about an event, discuss it with your children, comparing these new viewpoints with what they previously understood.

By embracing these approaches, worldschooling can profoundly enrich a child's understanding of history, fostering a more informed and empathetic worldview.

Seoul, the capital city of South Korea, was rated the most livable Asian city in 2015 for its high quality of life. It's the heartbeat and home to K-pop culture and the Korean Wave, also called *Hallyu*, a term referring to the global boom of South Korean popular culture from music to TV dramas and games to cuisine. A city where Buddhist temples, palaces, and sprawling gardens brush up against high-end shopping malls and sleek skyscrapers.

We stayed in Gangnam, an upscale district made famous by Psy's viral K-pop hit "Gangnam Style" in 2012, the first YouTube video to hit one billion views. Its tongue-in-cheek portrayal of Gangnam's lavish lifestyle captivated the world.

"Do you know what 'Oppa Gangnam Style' means?" I asked Finn and Aria, referring to the song's refrain.

They shook their heads. "No idea," Randy admitted.

"Apparently, it refers to the posh lifestyle here in Gangnam," I explained, having read up on this earlier. "Psy was making fun of the area's wannabes. The phrase 'Oppa Gangnam Style' literally means 'Big Brother is Gangnam Style,' symbolizing his ironic take on being fancy and high class."

Aria eyed me skeptically. "How do you know that?"

"Google. Where else?"

You could certainly tell the area was posh. Finn was beside himself, spotting fancy cars everywhere we looked—Ferraris, Corvettes, Porsches, a Maserati Gangnam dealership, McLaren Seoul, and Lamborghini Seoul Central. We thought his head was going to spin off.

The Cheongdam Fashion Street boasts one of the most luxury shopping areas in Seoul, with brands like Vera Wang, Gucci, Versace, and Cartier. Upscale restaurants and high-end hotels gave way to popular shopping and entertainment areas. To cap off our Korean pop culture tour, we visited K-Star Road in Gangnam, the leading place of Korean trends and fashion.

"I'd like the record to show that I'm not a K-pop fan," Finn declared, apropos of nothing.

"Fine," I replied. "But let's get a photo with these GangnamDols (a compound word meaning 'Gangnam,' 'idol,' and 'doll') anyway. They're adorable."

"Ugh, do we have to, Mom?"

"Yes! It's a fun memory. Say, 'BlackPink!'" I encouraged them, snapping a photo of them beside the colorful bear dolls, each representing a different K-pop group.

Our walk ended at a large bronze statue featuring the famous hand motion from "Gangnam Style."

"Just one more picture, OK?" I wheedled.

Finn stared me down. "One more for the whole trip?"

I laughed. "Nice try! One more for our K-pop tour."

Begrudgingly, he and Aria posed, and I captured the moment as a nearby French couple sang and danced, "Oppa Gangnam Style" enthusiastically under the statue.

One rainy afternoon, after a morning of journaling and math assignments, we pulled on our windbreakers and headed to the metro to visit the War Memorial of Korea.

The Statue of Brothers stands outside the museum. On top of a granite dome, two soldiers are depicted in an embrace, capturing a scene in which one brother—a Republic of Korea officer and his younger brother, a North Korean solider, meet on the battlefield and hug in reconciliation, love, and forgiveness. Below them, the dome is split down the middle, a crack representing the division of Korea and hope for its reunification.

We stood in the drizzle, and I felt a pang of sadness imagining the families torn apart by a war that split a land in half and which is still not over.

The museum's outdoor exhibition space featured armored vehicles and tanks, U.S. B-52 bombers, warships, and submarines used in World War II, the Vietnam War, and the Korean War. Inside were war memorabilia, maps, battle records, and statues detailing the history of the Korean War, the progression of hostilities, and eventual establishment of a truce. We watched black-and-white documentary footage with English commentary of main battles and events.

As we headed into the rain hours later, a local man stopped us and asked if he could ask us a few questions for his YouTube channel. We nodded. "Where are you from?"

"The United States," Finn replied.

He beamed, as though we gave the right answer. "We love Americans! I am from Seoul. You helped save our country in the war. Thank you! The United States is a great country. How do you like visiting here?"

"Korea is beautiful. We are enjoying our time here," Randy replied.

"How long are you traveling in our country?"

"Two weeks."

The man smiled again. "I hope you enjoy your time in Korea. Thank you again."

"That was weird," Finn muttered once we were out of earshot. "We didn't fight in the war. Why was he thanking us? We, personally, had nothing to do with the Korean War."

"Which, of course, isn't even called the Korean War here," Randy noted. "South Koreans call it Six-Two-Five, referring to the date it started on June 25 (6-25), 1950. Same as how, in Vietnam, they don't call it the Vietnam War, they call it the American War. This is just a small reminder of the fact that there are two—or more—sides to everything."

As we walked into the rain, we talked about the complex nature of many of the wars the United States got involved in over the years and the range of likely lingering reactions to those of us who came later.

"When you study about these places in the years to come, hopefully you'll remember our travels here and look at history from a more nuanced perspective," Randy said. Spoken like a true history buff.

"Is it raining again?"

"Sadly, yes."

"Is it really time to go?"

"Also, yes."

It was 5:30 a.m. on our last day in South Korea, cold and wet and dark. We were heading to the Korean Demilitarized Zone, the 2.5 mile (4 km) wide and 150 mile (247 km) long border that divides the Korean peninsula into North and South. The DMZ is one of the most volatile and heavily armed regions on earth, a tangible reminder that the war is technically not over. Hundreds of thousands of landmines litter the border, which is protected by barbed wire fences, outposts, and large numbers of troops stationed on both sides of the 38th parallel. We had booked an educational guided tour to deepen our understanding of the war and its aftermath.

As our bus made its way from Seoul, rain lashed against the windows. Without ponchos or umbrellas, we hoped for mostly indoor activities to avoid the downpour. Our first stop was Imjingak, a park along the Imjin River built in 1972 to honor those separated from their hometowns by the war. In the relentless rain, we huddled close, straining to hear our guide over the wind. Her heavily accented English made understanding even more challenging as she talked about the significance of the Freedom Bridge and other memorials.

"What is she saying about leper colonies?" I asked Randy.

"No idea. That doesn't make any sense."

"I know." I hopped back and forth from one foot to the other, trying to get warm. Aria stood on my leeward side, shielding herself from the wind.

"Ahhh, you know, I think she's saying refugees, not lepers," Randy whispered. I nodded. I was glad we had watched the war documentary since this part of worldschooling wasn't going great. Once our guide finished pointing out a few more statues and memorials, she said we could wander Imjingak on our own or get warm inside until the bus continued on. We ran for cover.

The tour continued at the Third Infiltration Tunnel, a grim reminder of North Korea's aggression. Discovered postwar, the tunnel's existence was initially denied by North Korea, then they falsely claimed it was a coal mine. We donned helmets, descending into the cold, dark tunnel, which runs through bedrock about 240 feet (73 m) below ground.

"This is so eerie," whispered Aria. "It's crazy to think of these tunnels being built right under South Korea."

"Right? And there are so many more believed to exist but still undiscovered," I added.

Our last stop was Dora Observatory. On a clear day, you can see North Korean troops patrolling over the border. With the rain and mist, we knew that wasn't likely. But we ran under the overhang and peered through binoculars over a high wall. Our guide described the Peace Village of Kijong-dong, a deserted North Korean town masquerading as a thriving community, a stark example of propaganda.

"They want to make it seem like life is good in North Korea," she explained. She was much easier to understand now that the rain had abated slightly. "But it's all for show, like a Hollywood set, never inhabited."

"Whoa," Finn said. "It's hard to see much, but the idea of a fake town is so bizarre."

We scanned the landscape, a serene yet distant green panorama, reflecting on the surreal reality of this divided land. We scanned the horizon more and were struck by how normal it all looked. It was unremarkable—green and hilly, a pretty landscape—so close and yet so very far away.

On our drive back to Seoul, our guide spoke of the South Korean dream of reunification, a dream shared by many in hopes of reconnecting with family and friends across the border.

"Do you think you'll see it in your lifetime?" someone in our group asked her.

"I hope so," she responded, a mix of optimism and realism in her voice. "Not anytime soon but maybe, someday."

ALMOND FAMILY REPORT CARD ON SOUTH KOREA

- *Top Marks*: South Korea offers a vibrant mix of ancient culture and modern, fun K-pop energy. Enjoy Seoul's lively nightlife, traditional Korean BBQ, selfie booths, and historical sites.
- *Needs Work*: Navigating South Korea's rich cultural landscape requires diligent research and planning. Having local insights is helpful to discover hidden gems.
- *Learning Tips*: An educational tour of the DMZ offers fascinating insights into the North-South Korea conflict, enhancing your understanding of the region's complicated history and geopolitical issues.

22

THE FAMILY MART GANG

Taiwan and the Philippines

Excerpt from Finn's Journal
May 14, 2023 | *Taipei, Taiwan*

WEEK 1
I have never lived in a big city before, so being in Taipei—especially on my own—is a totally new experience. There are so many new smells, of cigarettes and drain water and gas exhaust. There are also good smells—sweets and meats, cheeses, noodles, and rice. I'm not used to the noises of the city either, so I haven't been sleeping well this first week. It is odd being alone without my family, adjusting to my new homestay and Mandarin school.

My host mom isn't warm and welcoming. She just puts my breakfasts and dinners on the table, then leaves to do chores.

My new Mandarin school in Taipei seems good, and I like most of the teachers. I have also made friends, Leo and Julian. And Mom, Dad, and Aria stay to explore the city for a few days while I get settled, which is comforting.

On Sunday, I am invited by my host mom to go with her to a local church, and I accept because I think it will be a cool experience. In the end, it is awkward because it isn't a church at all. The service is at one of her friend's houses where they hold church every week. I am not used to going to church because I am not religious, plus everything is in Chinese, so I don't understand much that is going on. Even though I have taken two years of Mandarin, I haven't used it in a while, so it's rusty.

Luckily, I made plans with Leo and Julian to go to an arcade and watch a movie later in the afternoon, so I leave "church" a little early. I feel bad about that, but I really am not comfortable here. It just doesn't seem like the place for me.

Overall, the high parts of my first week in Taiwan have been meeting my new buddies and getting to explore the city. The low part is realizing that I'm not going to have a host mom who does much with me, so I really am on my own.

THE FAMILY MART GANG: TAIWAN/PHILIPPINES

To learn the language, you have to Live the Language

At the international arrivals terminal in Taipei, a man awaited us, holding up a sign that read, "Finn Almond." Even though I had been expecting it, the sight hit me like a gut punch. I took a deep breath and hitched on a smile. We waved and headed toward him.

"Mom, no crying, OK?" said Finn. "I am going to miss you all so much already. If you start crying, I might start with the waterworks too."

I raised onto my tip toes to kiss his cheek. "I promise. C'mon, let's get you set to go."

Randy headed to the ATM. "OK, buddy. Here's some money to get you started. The exchange rate is $30 New Taiwan Dollars (NTD) to $1 USD. I put 3,000 NTD on your debit card—about $100. If you need more, call me. I can add it remotely."

He handed a small wad to Finn, who pocketed the cash. "Thanks, Dad."

"And here's your passport. Don't lose it. We won't be able to leave in a month if you do."

"Got it."

"Tomorrow morning, when we meet you at your language school, we'll bring you a metro card and the spare iPhone loaded with a SIM card. You'll keep it for the month. Beyond that, I think you're set for now."

"Can I keep the iPhone after my month alone in Taiwan?"

Randy grinned. "Nice try. We'll discuss it after we see how this experience goes."

"I figured. But it was worth asking." Finn said. "Thanks, Dad."

Randy gave Finn a hug. "FaceTime us once you've settled into your homestay, OK?"

Finn nodded.

Aria reached into her pack and pulled out a bag of chocolates. "Here, Finny. This is for you. I'll miss you!"

"Aw, thanks, Aria. I'll miss you too. Love you all!"

Then he turned and walked with his driver into the drizzle of Taipei. He didn't look back. We watched until we couldn't see him anymore then turned to gather our bags and head out ourselves. We would be parting ways for the next month as we left Finn in Taiwan to live with a local family and take an immersive Mandarin language course.

THE FAMILY MART GANG: TAIWAN/PHILIPPINES

In many ways, this was the culmination of our worldschooling efforts and travel to date. He wasn't the kid who startled at noises in the medinas of Morocco from the start of our travels. After ten months on the road, our fourteen-year-old could navigate big cities on his own, figure out public transportation systems, and manage local currency conversions with ease. He ate just about anything and could sleep anywhere. He was resilient and able to roll with change.

I was going to miss him over the next four weeks, but I knew he would be good. He had this. He was ready.

When we first started planning Finn and Aria's worldschooling, we felt confident in our abilities to keep them on track in most subjects. Chinese, though, was another story. Having taken two years of Mandarin at school, Finn wanted to continue. It was his favorite elective and, while he could drop a level as it wasn't a mandatory subject, he preferred to track his cohort. We knew that this would require intensive lessons beyond what a language app could provide to bridge the year and prepare him for the school's placement exam.

Upon arriving in Asia, we initially considered China for Finn's Mandarin studies but faced visa challenges as Americans. Additional research led us to LTL—Live the Language—school, with locations in mainland China and Taiwan. Taiwan, a sweet-potato shaped island off southeastern China's coast, presented a compelling choice. It offered Mandarin immersion, a fascinating history, natural beauty, and a safe environment for Finn's solo stay.

We corresponded with LTL, arranging for Finn to stay with a local host near New Taipei City. We weren't particularly encouraged to meet his host family, so we did not, letting him experience that on his own and setting the stage for his month of independence and learning. We did plan to tour the school and meet his teachers the day after arriving.

After Finn left with his driver, Randy, Aria, and I hopped on the metro to check into our hotel. Our plan was to explore Taipei and surrounding areas for a week while making sure Finn settled in smoothly. Then, we would fly to the Philippines, and we'd reunite a month later.

CHAPTER 22

"This feels so weird without Finn!" Aria squealed as we settled into our room. It had two queen beds and felt oddly spacious for the three of us. She took a running leap and splayed out like a starfish on one of the beds. "It is nice to get my own bed, though. Finn kicks!"

That evening, we did a video call with Finn. He showed us his small but functional room in the homestay apartment, located in a suburb of Taipei. It had a bunk, a desk, and a closet. Down the hallway was a communal bathroom.

"How does your host mom seem?" I asked. "Are there any kids or is it just her?"

"She seems . . . quiet. She didn't say much. Just served dinner to me and left. I don't think she speaks English, and my Chinese is still pretty rubbish. So, I ate alone. I didn't see kids."

"Well, it's the first night," I replied, though I felt a knot tighten in my stomach. "Hopefully, it'll get better. Are there any other boarders?"

"Not sure."

"What'd you have for dinner?" Aria wanted to know.

Finn flopped on the bottom bunk. "Noodles with fish."

"Ugh."

"No, it was good. I like fish."

"Are you excited for your first day at LTL tomorrow?" I asked.

"Yeah. A little nervous but also excited."

I nodded, but before I could answer, Aria grabbed my phone and superimposed animal faces onto our chat, transforming herself into a rooster. Finn followed suit, giving himself a purple octopus head. The conversation devolved into incoherent cackling, and I left them to it.

"We'll see you at LTL at 10 a.m.," Randy interjected after a while. "Do you know how you'll get to school?"

"Not yet," Finn, the octopus, replied. "I think my host mom might be coming in with me, but I'm not sure. I'll figure it out. I think it's thirty minutes by subway."

"That sounds right. We'll see you tomorrow. Love you!"

"Love you too!" The octopus clicked off, and the screen went blank.

❖ ❖ ❖

It was raining again when we headed out the next morning. We stopped at a Family Mart—a popular convenience store found on nearly every corner—and bought umbrellas since the forecast was calling for daily rain. Then we caught the train to the Da'an district of Taipei.

The LTL Mandarin School's cheerful yellow and blue sign stood out against the gray residential street. It proclaimed, "To Learn the Language, You Have to Live the Language."

The reception area was warm and homey, with a tidy kitchenette, communal table and chairs, and a whiteboard with messages scribbled in Mandarin, English, German, and Italian. A plush yellow lion with big blue glasses—the school's mascot—sat atop the water cooler, under a sign promoting free bubble tea.

As we entered, friendly faces looked up and smiled. Finn was already there, sitting at the table, engrossed in a new Chinese workbook. His face brightened when he saw us, and I immediately went over for a hug.

"Ah, you must be Finn's family," the woman behind the reception desk said as she rose, smiling. "I'm Rionna. We've been eagerly awaiting your visit."

"It's nice to finally meet you," Randy said. "We're excited to see the school and get a sense of what Finn will get up to over the next month."

Rionna showed us around the school, with large classrooms for group learning and smaller nooks for private lessons. She went over Finn's schedule: daily two-hour individual lessons followed by four-hour group classes.

Before we left, we made sure Finn had everything he needed.

"Here's your metro card," Randy said, handing it to Finn. "It's preloaded and works as a debit card in local stores."

"And this is for you," I added, giving him a compact umbrella. "Fingers crossed the weather will clear up. But if not, you can stay dry."

"We'll be in Taipei a few more nights," Randy reminded Finn. "Text if you want to grab dinner after class."

Finn nodded, slid his metro card into his wallet and stuffed the umbrella into his faded gray daypack, then said goodbye and walked with his teacher to start his first set of lessons.

CHAPTER 22

The next few days in Taipei, a city of around 2.5 million, were a blur of exploration for us. Simultaneously, we got frequent updates from Finn. He was clearly enjoying his newfound independence and the novelty of having a phone. I was in the midst of admiring the intricate street art in the Ximending District when my phone rang.

"Hi, Mom!"

"Hey buddy, how's it going?"

"Great! Just finished morning lessons. Now I'm off to a stationery store."

"That's cool. Need something for class?"

"Yeah, I need a notebook for Chinese."

"Makes sense. Are you walking there?"

"Nope, I'm renting a U-bike. Just downloaded the app myself."

I could hear the distinctive click of a bike lock and the rustle of movement in the background. "Hang on. Okay, got the bike! I'll call you back in a bit."

"Sounds good. Be careful in traffic, okay?"

"I will. Bye!"

I smiled, returning my attention to the murals.

Fifteen minutes later, my phone pinged with a message from Finn. He had reached the stationery store and found what he was looking for. The photo he attached showed a notebook cover with a world map in sepia tones, prominently featuring Taiwan and neighboring countries. The words "To Travel Is to Live" stood out in bold English and Mandarin characters.

I texted back, "Love it! Perfect for you!"

"Yep. Talk to u later!"

On his first two nights in Taipei, Finn ate breakfast and dinner at his homestay, which was part of the lodging package. On our second-to-last night in the city, though, we met up for dinner at Din Tai Fung. This famous Taiwanese dumpling and noodle chain is renowned for its *xiao long bao*, pork-filled steamed dumplings with a rich soup broth.

Since Finn's journey from school to the restaurant via public transit took forty-five minutes, we put our names on the waiting list and passed the time exploring a nearby mall. When he arrived, there seemed a noticeable change about him—like he had grown taller or simply walked more confidently—despite it being just two days since we'd last seen him.

Over dinner, Finn told us about his experiences thus far. His group class included two other students: Leo, a twenty-year-old from France, and Julian, a twenty-two-year-old German. Both were studying Mandarin for three months and approaching their final weeks. The three of them had quickly become friends.

"We grab lunch together most days at the Family Mart and are planning to get together on the weekend to do something," said Finn.

"That's awesome. And how's your host mom? Any more talkative or outgoing?" I asked.

"No," Finn shook his head. "She's pretty quiet."

"Is there a host dad, or any other family members?"

"Not that I've seen. There may be other students staying there, but they're older and have different schedules."

"At least you've got Leo and Julian," I said.

"Yeah, and there's always something happening at night with the school. They do group outings to arcades, bowling, movies—it's cool."

Our conversation paused when our number flashed on the LED display at Din Tai Fung. Finn ordered water for us in Mandarin, along with a variety of specialties: steamed buns, crispy pot stickers with spicy sauce, and the famous soup dumplings. For dessert, we ordered hot chocolate truffles enveloped in mochi and dumpling wrappers, which Aria declared the best things she'd ever eaten.

After our meal, we stepped out into a clear night. We said goodbye to Finn, who headed toward his bus stop, while we walked in the opposite direction to our hotel.

On our last morning in Taipei, Randy, Aria, and I headed to the Chiang Kai-shek Memorial Hall. We arrived a few minutes before the changing of the guards. In front of the massive statue of the former Chinese leader, Randy gave Aria an overview of Taiwan's complicated history.

"In the 1600s, Taiwan was a Dutch colony. About forty years later, the Chinese took control. After China lost a war in the 1800s, Taiwan was given to Japan. But when Japan lost World War II in 1945, China took Taiwan back."

"That sounds like a lot of changes for Taiwan," Aria noted.

"Yep. And then there was more turmoil. In China, a civil war broke out. Chiang Kai-shek, the leader whose memorial this is, fought against Mao Zedong's Communists. Mao won, and Chiang Kai-shek fled to Taiwan, where he ruled for many years. This history is why China and Taiwan have such a tense relationship today. China sees Taiwan as a part of it that broke away and wants it back."

"But what about Taiwan?" she asked curiously.

"Taiwan doesn't agree. They say they've never been part of modern China, which started in 1949 under Mao. They have their own constitution and leaders. So, it's complex. There's no clear right or wrong, and few countries officially recognize Taiwan because China puts pressure on them. It's a delicate situation."

"Huh," she said, taking this all in, then fell silent as the two guards flanking the statue began to move. We watched as two new guards, clad in navy uniforms, filed in, somberly and slowly, to take their place in a meticulously executed ceremony.

That afternoon, we explored Lungshan Temple, in the bustling heart of the capital. Built in the 1700s, this temple, originally Buddhist, now embraced a mix of Taoist, Buddhist, and Confucian traditions. It was a sanctuary for over a hundred deities, each with a unique story—from the scholarly god of literature to the revered god of war, patron of police and gangsters.

As we stepped inside, the air was thick with incense and the murmur of prayers. People approached the altars with red wooden blocks called *jiaobei*. We watched an old woman intently toss her crescent-shaped blocks to the ground, seeking answers from the gods.

Aria's eyes lit up with recognition. "It's just like in *The Astonishing Color of After!*" she exclaimed. The novel we were reading, set in Taiwan, had described this custom. Worshippers would first introduce themselves to a deity, ask a yes-or-no question, and then cast the *jiaboei* like spiritual dice. The orientation of the blocks upon landing was believed to reveal the god's wisdom.

"Which way do they want the blocks to land?" Aria whispered.

"I guess it depends on their question and what they're hoping to find out," I murmured, equally captivated. "But no matter what, I think they're looking for comfort or direction."

"Me, too," she replied, her voice a blend of wonder and thoughtfulness, as we continued to observe the traditions playing out in the temple's time-worn halls.

Our day ended at Raohe Night Market, bustling with food vendors and an array of smells. Aria wrinkled her nose at the pungent aroma hanging heavy in the humidity.

"Is that stinky tofu?" she asked.

Finn, joining us, grinned. "Yeah, my teacher says it's an acquired taste. Want to try?"

"No way," Aria responded quickly.

"How about you, Mom? Will you try it?"

"You first, Finn." He shook his head, and we walked on.

We tried various local delicacies from the dozens of vendors lining the street, green scallion pancakes, Taiwanese pork belly buns, grilled corn with zesty seasoning, pancake fried chicken, and soup dumplings.

Hanging heavy in the air was the unspoken knowledge that we'd be saying goodbye this time for a while, as Randy, Aria, and I would leave Taipei the next morning to explore the central mountains then fly to the Philippines, while Finn stayed to complete his studies.

We walked to the metro station and boarded a train together a few minutes later. At his stop, Finn gave us all one last hug before stepping onto the quiet platform. He sat down on a bench and kept waving to us as our doors closed and our train pulled away and out of sight.

CHOOSING AN INTENSIVE LANGUAGE IMMERSION PROGRAM FOR YOUR CHILD

Selecting an intensive language immersion program for your child can offer a unique opportunity to enhance their linguistic skills and cultural understanding, but it can also be daunting. Here are some tips for navigating the decision:

- *Define Language Goals*: Determine what level of language proficiency your child wants to achieve. This will help in selecting a program that aligns with current skills and goals.
- *Program Reputation and Accreditation*: Research the program's credibility and success rate. Look for accredited ones with strong testimonials and proven track records.
- *Cultural Immersion Opportunities*: Choose a program that not only teaches the language but offers opportunities for immersion in local culture, traditions, and daily life.
- *Safety and Support Services*: Prioritize programs with robust safety measures and student support systems. Ask about handling of emergencies and ongoing support.
- *Accommodation Options*: Check whether the program offers homestay, dormitory, or independent living arrangements, and decide what's best for your child.
- *Consider Program Intensity*: Assess course intensity (e.g., one on one or group, number of hours, additional practice) to ensure it matches your child's learning style and stamina.
- *Financial Planning*: Budget for tuition, living expenses, and travel. Explore financial aid, scholarships, or grants that the program might offer.
- *Pre-Departure Language Preparation*: If possible, have your child start learning the language before departure. Language apps can be great—and inexpensive—for this.
- *Facilitate Independence*: Prepare your child for the experience of living abroad. Discuss and practice skills in independence, self-care, and problem-solving.
- *Regular Communication*: Make sure you arrange for regular updates, balancing the need to stay in touch with allowing your child to immerse in the experience.

Excerpt from Finn's Journal
May 21, 2023 | Taipei, Taiwan

WEEK 2
Over the weekend, Leo, Julian and I take a trip to the ocean. It's not very nice. There's weird foam on the beach, and it's littered with garbage. We get yelled at by a guard to get back from the sea because there is a tsunami warning. So that is scary. To top it off, at night when I head home, it's creepy walking through the alleyway to my homestay apartment. Frogs keep jumping at me in the dark, and the large spiderwebs on the walls creep me out.

On the plus side, this week at LTL, we're doing a lot of work on speaking Mandarin instead of just reading and writing. I like most of my teachers, except for one. She seems disappointed every time we take too long to answer a question and acts exasperated, like we have taken Chinese for years and are fluent and just acting stupid. The other teachers are great and helpful though.

Having Leo and Julian in my classes makes them a lot of fun. Leo is five feet seven inches and quiet but always available to go out and do stuff. Julian is five feet eleven inches. He is rarely available to hang out, but he is very nice. For lunch, the three of us almost always go to the Family Mart. I usually get gyozas and a chocolate M&M bar. After school, we play laser tag, watch movies, or go to the arcade. I try stinky tofu with some of my classmates one night at a night market. It is disgusting. The taste itself isn't horrible, but that smell makes it awful.

For breakfast and dinner at my homestay, it is still super awkward. I always sit by myself. So, I usually watch a show while eating. I try not to be home too much. Luckily, school and hanging out with my friends takes up most of my days anyway.

After saying goodbye to Finn, the rest of us caught a train south then rented a car to explore the foothills of Taiwan's central mountain range. At the Wen Wu temple by Sun Moon Lake, we got out to explore. I heard the tinkle of bells and went to investigate. Hanging in strands by the shrine, from every railing, even from the branches of a nearby tree were thousands of tiny golden bells. Each carried a plaque with crimson tassels and engraved with an inscription in Chinese characters.

I used Google Translate to understand the messages. One said, "For a happy marriage"; another, "For a prosperous career"; and another, "For good luck after graduation."

I lingered, mesmerized by the glinting bells, carrying peoples' wishes on the wind. In front of the main shrine, I closed my eyes for a second and sent up a mental wish for Finn to have a great month on his own, just in case anyone was listening.

"This doesn't feel right," Randy muttered from the driver's seat several hours later. "I'm going to turn around. Can you take a picture of that road sign we passed and use Google Translate to see what it says?"

We had continued east from the temple and arrived around twilight on a lonely road in the mountains. Thick fog hung heavy around us. We hadn't seen any other cars for a while, and the road had narrowed to one lane. It was unclear whether we were going the right way. Every street sign was in Chinese and, while some symbols were universal, many were unclear to us.

Randy made a U-turn. I translated a large road sign, but it didn't help. "Just truck guidelines," I said.

Randy pulled up to a ramshackle-looking building. "I'm going to check with the police." An officer, looking startled by our nighttime visit, communicated with Randy through messages typed and translated on Randy's phone. Randy conveyed to him that we were trying to get to Hualien, and asked if we were on the right road. The officer's reply revealed a crucial detail we'd missed: the road to Hualien was closed due to a collapse.

"Wow," I said, absorbing the news. "Looks like we're staying here tonight."

Aria, from the backseat, asked, "Where is here?"

"Good question. Let's figure it out," Randy replied, already pulling up a map.

We found a basic hotel, its rooms cold but equipped with electric blankets. "Reminds me of Nepal," Aria said happily, snuggling into the warmth.

"Dinner time," I cajoled, despite her protests to stay in bed.

There wasn't much in the tiny mountain town we'd landed in. But we found a local stand still open and grabbed a quick noodle dinner. The next morning, after a conversation with the hotel owner, who spoke a little English, we learned that the road was partially open for repairs and that we could, in fact, make it through during the day. We set out again, this time under clearer skies and joined by other vehicles, a reassuring sign.

After a few hours, we made it past the spot where huge landslides had taken out part of the road, and we continued toward Taroko National Park.

Marble cliffs plunged into a turquoise river that snaked along, past mountainsides dotted with cedar and pines. Near the north end of the gorge, we rounded a bend and spotted the red roofs of a beautiful shrine built into the cliff face above a waterfall. We hiked across the old Changchun bridge, descended a dank stairway, then walked through a narrow tunnel until we arrived at the temple. Called the Eternal Spring Shrine, it was built to commemorate the workers who died while constructing the highway. It was one of the most stunning spots I had ever seen.

Our final stop was the old mining town of Jiufen, with its narrow, cobbled streets and a unique blend of Japanese and Chinese influences. Perched on a mountainside, Jiufen offered panoramic views of the sea, its streets lined with teahouses and lanterns. At the Amei Tea House, we partook in a traditional tea ceremony. Aria carefully watched the intricate practice of serving tea, then took over, refilling our glasses with a flourish.

That evening, we video-called Finn. He regaled us with stories from recent days, from visiting Taipei 101, Taiwan's tallest building, to spending time at the batting cages and trying stinky tofu.

"Really?" I was impressed. It had smelled like death. "What did you think?"

"It . . . wasn't good, I'm not gonna lie. It didn't taste that terrible at first, but then you get the smell of it in your nostrils, it is not so great."

"Well, I'm proud of you for trying it. You're getting the whole Taiwanese experience!"

"Will you try it when you come to pick me up?"

"We'll see," I replied, noncommittally.

CHAPTER 22

Excerpt from Finn's Journal
May 28, 2023 | Taipei, Taiwan

WEEK 3
On Monday morning, I wake up feeling awful. I'm nauseous and cold even though it's 90 degrees F outside. I text Rionna to ask her to tell my teachers that I'm going to be out. Then I spend the day sleeping. On Tuesday, I still don't feel great, so I stay home again. I feel sad to miss two days of class. Even though I still have another two weeks of school, it's Leo and Julian's final week. They go bowling with our other classmates on Tuesday night. I wish I could have joined for that. (On the plus side, Leo texts to ask if I have been kidnapped or murdered since I have been out for a couple days. It's nice to know that he's concerned.)

It's tough to be sick in this homestay. My host mother tells me to stay in my room, so I don't spread germs. That makes it stuffy and lonely. For two days, the best part of my time is going out to the 7-Eleven around the corner for lunch, where at least I can get fresh air.

By Wednesday, I feel better and am happy to be out again. Leo, Julian, and I go to the movies to watch The Fast and Furious 10, *which is great, but I get in major trouble with Mom for being out till 1 a.m. and not texting to let her know where I am.*

"I feel kind of bad hanging out on a beach in the Philippines while poor Finn is sick miles away," I said. "I wish his homestay mom were more comforting."

"Yeah," Randy said. "Not to sound like the dad in *Calvin and Hobbes*, though . . . it is character building. And overall, it sounds like he's having a good time. Maybe not today, but in general."

"I know. It's just hard to hear that he feels crummy when we're apart."

Randy, Aria, and I had flown from Taipei to Cebu City then caught a ferry to Camiguin, a sleepy, pear-shaped island in the Bohol Sea. Nicknamed the "Island Born of Fire," Camiguin is home to seven volcanoes, waterfalls, springs, white sand beaches, and Spanish-era churches.

For the next two weeks, the three of us were island hopping, continuing our worldschooling with Aria in another new-to-us culture. We chose the Philippines because its proximity to Taiwan meant we were only a three-hour flight away should any emergency arise. It was also a country we'd never been to before, an archipelago of more than seven thousand islands in the Pacific Ocean. The country's official slogan is, "It's More Fun in the Philippines," and my belief in that reality was tempered only by a tiny tinge of guilt for the teen we'd left behind.

"We love you, Finn," I texted. "Hope you feel better soon. Talk tonight."

"*Xièxiè*," he wrote back. It meant "thank you" in Mandarin.

While Finn filled his days with Chinese lessons—after recovering from his cold—we rented a motor scooter to explore the lush island of Camiguin. One afternoon, we drove up a steep hillside to the Hibok-Hibok Volcano Observatory. The small blue building housed exhibits and information on the Pacific ring of fire's volcanic activity. Inside, we learned about Hibok-Hibok, an active stratovolcano with a history of eruptions, the most recent in 1953.

"Isn't it risky living near an active volcano?" Aria asked one of the resident scientists.

"No worries," he reassured her. "We monitor it closely."

Later that evening, we were cuddled into bed. Aria was reading a new worldschooling book, a young-adult novel called *Patron Saints of Nothing*. Set in the Philippine capital, Manila, it is a coming-of-age story set against the backdrop of President Duterte's controversial war on drugs, which started in 2016. I texted Finn to see what he was up to and say good night.

9:00 p.m., me—"*Finn, did you have a nice day?*"

9:01 p.m., Finn—"*Yeah. I'll be home 10:45-ish. We just ordered dinner. And I'm a ways away.*"

9:03 p.m., me—"*You're out late. OK, text me when you get home. Love you tons!*"

10:45 p.m., me—"*Finn, you almost home?*"

11:30 p.m., me—"*Finn, are you still not back home?*"

11:45 p.m., me—"Hello???"

11:46 p.m., me—"Finn?"

12:15 a.m., me—"Finn, text me when you get this!"

I poked Randy, who had gone to sleep. "Wake up. I still haven't heard from Finn. It's past midnight."

"Mmm . . . Well, what do you want me to do about it? He's out with his buddies."

"I know that, but I want to be sure he's safe. I asked him to text when he gets home."

Randy rolled over, mumbling. "So, he's probably not home yet."

"Right, but it's past midnight, and he's fourteen years old. We wouldn't be OK with him staying out past midnight in Colorado, let alone in a foreign country."

"But we're not home in Colorado. We're in the Philippines. And he's in Taiwan. What do you want me to do right now?"

I sat up in frustration. "At least be concerned so we're anxious together!"

Aria popped her head up from the bed next to us. "Is everything all right, Mama?"

"It's fine, go back to bed, honey. We're just waiting to hear from Finn."

"Is he OK?"

"Yes, I'm sure it'll be fine; it's just late."

Randy got up in a huff and grabbed his phone. He banged out a message.

12:45 a.m., Randy—"Yo, Finn. Text your mom back ASAP. She's wigging out."

I blew up. "Why do you have to lay this all on me? Why can't you tell him he needs to text us back because WE'RE wigging out?"

He lay back down. "Because I'm not wigging out. I'm sure he's fine."

"You know—" I started, then a new text came in.

1:02 a.m., Finn—"I'm so sorry for keeping you up late. Phone died so had to plug it in. I'm home now."

Randy smirked. "See? I told you he was fine."

I glared at him, gave Aria a kiss, and went to sleep in a huff.

❖ ❖ ❖

THE FAMILY MART GANG: TAIWAN/PHILIPPINES

Excerpt from Finn's Journal
June 2, 2022 | Taipei, Taiwan

WEEK 4
Since Julian and Leo finished their Mandarin lessons, I have private sessions all week, which is less fun. I do feel like I am learning a ton, though, and I submit my Mandarin placement test, so I'll know soon what level I can go back into at home in the fall.

One tough point of the week is, when I take a shower in the shared bathroom of my homestay, I step on a live rat. It's disgusting and makes me not want to take a shower there ever again. . . .

It helps seeing my family again on Thursday though! At the end of my last week, I feel a little sad since it's the end of my adventure in Taiwan, but also elated that I'm done, because my brain is hurting after six hours of Chinese classes daily.

Overall, my time in Taiwan has been an amazing experience. I have really, really enjoyed it. There were difficult times, but also a lot of high points. I won't rush back to Taiwan anytime soon, but I'd love to visit in the future. . . .

UPDATE: I find out that not only did I pass my Mandarin test, I skipped ahead three levels! I will be able to choose whether I rejoin my freshman class or study with the juniors. I am proud of that. All this work paid off.

"Come on, Mom, it's not *that* awful. It doesn't even taste like much if you tell your brain not to smell it."

We had returned to the night market on our last night in Taipei after reuniting with Finn, who finished his studies that morning. Rionna gave us the lowdown of the month.

"Finn, Leo, and Julian were inseparable," she said then added with a smile, "We called them 'The Family Mart Gang.' Every afternoon, the three of them would run over there at lunch to stock up on *gyozas* and big piles of snacks for their afternoon classes. Finn fit in so well and did great in his studies."

Later, at the night market, we did a last culinary circuit of Taiwan. I let Finn pull me to stand after stand and finally, laughingly, gave in when he implored me once more to try stinky tofu. It came in a cardboard carton with a dozen squares. I popped it open, trying not to sniff too deeply. I grabbed one of the dense squares with my chopsticks and took a tiny nibble.

"I feel like I need to plug my nose," I noted, chewing deliberately.

"It's supposed to a delicacy," Randy offered helpfully, though I noticed he didn't make any moves to try it himself.

"It's not . . . horrible," I said slowly. But then the flavor settled on my tongue, and I willed myself not to gag. "Oh, wait . . . No. Ugh, it's like I haven't brushed my teeth for ages."

I kept chewing, bravely trying to keep it down. "Well, I tried it—gah! I'm not gonna lie, that is a strong, awful flavor."

"Thanks for trying it, Mom," Finn said, grabbing my hand. "It's not my thing either."

I chugged soda to help wash the dirty-diaper taste out of my mouth.

"Come on," Finn gestured to the corner, where he had spotted a Family Mart. "Let's get Taiwanese treats for dessert; I'll show you my favorites!"

We let him pull us through the crowd, past the squid and scallion vendors, the stalls piled high with durian, pineapple, and mango, through the warm night air toward the neon lights of the convenience store.

He marched confidently ahead, and we were only too happy to follow, knowing he would steer us well and find us a sweet ending to our Taiwanese adventure.

ALMOND FAMILY REPORT CARD ON TAIWAN

- *Top Marks*: Discover Taipei's vibrant street art scene, sample local delicacies from vendors at a night market, explore historical sites like Chiang Kai-shek Memorial Hall, and engage in customs like traditional tea ceremonies.
- *Needs Work*: Urban density and language barriers can be overwhelming. Use translation apps and local guides for easier

navigation. Plan routes carefully to manage travel challenges, especially in rural areas outside Taipei.
- *Learning Tips*: Enhance your understanding of Taiwan with an immersive Mandarin language course and dive into its complex history through documentaries or books.

ALMOND FAMILY REPORT CARD ON THE PHILIPPINES

- *Top Marks*: Explore the Philippines' stunning beaches and underwater world through scuba diving or snorkeling. Island hopping and experiencing local festivals also highlight the cultural vibrancy of this diverse archipelago.
- *Needs Work*: Transportation can be unpredictable, requiring flexibility and patience with the laid-back island lifestyle and infrastructure.
- *Learning Tips*: Take advantage of the Philippines' status as a major English-speaking nation to enhance your visit. Chat with locals, known for their big, warm personalities, to gain deeper insights into their culture.

㉓

UNDERWATER CLASSROOM

Indonesia

Excerpt from Aria's Journal
June 8, 2023 | Bali, Indonesia

Today is a very school-focused day. I do math, science, P.E., reading, language, and writing. For math, I take two tests. They are end-of-year tests. After I finish those, I take a placement test to figure out if I'll be in Algebra A or Algebra B when I get back to Colorado. Algebra B is more advanced than A. For science, we watch a documentary about ways the environment is getting destroyed by careless humans causing global warming. We need to be more careful with our earth! For P.E. (or physical education) I swim in the pool. Best P.E. ever! Then I read the book Finn and I were assigned to read in Indonesia. It's called The Rainbow Troops. It's a very good book. For language, I work on my Spanish on Duolingo, and finally, last but not least, for writing I do a journal entry (this one!). To end the day, we walk past rice paddies to the beach. Finn and I body surf in the waves before dinner at a little restaurant near the beach. I order cheese ravioli. This is a terrible choice! Dad says I should know by now to order local specialties, and I agree with him. Tomorrow I'll get Nasi Goreng.

UNDERWATER CLASSROOM: INDONESIA

"All right, everyone, that's us," Randy called out. Our flight to Bali was boarding.

Aria had to be pried away from the guidebook; she was reading aloud about our destination, one of Indonesia's more than seventeen thousand islands between the Indian and Pacific oceans.

"Indonesia is the world's largest Muslim-majority nation, the third largest democracy, and the fourth most populous country," she recited while lining up at the gate. "The official language is Indonesian; the capital is Jakarta. Bali is the only Hindu-majority province in Indonesia.

"Ooh, and it says here that Indonesia is home to vast wilderness areas," she continued, "which support one of the world's highest levels of biodiversity above and below the sea."

Finn pumped his fist. "I'm excited to scuba dive again when we get to Flores!"

"Me, too," agreed Randy. "But for now, let's catch our plane to Bali."

Stepping outside into the airport in Denpasar, Bali's capital city, we were greeted by a blast of tropical heat. "Welcome to the island of gods," Randy said.

Our first stop in the Southeast Asian archipelago was Ubud, a cultural haven in Bali's uplands surrounded by verdant rice paddies and dense forest. Once a quiet mecca for hippies seeking meditation, healthy foods, and solitude, Ubud was thrust onto the tourist trail in 2010 as the "Love" spot in Elizabeth Gilbert's *Eat, Pray, Love* bestseller.

After a day of exploring the town, lined with art galleries, Hindu temples, yoga studios, and organic cafés, we walked to the Pura Dalem temple to experience a traditional Balinese Kecak and fire dance. One of the island's most iconic performances, the "monkey chant" dance is an adaptation of the Sanskrit poem, Ramayana, which tells the story of King Rama who must save his kidnapped wife, Sita. The performance draws from themes from Sanghyang exorcism, an ancient ritual to repel evil spirits.

Against the dark night, a hundred men flowed in from the temple to sit around a statue lit with candles. Wearing checkered sarongs, they chanted and raised their arms toward the flames. They had no musical instruments, only the rhythms of the men clapping and intoning in sync as the story of Ramayana unfolded.

In the Sanghyang Jaran, a sacred Balinese trance dance, a man riding a hobbyhorse galloped around a bonfire made from coconut husks. Eyes closed, seemingly oblivious to the heat and flames, he kicked then trampled the hot coals, his bare feet pounding the ground and embers in a relentless stomp.

"He's not even flinching!" exclaimed Aria, eyes wide with a mix of fear and fascination.

Even as we leaned back from the heat emanating from the fire, the dancer continued his wild romp across the red-hot embers, spurred by the chanting of the men encircling him.

When the chorus stopped, the dancer collapsed, as if wrenched from his dream-like state. Chest heaving, his blackened feet splayed before him on the ground.

"Will he be OK?" Finn asked.

"I'm sure he will," I said. "This dance is a sacred tradition and part of the religious and artistic expression among the Balinese people. It's believed to invite the spirits to enter the dancer's body, which puts them into a trance. It dates to ancient times when it was believed that dance could end sickness and disease."

But I was a bit shaken too, and the memory of the dancer with blackened feet and heaving chest lingered in my thoughts long after.

In the center of Ubud, a dense forest of banyan and nutmeg trees is home to a thousand long-tailed macaques who roam freely among three ancient Hindu temples deep in the heart of the jungle. The Sacred Monkey Forest Sanctuary is both highly touristy and deeply holy, and for anyone who finds cantankerous, mischievous monkeys a hoot, it's a unique primate-watching experience.

"Keep your stuff close," Randy cautioned as we entered the forest. "Don't make eye contact with the monkeys. Put your sunglasses and anything dangling away so they're not tempted to steal them. And no feeding them."

We wandered the heavily wooded paths past fourteenth century temples thick with moss and entwined with tree roots, serene reminders of Bali's spiritual heritage. The original vision of the thirty-acre site was conservation and prayer in line with the traditional Hindu philosophy of life—*Tri Hita Karana,* or harmony between people, nature, and God. While vestiges of its sacred nature remain, since mass tourism took off on the island in the 1970s, the site has become overrun with visitors keener to feed and take selfies with the macaques than to commune with nature and the spiritual spaces. So, despite signs prominently warning not to touch or engage the primates, monkey assaults are common.

We sat on a bench in front of one of the temples, studying its stone facades and intricate carvings depicting scenes from Balinese mythology.

"Look at how detailed these carvings are," Randy said.

"I'm too distracted by the monkeys," commented Finn, pointing to one with a little mohawk, perched atop a stone gargoyle.

Suddenly, a terrified shout drew our attention. One brazen macaque leaped onto an Asian woman wearing a pastel yellow dress. With adept movements, the monkey scrambled up her skirt, onto to her shoulder, then launched itself off her head onto a low-hanging branch before vanishing into the dense underbrush.

"Wow, that was quick!" Finn exclaimed, impressed by the monkey's agility.

"What did I tell you—they're brazen," Randy said. "And they can be dangerous. But they're regarded with reverence, reflecting the Balinese belief in the sacredness of all creatures."

Aria looked doubtful and attached herself to us like a small burr, clearly not wanting to be next on the monkeys' list of human ladders. Her head on a swivel, she kept on the lookout for other wayward macaques as we wound our way through the park.

We spent our last few days in Bali at the beach in Seminyak, on the southern shore. One evening, the kids played at low tide on the wide, gray sand beach, doing cartwheels and handstands against the setting sun. Randy and I sat quietly and watched them, silhouetted against a tangerine sky. I let my mind wander.

Phrases like "when we're back home" had started to creep into our conversations in recent days. We found ourselves spending more time signing Finn and Aria up for fall soccer than booking our next Airbnb. We all shopped for small, local souvenirs for friends and family, now that we only had a few more weeks to carry them. Finn researched requirements for getting his learner's permit, eager to begin driving upon our return to Colorado.

As our year-long trip entered its final month, and we all started giving more mindshare to reentry, we still wanted to stay present and soak in the moments together on the road—like endless games of Bridge or Hearts over Indonesian lunches of *Nasi Goreng* (Balinese fried rice), chicken satay, and *krupuk* (prawn crackers common to Southeast Asia); aimless wandering amid the rice paddies; wrapping up worldschooling assignments and penning journal entries; and breathing in the sea air and wading in the waves of the Indian Ocean, in no hurry at all to be anywhere except where we were right then.

As Billy Joel said, "this is the time to remember, 'cause it will not last forever / these are the days to hold on to / 'cause we won't, although we'll want to."

UNDERWATER EXPLORATION: A GATEWAY TO MARINE LEARNING

Underwater exploration—whether through snorkeling, scuba diving, or marine observation—can offer educational adventures for families that don't have to break the bank. Here's what these activities offer:

- *Marine Biology Insight*: Get up-close with marine life, understanding their behaviors and ecosystems.
- *Conservation Awareness*: Learn about ocean conservation by observing the beauty and fragility of underwater habitats.
- *Climate Change Awareness*: See firsthand the impacts of climate change on marine environments.
- *Natural Diversity*: Experience the ocean's biodiversity, emphasizing the importance of preservation.

Budget-Friendly Tips for Parents:

- *Start with Snorkeling*: Affordable, accessible, and perfect for beginners.
- *Use Local Resources*: Local beaches are great for first experiences.
- *Educational Discussions*: Talk about the marine life and ecosystems encountered.
- *Observation Logs*: Encourage kids to record their findings in journals or sketchbooks.
- *Explore Diverse Environments*: Visit beaches, lakes, or aquariums for a range of experiences.
- *Supplement with Resources*: Enhance learning with videos, books, and apps.
- *Environmental Respect*: Teach the importance of respecting marine habitats.

On the island of Flores, one of the Lesser Sunda Islands in the eastern half of Indonesia, our worldschooling adventure took a deep dive, quite literally. We planned to spend several days scuba diving in Komodo National Park, part of the coral triangle known for its rich marine biodiversity.

Randy had booked us into bungalows at the Scuba Junkie resort on the edge of the national park. Every morning, we headed out on the dive boat and returned late in the afternoon after three dives at different spots in the area.

Each underwater experience was unique, from thrilling rock walls and challenging drift dives to muck dives, which at first seemed uninteresting but as we learned to train our eyes to look deeper, were rich with some of the ocean's most curious species. Across patches of sand, we spotted rare sea critters and tiny animals hiding in plain sight—nudibranchs and cuttlefish, pygmy seahorses, tiny shrimp and box-like cowfish, zebra crabs, and the fabulously named wunderpus, a little, spotted octopus like something from science fiction.

"That was the coolest thing ever," Finn said when we surfaced. "Like finding hidden treasure."

Our guide, Jaka, nodded. "The black sands here, which come from ancient lava streams, are rich in nutrients. They're home to hundreds of species not found anywhere else on the planet. . . . Everyone wants to see the big animals in the sea, but sometimes the tiny ones are the strangest and most fascinating. And since they're so hard to spot, it makes discoveries more memorable."

On one dive, we watched for long minutes as an octopus camouflaged itself against a coral. When he moved, we could spot his sleek body, but as soon as he reattached to the coral, he instantly assumed its rugged texture and color, blending seamlessly into the background. We delighted in a group of surgeonfish swimming playfully in our bubbles. And we were entranced by a feather star, which looked like a delicate flower swimming serenely along. Jaka told us the marine invertebrate dates back 200 million years and is considered a living fossil.

At the Cauldron, also known as the Shotgun, it felt like we descended into the heart of an underwater storm. The dive site is in an underwater channel that creates a strong, swirling current funneling between the two islands above. That creates a veritable playground for sharks, manta rays, and other marine life. After reaching our target depth, Jaka tethered us into a line attached to a rock wall to watch as dozens of reef sharks circled the cauldron in languid circles, just feet away from us.

Farther on, sea turtles burrowed into the coral or swam gracefully toward the surface, as though flying. And, just before we ascended, we spotted a huge manta ray—the largest ray in the world—glided along, its massive fins sweeping up and down like wings until it disappeared into the murkier waters.

"It's all like a real-life lesson in marine biology," Randy pointed out at the end of another packed dive day. Jaka nodded.

"Best job in the world, dive master," he said. "I learn new things every day. Want to know some life lessons from sea turtles?" Jaka asked Finn and Aria. They nodded eagerly.

"OK, here they are: (1) Sometimes you have to dig yourself out of a hole you didn't dig. (2) Make time for the beach. (3) Slow down. (4) Come out of your shell. (5) Age gracefully. (6) Life is better with a friend. (7) Enjoy the views. (8) Travel far."

He smiled at us. "I think you're well on your way."

In the evenings, to continue our immersion in nature and conservancy, we turned to legendary naturalist David Attenborough. Curled up on our bed as a family, we watched his documentary *A Life on Our Planet*. It's both an ode to the breathtaking diversity of earth's ecosystems and nature's beauty and a dire warning about the stark realities of climate change.

As Attenborough talked about vanishing landscapes and endangered species, we couldn't help but reflect on our recent scuba experiences.

"I feel so lucky to have seen what we saw underwater," Finn said, recalling the vibrant coral reefs and rich wildlife.

Aria, looking concerned, added, "Attenborough said those corals are dying because of the warming seas. That's scary."

The film left us all with a sense of awe, disquiet, and renewed responsibility. It emphasized that every action counts in preserving the planet's biodiversity. As we switched off the TV, Aria sat back, arms crossed. "We need to do more to help our planet."

Randy and I nodded. "Maybe you and Finn can spend time thinking about what those things can be. There's no doubt a lot more we can—and should—do."

Our last stop in Indonesia was to the remote island of Komodo, home to the legendary Komodo dragons, the largest lizards on earth.

"Remember, stay close and follow the guide's instructions," Randy told the kids, as we stepped onto the rugged island, a land seemingly lost in time. We walked past a wooden sign saying "Hati Hati Lintasan Komodo," which thankfully also had an English translation underneath: "Watch out Komodo Crossing." Approaching a white hut on the beach, we greeted a guide who was required to take us through the park.

He carried a six-foot long wooden staff, forked at the end.

"Is that in case a Komodo dragon charges us?" Finn wanted to know.

"Yes," the guide said simply and, I thought, not very reassuringly.

"Would that pole *actually* stop a big dragon from attacking us?" Aria pressed skeptically, clearly thinking as I was that it'd be like to trying to hold back a giant with a toothpick.

"Yes," he replied again, without bothering to elaborate.

As we continued along a path through the dry forest, on the lookout for dragons, he explained more about these huge lizards.

"They're considered dangerous but not deadly. Partly because they're ectotherms, which means they need to bask in the sun to recharge, like batteries. But even when their energy levels are full, they use most of that for mating and foraging. Primarily, they like to lounge."

"Finn," I said, swiveling to grin at him. "You may have found your spirit animal."

He ignored me.

"Look, there, there!" Our guide said in a whisper-shout, pointing to a lizard lazing in a shaft of sunlight beneath a den of gnarled mangrove branches. Its scaly skin, reminiscent of ancient armor, glistened as the creature lazily flicked its tongue, tasting the air.

"That's a little guy," he said of the six- or seven-foot beast. "You'll see bigger creatures inland. Come, let's continue into the forest."

As we trekked further, we saw a couple more dragons, one crashing through the underbrush, another half sleeping, half eyeing us in the shade. "They may look lazy, but they can run very fast when they need to," our guide cautioned, keeping a watchful eye.

We followed him along a sandy path while he talked more about the animals, which are endemic to the Indonesian islands of Komodo, Rinca, Flores, and Gili Motang. "Komodo dragons reach up to ten feet in length and weigh more than 150 pounds," he explained. "They have a unique hunting method, relying on their strong jaws, sharp claws, and a venomous bite."

We learned about their solitary nature, their powerful sense of smell, and their ability to consume large prey, like deer and water buffalo. "They can eat up to 80 percent of their body weight in one meal," the guide added.

Before reaching the wharf again, we spotted a baby dragon peeking out of a hole high in a hollow tree.

"Once they hatch, the young receive no protection or care from their mother," our guide said as we watched the tiny head peeking out from the hollow. "In fact, they must swiftly climb the nearest tree to escape being preyed upon by adult Komodo dragons, who see the hatchlings as an effortless snack. It's quite a harsh reality, isn't it?"

"Whoa," Aria said, and Finn nodded.

"Feeling pretty good about us as parents right now, aren't you?" I asked, smirking.

On the long boat ride back to Flores, I watched the kids napping on the wooden benches and recalled a couple quotes I had read from Attenborough that resonated with me.

"Bringing nature into the classroom can kindle a fascination and passion for the diversity of life on earth and motivate a sense of responsibility to safeguard it." I thought of Finn and Aria's indignation in seeing pockets of bleached coral under the sea, so washed out and devoid of life in comparison to the healthy coral reefs we had the privilege of diving through. Their anger at the idea of habitat destruction. Their incredulity and sense of wonder about the vast array of animals above and below the sea.

I hoped they'd remember the lessons learned on the road once we were back home, percolating and blooming over time. Because, as Attenborough says, "The final chapter is ours to write. We know what we need to do. What happens next is up to us."

> **ALMOND FAMILY REPORT CARD ON INDONESIA**
>
> - *Top Marks*: Located in the Coral Triangle, Indonesia is a diver and snorkeler's paradise, with some of the world's most pristine marine biodiversity. Sites like Komodo National Park or Raja Ampat are incredible underwater classrooms.
> - *Needs Work*: While Bali's allure is well earned, its popularity can lead to crowded experiences. With thousands of islands, advance planning is crucial to navigate Indonesia and discover its lesser-known gems.
> - *Learning Tips*: Delve into marine biology and participate in conservation initiatives with community guides to expand your appreciation of the local ecological diversity.

24

SEVENTH CONTINENT

Australia

Excerpt from Finn's Journal
June 24, 2023 | Port Stephens, Australia

This morning, we hop on a boat to go whale watching. Our first sighting is a blow in the distance. We take off toward it and suddenly see a whale breach. It is far off and hard to see clearly, so I feel a little disappointed at first that I mostly missed it . . . but luckily, it turns out there are two whales nearby. And they are super active! They show off and play near our boat. They breach and slap their fins and dive and jump right next to us for more than an hour!

When we get back to shore, we drive to a Koala Sanctuary, where we stay the night in a tent camp. The sanctuary is a huge area where they take care of sick or injured koalas and rehabilitate them in their natural habitat. We walk along a boardwalk to check out the koalas. Mostly, they're curled up in furry balls in the trees, asleep. But one, named Basil, is awake and munching on eucalyptus leaves. He's so cute. He and his mom, Rosemary, were brought to the sanctuary after they got trapped in the middle of a busy road. Basil's leg was injured, and his mom's arm broken when she was hit by a car. She ended up OK and was released back into the wild. Poor Basil's back leg has permanent damage, so the guide tells us he needs to climb three-legged. He'll never be able to be released, which I think is sad but also not too bad since he seems happy with his eucalyptus leaves and cozy home here.

"You know what I'm looking forward to in Australia?" I asked Finn and Aria as I set my seat to its upright position in preparation for landing in Sydney.

"No, what?"

"Spending *koala-ty* time together." I gave them a big, toothy grin. They don't even glance up from their iPads.

"No. We are not starting with the puns again," said Finn flatly. "The only thing worse than dad jokes are mom jokes."

"Fine. You'll *roo* the day you told me to stop, though."

Continuing to tune out my humor, they turned their attention out the windows as we touched down on the oldest, driest, and flattest continent in the world, home to some of the strangest and most fascinating animals on the planet. Our lessons in zoology and evolutionary biology were about to continue—this time, above the waves.

When the ancient supercontinent of Gondwana broke up hundreds of millions of years ago, one of the chunks that splintered off contained the landmasses of present-day Australia and Antarctica. By 30 million years ago, Australia had fully separated and drifted north. Its physical separation, coupled with land formation and climate changes, led to the unique flora and fauna found there today. More than 80 percent of its plants, mammals, reptiles, and frogs are endemic to the continent, found nowhere else on the planet.

"Can you think of any other places we have been in our travels where isolation brought about unique evolutions in plants and animals?" Randy asked.

"Komodo with its dragons. Oh, and the Galapagos!" Finn promptly replied.

"Yep," Randy said. "Do you remember learning about the naturalist Charles Darwin?"

They nodded, so Randy continued. "When he traveled to the Galapagos on the *Beagle* in the early 1800s, he noticed that the animals were similar from island to island, but with differences that made them perfectly suited to where they lived. That led him to think about the origin of species. As he observed the plants and animals, he began to wonder if they migrated from South America to the Galapagos and evolved as they adapted to their new environments. That idea—that species could change over time—led to his theory of evolution.

"One thing you might not know," added Randy, "is that Darwin *also* visited Australia on that round-the-world voyage. He studied the wildlife here too, like the duck-billed platypus, which was so crazy that British biologists thought it was a hoax. What Darwin saw here—along with his Galapagos observations—contributed to his theories years later on evolution."

Aria interjected, "I'd love to see a platypus. They do sound so bizarre."

At the top of our plans for our week in Australia was seeing and learning more about its native animals. Kangaroos and koalas were big draws, as were dingoes and wallabies. We were less enthusiastic about the deadly creepy-crawlies that sometimes get outsized billing, but we also knew the risk of being attacked by a dangerous snake, spider, or crocodile was small.

"We'll see what we see," Randy said. "For this afternoon, we're going to meet Katja at Manly beach. Exotic animals will need to wait for another day."

Manly, one of Australia's most famous beaches, is best known for hosting the world's first surfing contest in 1964. The stretch of golden shoreline, lined with towering Norfolk pines, spans 1.24 miles (2 km) from South Steyne to Queenscliff. There, a hidden reef, known as a bombora, generates the coveted waves that attract elite surfers. We walked along the boardwalk, feeling the cold wind against our faces. June is the start of winter in the southern hemisphere, and it was crisp along the shore. We watched the surfers and kayakers in the waves, undaunted by the cool temperatures.

We were excited to meet up with a friend of Randy's, Katja, who spent a year decades earlier as a high school exchange student in the United States and became close to his family. Originally from Germany, she had lived in Australia for years, and we were looking forward to exploring with her.

Tall, blond, and bubbly, she greeted us warmly and welcomed us to Australia. We wandered along the sand, catching up on twenty years' worth of news, then climbed the rocks overlooking Manly Beach to take in the sunset. Randy and Katja chatted while I found my mind drifting again, as it had in recent weeks.

Arriving in Australia felt like we had stepped one foot back home while the other was still on our travels. Being in an English-speaking country again, reuniting with an old friend, and experiencing a similar culture felt deeply familiar but with subtle differences. It was like looking at a doppelgänger you recognized but knew from the subtle nuances wasn't the original.

Increasingly now, we were starting to think in terms of "lasts." Last time we'd struggle with a language barrier. Last haircut in a hole-in-the-wall shop or from someone right off the street. Last toilet-shower bathroom combo or outhouse (that one we wouldn't miss). Last virtual math chapter to complete. Last major foreign city we'd explore, at least on this adventure.

Knowing our trip was winding down made me appreciate each experience more. I snapped a photo of Finn, sitting on a rock by himself, gazing out at the waves. Then I snapped one of Aria tilting her head back, mid-belly laugh; and then a selfie of Randy, Katja, and me. I wanted to capture it all—the sensation of the wind against our cheeks; the sound of the waves against the breakwater and the caws of the gulls circling overhead; the salty scent of the sea; the heady sense of freedom; and the gift of time. After taking one more photo of the setting sun over the surf, I pulled myself back to the present to rejoin the conversation.

ENRICHING FAMILY TRAVEL: CONNECTING WITH FRIENDS AND FAMILY ON THE ROAD

Connecting with friends, family, and old acquaintances around the globe can deeply enrich a journey of any length. Here's how to enhance your adventure with these meaningful interactions:

- *Coordinate with Loved Ones:* Plan parts of your trip with friends or family. Shared experiences can strengthen bonds and create lasting memories.

- *Reconnect with Old Friends Abroad*: Meeting up with friends in the countries you visit adds a personal touch and local perspective to your travels.
- *Enjoy Diverse Cultural Insights*: Engaging with people—especially friends and family—from different backgrounds broadens your children's understanding of the world.
- *Share Responsibilities and Costs*: Traveling with others can lighten the load, from childcare to splitting costs on accommodation and transportation.
- *Offer Emotional Support*: Having a familiar network nearby can be reassuring, particularly in unfamiliar settings.
- *Explore New Activities*: Friends or family might introduce you and your children to unique activities or destinations, enhancing your travel experience.

We spent the next few days exploring Sydney and taking in its iconic sights, like the world-famous opera house at the mouth of Sydney Harbor and Circular Quay, which was the landing site for the first ships carrying European convicts to Australia. We wandered around the fabulously named Woolloomooloo Bay and Finger Wharf, the longest wooden-piled wharf in the world. We watched people play chess in Hyde Park, then walked along its southern edge to the ANZAC Memorial, honoring the Australians who fought and died in World War I.

"I could see living in Australia someday," said Finn. "I really like Sydney."

"It is a very livable city," I agreed.

A few days later, we headed north in our rental car toward Port Stephens. The seaside town, about two and a half hours from Sydney, is a renowned whale watching destination located in the middle of Australia's "Humpback Highway." From May to November, tens of thousands of humpbacks, southern right whales, blue whales, and orcas travel along Australia's east coast on a massive migration from Antarctica to give birth and raise their young in the warmer waters.

On a cool, clear morning, we boarded a cruise vessel called the Hinchinbrook Explorer and motored into the bay. Bundled up in multiple layers against the biting wind, we stood with other passengers at the bow of the ship, scanning the horizon. Not long after we entered the open ocean, we spotted a pair of humpbacks on the starboard side.

The duo swam close to the ship, breaching in tandem like synchronized swimmers excited for an audience. They lay on their sides and raised long pectoral fins high into the air, then slammed them onto the surface, sending up plumes of frothy white water. The ship's guide explained that this was how whales communicate with each other.

"The females slap their fins to attract males. And pairs of whales, like these two, may 'pec slap' as part of their mutual flirtation. You're lucky to witness a show like this, especially at such a close range."

Every few minutes, a collective "ooh" rose from the decks as we watched, entranced, as the massive creatures launched themselves again and again into the sky, their black bodies punching up against the blue, then crashing under the waves again. The sea would turn still for long minutes, and we'd think they dove deep, before we spotted a tail or fin or full-body breach as the show continued.

On our return trip past Cabbage Tree Island, we spotted fur seals sunning themselves on the rocks and swimming in the shallows. And, just as we were about to head back into the harbor, a playful pod of bottlenose dolphins darted up and kept pace with us for a while, leaping and splashing alongside our hull, as though racing the ship.

"That was amazing," Aria said as we disembarked, her face shining from the wind.

"Unbelievable," I agreed. "It's hard to imagine humans hunting humpbacks, isn't? Did you hear the guide say that, in the 1960s, the global population of humpbacks was only around five thousand because of commercial whaling? Good to hear that the humpback populations have mostly recovered and aren't a threatened species anymore."

Aria nodded, thoughtfully. "Much better to watch than attack them."

"Agreed."

"Mom, look! A koala crossing sign!" Finn called out, tapping my shoulder from the backseat. He knew that I loved taking photos of all the different wildlife crossing signs we saw in different countries. I had built up quite a collection—oryx, eland, zebra, giraffe, and elephant crossing signs across Africa; a camel crossing in Jordan; guanaco in Chile; bear in Japan; sheep and monkey in Taiwan; kangaroo in Sydney . . . and now, a koala crossing sign.

We glanced around eagerly to see if we might spot the real thing.

"I wonder how often you see koalas in the wild," Aria mused.

"The website for the koala sanctuary said it's not super common. Kangaroos, snakes, and spiders are often spotted in the bush. But koalas, not so much."

We were headed to the Port Stephens Koala Sanctuary and hospital, a facility dedicated to the rehabilitation, preservation, and conservation of koalas in the wild. We pulled onto the property, set on twenty acres of bushland. Our glamping tent for the night was set on a raised wooden platform and had a deck that overlooked the expansive property.

As we explored the grounds, a kookaburra, perched on a low wooden fence, fixed me with an intense glare. The native bird, known for its distinctive "laughing" call, seemed to be sizing us up, and I was afraid it was finding me lacking.

"Watch it," Randy warned. "He doesn't look happy to see you."

I gave the bird a wide berth, feeling its sharp gaze follow me as we wandered toward the koala enclosures.

"They're so cute," Aria murmured, wide-eyed. The koalas nestled high into the treetops, tucked into nooks, or hidden among clumps of eucalyptus were hard to spot from the skyway. "Look, I see one! This sign says he's named Solstice! What a sweet little guy."

The next morning, we met one of the sanctuary's guides for an early morning immersive "walk and talk" to learn more about koala behavior, their habitat, and conservation efforts.

"Are they bears?" Aria wanted to know.

The guide shook her head. "No, even though they're sometimes called 'koala bears,' they are marsupials—mammals that have pouches for the development of their offspring."

"Look, that one's awake!" Aria whispered excitedly as we traversed the wooden walkway again, pointing at a koala munching on eucalyptus leaves. Most of the marsupials were asleep, so it was thrilling to find one awake and having breakfast.

"Koalas can eat a pound or more of eucalyptus leaves every day. Eucalyptus is toxic, so their digestive systems work hard to digest it, extracting the needed nutrients. That's why koalas sleep so much—up to twenty hours a day," the guide said.

Finn nodded appreciatively. "That's my kind of lifestyle."

The guide went on to talk about conservation efforts for koalas in Australia. "There are many threats we're trying to address, from habitat loss to disease, and climate change. Conservation initiatives include preserving and expanding koala habitats, planting eucalyptus trees, and creating wildlife corridors for safe movement. Sanctuaries like this one play an important role in rehabilitating injured koalas and raising public awareness about their plight. Community involvement in conservation efforts, along with government policies aimed at protecting koala habitats, are key to ensuring their survival."

We stayed for a while longer after the tour ended, captivated by the koalas engrossed in their breakfast routines: pulling a branch to their nose with a forepaw, sniffing it, then munching one leaf at a time, unhurriedly until eventually we walked on.

Before returning to Sydney, we made one last stop at Featherdale Wildlife Park, home to the largest collection of Australian animals in the world. A cacophony of bird calls greeted us as we entered the park, echoing through the gum trees. In the distance, we could make out the laughter of kookaburras. "They're following you," Randy teased me.

An earthy scent of eucalyptus and pine floated on the breeze. We strolled through the enclosures, the kids crying out as they saw animals they recognized from books or movies.

"Look, a Tasmanian devil!" Finn shout-hissed to Randy and me, trying to keep his voice down as he pointed toward the squat, thick creature. It looked more like a rat than I imagined, not surprisingly resembling nothing like its Looney Tunes namesake.

"Check it out," Finn read from a placard. "The Tasmanian devil is the world's largest carnivorous marsupial. It got its name from early European settlers who heard its unearthly screams and growls from the bush. When they finally found the dog-like animal with red ears and sharp teeth, they called it 'The Devil.' Cool!"

The park's collection of wallabies, wombats, dingoes, emus, penguins, reptiles, and birds captivated us for hours, along with other animals we'd never heard of like quokkas, bilbies, echidnas, and cassowaries. But nothing was quite as exciting as the animal Finn and Aria had been most looking forward to seeing: kangaroos.

"Ohhh, it looks like we can actually feed these," Aria noted, watching as other visitors bought cups of pellets for the kangaroos, who hopped over to eat it out of their hands. "Can we try it, please?"

We nodded, and she trotted off to buy some of the approved food. As she held out her hand, a kangaroo approached, no stranger to the ritual. Aria giggled as it nuzzled her palm.

We watched as the animal ate his fill then hopped away. He hunched over on his hind legs, stretching out his arms in the dirt, then plopped over onto his back, belly up, and closed his eyes.

"Ha-ha," Finn said. "I get it, buddy. That's how I feel after eating sometimes too."

Back in Sydney, Finn and Aria's worldschooling journey reached its end—at least for this adventure—as they completed their school's placement tests to be able to rejoin their classmates in ninth and seventh grades in the fall. They finished book reviews for me of Bill Bryson's *In a Sunburned Country*, our literature assignment for Australia, and put finishing touches on a short essay about endemic species.

Our adventure in the Land Down Under culminated with a hike up the Barrenjoey headland a few days later. We climbed the steep Smugglers Track to a lighthouse perched atop the hillside. From the crest, we were rewarded with sweeping views—the endless Pacific to the east, Hawkesbury River to the north, and the Pittwater and Broken Bay to the west.

We trampled through thick brush to a rocky outcropping, the kids enjoying a game they made up of "throw the thistle at each other," which basically consisted of them hurling prickly plants at each other as hard as possible and giggling madly. Standing on the edge of the cliffs, watching the late afternoon sun glint like sequins across the ocean, I thought of one of Bill Bryson's lines about Australia. As usual, he summed it up perfectly: "The sun nearly always shines. There is coffee on every corner. Life doesn't get much better than this."

> **ALMOND FAMILY REPORT CARD ON AUSTRALIA**
>
> - *Top Marks:* Australia's got it all, from the vast Outback and sun-drenched beaches to the bustling cities of Sydney and Melbourne. Whether you're surfing, road tripping, or café hopping, your experiences will depend on how much time you have.
> - *Needs Work:* With so much to experience, you need to prioritize ahead of time any must-sees and carefully plan your route and transportation.
> - *Learning Tips:* Visit a wildlife sanctuary to learn about Australia's conservation efforts. Watching koalas or feeding kangaroos—when expressly permitted and with approved food—isn't just fun; it can be educational.

EPILOGUE

Homeward Bound: French Polynesia and the United States

It seems that the more places I see and experience, the bigger I realize the world to be. The more I become aware of, the more I realize how relatively little I know of it, how many places I have still to go, how much more there is to learn.

—Anthony Bourdain (*No Reservations*, Season 2, Episode 3, "Peru")

In the end, we only regret the chances we didn't take.

—Unknown

EPILOGUE

In French Polynesia, the last stop on our thirteen-month odyssey, we learned of a fruit that comes from the fish-poison tree. The locals call it *hotu pāinu*. The tree grows by the ocean, and its almond-like fruit disseminates by floating on the waves. For centuries, the Tahitians used its nuts, which contain ichthyotoxins, to catch fish. Because of the way the fruits bob along the sea's surface, the islanders called them *hotu pāinu*, which literally means "floating drifter." They also use the term as a derogatory name for foreigners—people without attachment.

"*Hotu pāinu* has a strong meaning in Polynesia," our guide, Cindy, told us on a jungle hike near the southern tip of Tahiti. We stood, looking at the pale-yellow tree as she spoke. She held out one of its green fruits, about the size and shape of a fig. After we had a chance to see it, she tossed it into the waves. It plunged under briefly then shot to the surface like a cork, before being swept away by the swells.

"Here, when we give birth, we plant the baby's placenta in the soil," she explained. "This is called *te pūfenua*. It signifies the deep connection between our people and the land. From their earliest moments in the world, a baby is connected by its parents to the earth, the source of life. That's why we say, for anyone not from here, that you are *hotu pāinu*. If you don't live by the tree that carried you, you are aimless, like a fruit carried by the wind. For us, there is nothing worse than being far from your home, adrift, and rootless."

In late June 2023, we began making plans for the long journey east, toward home. As we priced out routes from Sydney to Denver, Randy realized we could squeeze in a final stopover in French Polynesia, a sprawling set of volcanic and coral islands and atolls in the South Pacific, halfway between Australia and California. We worried a stint in these pricey French islands would blow up our backpacker budget, but after some research, we decided we could make it work. By avoiding the most expensive, storied destinations like Bora Bora; seeking inexpensive Airbnbs in less touristy areas; making our own meals; and prioritizing free activities—with a notable exception to reserve some budget for scuba diving—we calculated we would be able to swing it.

It was a special last port of call, each spot in the remote archipelago more stunning than the last. We spent two weeks island hopping from Tahiti to the far-flung atoll of Fakarava to the heart-shaped island of Mo'orea.

For their last worldschooling book of the trip, Finn and Aria read the adventure classic *Kon-Tiki*, by Thor Heyerdahl, chronicling the author's incredible journey across the Pacific from South America to the Polynesian islands on a balsa-wood raft in 1947. Looking across the waves into the vast expanse of open water, it was easy for us to imagine the sense of adventure that compelled Heyerdahl and his crew to set forth across the South Seas so many years ago on a grand voyage of discovery.

Our days in Polynesia were spent hiking to waterfalls, watching double rainbows arc over the distant mountains, diving with hundreds of sharks, biking on rusty old two-wheelers down desolate dirt roads, snorkeling with Manta rays, learning how black pearls are cultivated, and walking along soft pink sand beaches.

On the last night of our trip, Finn and Aria wrote their final journal entries. We packed our backpacks with clothes now more dirty than clean. We tucked our travel essentials into their spots in our day packs, a routine by then as common as brushing our teeth. Then, after lining up our four well-worn packs by the door of our Airbnb, we fell asleep for the last time in a foreign bed in a far-off land, at least for the foreseeable future.

The next day, all of us practically bouncing with anticipation, we flew from Papeete to San Francisco. I teared up when we exited the plane onto U.S. soil and saw the sign reading "Welcome to the United States of America." When the customs officer stamped our passport, he smiled and said, "Welcome home." I grinned, too, overcome with emotion to say much in return.

Later that afternoon, we flew on the last leg from San Francisco to Denver. I looked out the window and down at the land below us as I had on so many other flights over the last year, this time feeling the thrill not of the unknown but of the deeply familiar. The Rocky Mountains spread out before us, like open arms beckoning us back.

Our friend Adrian met us at the arrivals terminal, filming us as we bounded toward the baggage carousel, and exchanged hugs. His wife, Nicola, and their kids were waiting for us at our house, cheering as we pulled into the yard. That quickly turned into an impromptu play date with the kids all hanging out at our house like old times and the adults reconvening an hour later for drinks and appetizers on our deck in the late afternoon sunshine. A spontaneous gathering—just as we always loved them.

Neighbors soon wandered over to join us. Friends had left welcome baskets and stocked our fridge full of homemade chili, guacamole, watermelon, and beer. We weren't jet lagged as we had slowly been migrating east, the time difference from French Polynesia to Colorado only four hours. So, we laughed and talked and toasted and caught up, well into the night—like no time had passed.

EASING BACK HOME: TIPS FOR FAMILIES POST EXTENDED TRAVEL AND WORLDSCHOOLING

Readjusting to your regular life after a long period of travel and worldschooling can be challenging. Here are some strategies to help families transition home smoothly while keeping the spirit of your adventures alive:

- *Ease into Routine*: Allow your family a buffer period to readjust. Avoid jumping straight into your old routines and take time to acclimate.
- *Continue Travel Rituals*: Keep some travel habits going to keep a sense of wanderlust and adventure, from exploring new places locally and naming future travel wish-list spots, or having family movie nights to learn about far-away places.
- *Manage Expectations in Sharing*: Encourage your children to talk about their experiences but be aware that not everyone may relate to or show interest in your travels, and that's perfectly okay. Each person connects with stories differently.
- *Reconnect with Your Community*: Get involved in local activities and events to reestablish ties with your community.
- *Reflect and Process*: Hold regular family discussions about your travels to help process the transition and preserve your experiences.
- *Stay Connected with Travel Contacts*: Keep in touch with friends you met while traveling to keep a global connection.

- *Be Patient with Adjustments*: Recognize that each family member may adapt at their own pace.
- *Seek Professional Support If Needed*: If the transition proves challenging, consider seeking advice from counselors or educational professionals.

Transitioning back to normal routines after any big adventure can be a gradual process. By keeping elements of your travels alive, staying connected, and being patient, your family will integrate the richness of your experiences into your everyday life.

"How does it feel to be home?" This was the number one question we were asked over and over in the days and weeks after returning to Colorado. Most people seemed to expect us to reply that it was bittersweet—or that we felt sad at the closing of such a big chapter in our lives, something we had planned and saved toward for so many years.

It wasn't either of those things, though. None of us had mixed or negative emotions upon our return. Since setting off for Casablanca more than a year earlier, we had spent four hundred days on the road. We traveled 102,000 miles (about 164,153 km), exploring twenty-seven countries across all seven continents. We took sixty-five flights on thirty-eight airlines and stayed in 141 accommodations. We did three multiday treks, one Antarctic crossing, and thankfully, managed to pull it all off with only one big emergency (Randy's scorpion sting in Jordan), one bout of altitude sickness, and a few stomach bugs. I had taken over a hundred thousand photos, which I whittled down into country albums totaling fifteen thousand edited favorites. We had memories for a lifetime.

We loved our time together traveling the world, swapping classrooms for countries, immersing ourselves in different cultures, learning languages, experiencing the kindness of strangers, and making new friends, exploring the farthest corners of our planet, and becoming closer as a family. The trip that we first envisioned years ago as a crazy idea had exceeded our wildest expectations.

At the end of it all, though, we were ready to be home; to reintegrate back into a life that we worked hard to build in a state that fits our interests and is as beautiful as any place we visited; to return to family and

EPILOGUE

friends; and to reunite with classmates in brick-and-mortar school. Finn couldn't wait to start driver's ed and get his learner's permit, confident that he knew everything he needed to know after a couple of lessons in Namibia and Greece. Aria was eager to dive into the theater program at school and play soccer on a club team. We were all excited for the winter season to head to the slopes again.

So, the answer we gave to how we felt upon our return was, simply, gratitude. We felt deeply grateful for the time we had to explore and worldschool our two children through a formative year of their lives. And we were grateful to come home to begin a new chapter, this one rooted in the wide-open spaces and rugged mountains of the American West.

In the waning weeks of the summer of 2023, Finn and Aria relished reconnecting with friends. They seemed to get extra enjoyment from errands like back-to-school shopping or chores like making up their rooms, happy to have rooms of their own again. When the fall school semester started, they slid back into their classes without a hitch. They each placed into advanced math courses. Finn's time in Taiwan not only bridged the year, but he advanced three levels in Mandarin. And in every other subject, they carried on without a hitch.

I returned to my former employer, McKinsey & Company, ten days after we got back. Having a leave of absence was extremely helpful for our peace of mind, knowing that one of us would have a steady paycheck and health insurance immediately upon return. Randy spent time in our first few months home caring for his mother and uncle, whose health had taken a turn, while looking for a new job. The labor market was not as strong as it had been before we left, especially in the tech sector (where Randy focused), but we had planned conservatively and had a runway for him to find his next opportunity.

In November, wanting to embrace a bigger life, we got a new dog, then in the spring, two tabby cats. The kids were allowed to name them; our only criterion that the names had to relate to our world travels. Finn named our Alaskan Klee Kai puppy "Tokyo Sakura," remembering our time in Japan among the cherry blossoms. Aria dubbed one of the kittens "Messi," ensuring we'd never forget the World Cup season we spent in Argentina watching the blue-and-white team win thanks to the brilliance of Lionel Messi. And Randy and I named the other kitten, Rio. In the depths of Colorado winters, we could look at him and smile, remembering the warmth and beauty of Brazil. *Saudade.*

Over time, friends stopped asking about the trip. Our family conversations around the dinner table switched from swapping stories from the road to recounting highs and lows from our days. Life slipped into its normal rhythm. Tokyo, Rio, and Messi—not to mention our teen and tween—kept us busy.

Did we feel a massive sense of transformation after having taken such an epic trip? The honest answer is yes and no. On a day-to-day level, not much changed dramatically for us. On the outside, except for minor changes, our life looks much the same as it did before we embarked for Africa and beyond. At times, the kids display maturity and worldliness beyond their years, but most of the time, they're just normal teens, content to spend time with their friends or immerse themselves in a book or video game.

We made small shifts to do our part to make the world a better place, though they're more like tiny drops of water in a pond than any wave. We took up composting—for a time. After a big earthquake rocked Morocco, we checked on our friend Ayoub and donated money to local aid organizations; and after a powerful quake hit the Hualien region of Taiwan, Aria set up a lemonade stand and donated her earnings to relief efforts. We kept in touch with Three Sisters Trekking in Nepal and our friend Pradeep and his school in India, pledging to donate annually to both organizations to continue supporting their causes.

I forged deeper partnerships with two nonprofit organizations that focus on study abroad opportunities, arranging to donate part of the proceeds of my book to IES Abroad scholarships for disadvantaged students to experience the power of travel, as mine had the privilege to do. And I became a board member of the Global Livingston Institute, a Denver-based organization whose global classroom engages students and communities to think critically about international development and engage in immersive cross-cultural learning in East Africa.

While overtly, Finn and Aria don't seem that different, we hope the experience they had burrowed into their souls, like a seedling that will sprout over time. When they study world history, geography, and religions in the future, they'll have a deeper appreciation and can further their understanding from a place of recognition. In learning about climate change or oxidation in science, they might think back to the glaciers they witnessed firsthand or recall the rust-colored hues of the Namibian sands. When they meet someone from a different culture, they'll build relationships from a more expansive—and hopefully more inclusive—worldview, and they may explore different career paths than they otherwise would have had they not been exposed to the different ways of life and of being happy on the planet.

Time will tell what larger changes will emerge. For now, we are content to simply have small moments that make us remember the experiences we had together, like passing a Greek restaurant and reminiscing about gyros at the seaside in Amorgos or getting caught in the rain and smiling at the memory of our cold-but-unforgettable trek in the Himalayas.

Months after we returned home, a friend confessed that she was surprised that we came back at all. Knowing how much we love to travel and what adventures we had, she had predicted we would choose to stay endlessly nomadic and keep on going.

I smiled and shook my head. That was never something we wanted, and probably why it wasn't bittersweet to return. We didn't leave home to escape life. We left to experience it, together, in a different way.

Travel and adventuring and roaming the wild places will always be core to who we are—but we never wanted to drift forever. Our aim was to give our kids roots in addition to helping them spread their wings. We were excited for the next chapter of our lives, enriched by the learnings from the Everywhere Classroom, at home.

In short: *hotu pāinu* no more.

ALMOND FAMILY REPORT CARD ON FRENCH POLYNESIA

- *Top Marks*: Though remote and hard to reach, French Polynesia is worth the journey, its clear waters, lush landscapes, pristine underwater world, and laid-back atmosphere epitomizing paradise.
- *Needs Work*: It's beautiful, but French Polynesia can hit your wallet hard. To keep costs down, choose lesser-known islands over pricier ones like Bora Bora, stay in guesthouses in less touristy areas, cook your own meals, and prioritize free activities.
- *Learning Tips*: Immerse in local culture and support local, sustainable tourism to preserve this stunning environment for future travelers.

APPENDIX
Worldschooling FAQs

What are the regulations around homeschooling or worldschooling?
The legal and social landscape for homeschooling or worldschooling varies significantly across different countries. Those with prevalent homeschooling movements include the United States, Canada, the United Kingdom, Australia, and New Zealand, though specific regulations vary, even by state or province. Some countries have highly regulated homeschooling programs as extensions of their compulsory school system. Others, like Germany have deemed it illegal entirely. Lastly, there are some places, like Argentina, where it's not restricted by law, but it's not socially acceptable either so, in practice, it's largely nonexistent. Thoroughly research and understand the legal landscape early to align your travel aspirations with relevant regulations.

How long do you need to travel to use the world as a classroom, and is there a minimum budget needed?
You don't need a lengthy trip to benefit from worldschooling; even short trips near or far from home can offer enriching educational experiences. The key is in thoughtful planning of activities that support your educational goals, whether for a weekend getaway or a year-long odyssey. As for budget, worldschooling is adaptable to different financial situations. With smart planning, you can access free or affordable educational

resources and find accommodation and transport options to suit your budget. This flexibility allows families of various means to experience the Everywhere Classroom.

How did you decide which subjects to focus on while traveling?
We developed a curriculum that maintained a strong foundation in core subjects, ensuring no educational gaps for Finn and Aria. We aligned subjects like history and literature with our travel destinations to make learning more relevant and engaging. For structured subjects like math, we sourced materials through a site called teacherspayteachers.com to maintain consistency with their school curriculum.

What preparations did you make for worldschooling before leaving?
We coordinated with our children's teachers and identified a starter list of books, documentaries, and online resources tailored to our itinerary. Along the way, we tapped into insights and recommendations from the worldschooling community on social forums, which provided valuable additional tips and advice along the journey.

How did you integrate cultural experiences into your educational plans?
We consciously sought out places that were farther afield than many tourists visit for more authentic cultural experiences (this kept costs lower, too). We stayed in guesthouses and homestays to interact with locals and frequently used community guides. We planned visits to historical sites, museums, and cultural events and layered in relevant lessons or readings to give a layered, immersive experience.

What was a typical worldschooling day like during your travels?
Every day was different, but we tried to balance structured academic time with exploratory learning in each location. We dedicated periods each day for journaling or completing assignments, while also taking advantage of the unique learning opportunities all around us, presented by our travels.

APPENDIX

How did you handle educational resources while traveling?
We relied heavily on digital resources, which allowed us flexibility and access to a wide range of materials. Each child had access to devices for e-books, educational apps, and audiobooks. We planned for internet connectivity issues by downloading materials when we had access and frequently printed out worksheets and tests for hands-on subjects like math.

How did you manage different learning styles and paces between your children?
It was an ongoing process. As we grew to better understand their learning preferences, we did our best to tailor our approaches, using a combination of interactive activities, digital and audio books, and assignments. We continually evaluated and adjusted based on their feedback to keep them engaged and learning effectively.

Do you have a full list of books and documentaries that your kids read and watched, by country?
Yes, I've compiled a list of the materials we used, organized by country, on my website, andialmond.com. This includes book reviews from Finn and Aria to give a sense of how these resonated with a teen and tween.

What impact did worldschooling have on your children's education after returning home?
When we finished our travels, both children took assessments from their school in Colorado to gauge their academic standing. They reintegrated smoothly into all their classes, and, in some areas, like math and Mandarin, achieved advanced proficiency.

How has the worldschooling experience influenced your children's long-term educational paths?
It's too soon to know how our worldschooling adventure will shape our kids in the long run. Day to day, they can seem like any other teenagers—juggling homework, hanging out with friends, and occasionally

needing to be reminded to get off their phones. But we're confident that the seeds we planted during our travels will grow into a lifelong curiosity about the world and give them a deeper foundation on which to continue learning.

Would you recommend worldschooling to other families? What advice would you give?
Absolutely. We recommend worldschooling for any family looking to broaden their children's horizons. As we have hopefully shown, using the world as a classroom is doable on travels of any budget and length, near or far from home. Effective planning, leveraging the vast array of online and community resources, and staying adaptable are key to a successful experience. It's a rewarding way to educate your children while exploring the world together.

Where can I learn more about different worldschooling options?
Thanks to a plethora of online resources, exploring worldschooling options and finding practical guidance is easier than ever. Forums, social media platforms, and educational websites offer detailed insights into how families can tailor educational approaches to travels of any length. Tools like Khan Academy, Coursera, and various virtual academies provide structured learning paths that are accessible from anywhere in the world. And joining the growing travel and worldschooling community through outlets like Instagram enables meaningful connection with others who share like-minded aspirations or are on similar journeys. Follow us on Instagram @4almondsabroad, and let's continue exploring together.

ACKNOWLEDGMENTS

When I set out to write a book about our travels, I thought it would be a snap. I'm a writer by nature, a former journalist by training, and the subject matter was personal and timely. How hard could it be? Turns out, a heck of a lot tougher than I expected. Distilling the adventures of thirteen months on the road into concise, relatable stories and extracting worldschooling lessons applicable to travels of any length and budget was challenging. Thankfully, I had a great group of people who believed in the project and were sounding boards from idea to hard copy.

To start with, this book might never even have been conceived if it weren't for the brilliant Raju Narisetti, who, upon hearing about our travel plans, promptly asked me, "What's your intended output?" I'd expect no less ambitious a nudge from McKinsey's leader of global publishing, a mentor, and friend. Thank you, Raju, for the push and advice along the way.

To Lindsay Pollak, who helped me figure out Instagram Stories as I first bumbled my way into social media to share our travel tales, read an early draft of my intro, and acted as thought partner and champion throughout the process. All In 4 Eva, my dear friend.

Christen Karniski and the whole team at Rowman & Littlefield, thank you for seeing the potential in my manuscript and helping take it from draft to final version. I'm honored to be part of the R&L family!

To my fantastic agent, Kim Peticolas. I feel so lucky to have met you before setting off on our journey at that Starbucks in Broomfield. You believed in this project from the get-go—even when I started doubting it, helped me shape the worldschooling angle, and were instrumental in guiding me at every stage. I couldn't have done this without you.

I love that this endeavor reconnected me with the ever-inspirational Kim Beck, who unconditionally leaped into helping me brainstorm early days marketing plans and book pitch approaches. I'll never forget our first conversation; we were in Ushuaia, Argentina, about to board the ship for Antarctica, and you hopped on a quick chat to talk through what I was envisioning and went a mile a minute with ideas. I truly appreciate your infectious enthusiasm, Kim. You're the best!

Through our travels in South Africa, we met up with Tracy Lindner, a former colleague of Randy's who was art director at the start-up they worked at more than a decade earlier. We had fun picnicking on the beach in Cape Town and catching up on life. So it felt fitting when, more than a year later and needing a brilliant book cover design, I called on Tracy. She, who shared my sensibility on typography, immediately brought her creative energy to design a gorgeous illustration that I love. Thank you, Tracy!

To Carole Almond, for joining us on safari in Africa—and bringing us homemade chocolate chip cookies all the way from Colorado! Even though those experiences didn't make this book, they are no less memorable and special, and I'm so glad we got to have them together.

To Shay Hulser for being a great sport and travel partner as we explored Japan. It was wonderful to have you be a part of our world travels; we'll treasure our memories of snow monkeys and Bless wine bar encounters, sakura blossoms and horse meat surprises.

To my dad, Fred Hulser, for always being there for me as my biggest champion and supporter. You eagerly read every early chapter draft and gave comments and encouragement. I will cherish the time we had zipping across Japan, failing at meditation but succeeding in life. You're the best father in the world. Thank you for everything. I love you so much.

ACKNOWLEDGMENTS

Finn and Aria, thanks for always being up for something new, putting up with your crazy parents and our wild ideas, embracing the experiences of a year-long backpacking odyssey and throwing yourselves into the discomforts along the way. It was an honor to be your worldschooling teacher, even in the times Daddy or I wanted to throw a book at you. I wish you could see yourselves through my eyes—the growth across the arc of our travels has been something to behold. I'm so proud of you both and excited to see the paths you blaze in life.

And, lastly, to Randy, my fellow drifter (off to see the world). I'm forever grateful to have found my soulmate at age twenty-two and for all the adventures we have had—and all those yet to come. After all, there's such a lot of world to see. I love you, always and forever. Is it time for our next trip yet?

ABOUT THE AUTHOR

Andi Almond, born in San Juan, Puerto Rico, is an accomplished author, illustrator, and former Associated Press journalist. She has written two educational children's books and is an active member of the growing worldschooling and travel communities. With a popular Instagram presence @4almondsabroad, Andi frequently collaborates with influencers and speaks on family travel, adventure, and educational enrichment topics across various platforms.

Dedicated to making travel more accessible for all, Andi partners with organizations that promote study abroad experiences and donates part of her book sales from *The Everywhere Classroom* to scholarships for IES Abroad. She is a board member of the Global Livingston Institute, a Denver-based nonprofit whose Global Classroom program provides immersive cross-cultural experiences and fosters international connections for students.

Her prior books include *Henry in the Caribbean*, a learning adventure, which follows a cat's journey across the Caribbean to find his family, and *Henry and a Special Friend: An AIDS Awareness Book*, commissioned by the Puerto Rico Committee for UNICEF to promote HIV/AIDS education. It has been translated into multiple languages including Spanish, French, Haitian Creole, Thai, and Burmese.

Andi's day job is as a global communications leader at McKinsey & Company. When not traveling, she calls Boulder, Colorado, home with husband Randy, their children Finn and Aria, and a lively mix of pets, including their Alaskan Klee Kai puppy Tokyo Sakura and two tabby cats, Rio and Messi. You can follow their adventures near and far from home on Instagram (@4almondsabroad) or visit her website at andialmond.com.